商务外语
人才能力标准

张蔚磊 著

中国人民大学出版社
·北京·

图书在版编目（CIP）数据

商务外语人才能力标准 / 张蔚磊著. --北京：中
国人民大学出版社，2025.3
ISBN 978-7-300-32113-4

Ⅰ.①商…　Ⅱ.①张…　Ⅲ.①商务—外语—人才培养
—研究　Ⅳ.①F7

中国国家版本馆 CIP 数据核字（2023）第 163085 号

商务外语人才能力标准

张蔚磊　著

Shangwu Waiyu Rencai Nengli Biaozhun

出版发行	中国人民大学出版社	
社　　址	北京中关村大街31号	**邮政编码**　100080
电　　话	010-62511242（总编室）	010-62511770（质管部）
	010-82501766（邮购部）	010-62514148（门市部）
	010-62511173（发行公司）	010-62515275（盗版举报）
网　　址	http://www.crup.com.cn	
经　　销	新华书店	
印　　刷	唐山玺诚印务有限公司	
开　　本	720 mm × 1000 mm　1/16	**版　　次**　2025 年 3 月第 1 版
印　　张	16.25	**印　　次**　2025 年 3 月第 1 次印刷
字　　数	260 000	**定　　价**　82.00 元

序　言

欣闻上海对外经贸大学张蔚磊教授的新著《商务外语人才能力标准》即将出版，甚为高兴。几十年来，她笔耕不辍，刻苦钻研，坚持研究，令人甚为钦佩。我为她取得的研究成果以及新著的出版感到非常欣慰，可喜可贺！

党的二十大报告指出，我国要加快建设贸易强国，坚持社会主义市场经济改革方向，加快构建国内国际双循环相互促进的新发展格局，积极建设覆盖全球的伙伴关系网络。我国要深入实施科教兴国战略、人才强国战略、创新驱动发展战略，构建中国特色哲学社会科学学科体系、学术体系、话语体系。建设贸易强国和覆盖全球的伙伴关系离不开商务外语人才。新时代如何培养高质量的商务外语人才，实现人才强国、创新驱动发展，值得我们深入研究。数字经济、数字贸易背景下对商务外语人才提出了哪些新要求？百年变局对商务外语人才的能力提出了哪些新要求？在此背景下，我们亟须研制出一套我国新时代的商务外语人才能力标准。

人才培养离不开能力标准，一个清晰的能力标准体系可以为人才培养指明方向。《商务外语人才能力标准》一书不仅是对商务外语教育的一次深入探讨，还是对我们如何培养适应全球化时代的商务外语人才的一次全新思考。本书共参考了 22 个国际量表，这 22 个量表来自 7 个国家和区域，涉及 6 类不同机构。本书设计了 5 个能力量表，共包括 1 133 条描述语。

本书为商务外语人才能力标准的深入研究，提供了一个全面的解决方案。这个方案不仅涵盖了语言技能，还涉及文化理解、商业洞察、创新思维和自主学习等领域。这不仅为商务外语专业的学生指明了一个能力提升的方向，还为教育者、测评机构和企业提供了一个明确的评估标准。随着全球化的加速和跨国业务的繁荣，商务外语人才的培养显得尤为重要。这类专业人才不仅需要精通语言技能，还需要具备深度的商业理解力，能够在跨文化环境中进行有效沟通，从而解决问题。然而，如何明确并衡量这些必要的能力，一直是教师和企业面临的挑战。本书中的评价描述语可以帮助教师设计有效的问题和活动，并评估和提升学生的这些关键能力。例如，通过模拟商业场景，学生可以在实践中学习和应用语言技能，同时也能深入理解商业运作和文化差异。

本书的另一个重要贡献是其实用性和可操作性。作者尽量避免抽象和理论化的论述，而是以清晰、具体、实用的方式，介绍如何评估和提升商务外语人才的各种能力。这使得本书不仅适合教育者阅读，还适合商务人士和企业人力资源部门参考。我期待更多的教育者和商务人士能够读到这本书，并从中获得启示。

是为序。

北京语言大学教授　王立非

2024 年 9 月

前　言

　　党的二十大之后，我们迎来了发展的新机遇。党的二十大报告提出了十多个强国目标，即教育强国、科技强国、人才强国、文化强国……其中，教育强国是根本。2023年，中国高等教育在学总规模4 763万人，全世界第一；2023年我国高等教育的毛入学率是60.2%，标志着我国已经进入高等教育的普及化发展阶段。传统统一规格的人才培养模式已经无法满足社会发展的需求。截至2024年，我国开设商务英语专业的院校高达400多所。在这个大背景下，我们要思考如何更好地开展新文科、跨学科教育，提高外语人才培养的质量，着力培养拔尖创新人才。人才培养离不开能力标准，一个清晰的能力标准可以为人才培养指明方向。

　　商务外语人才能力标准研究旨在探索我国商务外语专业人才的能力量表的构建，尝试建构一个科学的、动态的、开放性的指标体系。该指标体系既要具备国际标准的共同要求，又要具有中国特色，符合中国国情和国内外经济社会对商务外语人才能力的要求。

　　鉴于国家语言和语种的规划和布局，在我国，关于商务外语和商务外语人才培养的研究，大多聚焦在英语领域。因此，本书采用由特殊到一般的推理方法，以商务英语为典型样本，探讨商务外语人才能力标准的共性。

　　2014年，教育部组织编制了《高等学校商务英语专业本科教学质量国家标准》。2018年，教育部高等学校教学指导委员会发布了《普通高等学校本科专业类教学质量国家标准（外国语言文学类）》（以下简称《国标》），《国标》是商务英语本科专业准入、建设和评价的依据。各高等学校可根据该标准、相关行业标准和人才需求，制定本校的商务英语专业培养方案。《国标》指明了培养目标：商务英语专业旨在培养英语基本功扎实，具有国际视野和人文素养，掌握语言学、经济学、管理学、法学（国际商法）等相关基础理论与知识，熟悉国际商务的通行规则和惯例，具备英语应用能力、商务实践能力、跨文化交流能力、思辨与创新能力、自主学习能力，能从事国际商务工作的复合型、应用型人才。《国标》对商务英语专业的培养规格作出了清晰的界定，在培养规格中明确了能力要求：商务英语学习者应该掌握英语应用能力、跨文化交际能力、思辨与创新能力、自主学习能力和商务实践能力五大能力。

2020年教育部高等学校外国语言文学类专业教学指导委员会正式发布《普通高等学校本科外国语言文学类专业教学指南》（以下简称《指南》）。《指南》是继2018年《国标》之后的又一纲领性文件。《指南》明确指出商务英语专业的人才培养目标是：培养具有扎实的英语语言基本功和相关商务专业知识，拥有良好的人文素养、中国情怀与国际视野，熟悉文学、经济学、管理学和法学等相关理论知识，掌握国际商务的基础理论与实务，具备较强的跨文化交际能力、商务沟通能力与创新创业能力，能适应国家与地方经济社会发展、对外交流与合作需要，能熟练使用英语从事国际商务、国际贸易、国际会计、国际金融、跨境电子商务等涉外领域工作的国际化复合型人才。在培养规格中对能力要求也作出了明确指示：本专业学生应具有良好的商务英语运用能力和跨文化商务沟通能力；具有思辨能力、量化思维能力、数字化信息素养；具有基本的商务分析、决策和实践能力；具有良好的团队合作能力，较强的领导、管理、协调和沟通能力；具有终身学习能力；具有良好的汉语表达能力和基本的第二外语运用能力。

《国标》提出外语类专业准入、建设和评估的基本原则与总体要求，《指南》则为各专业创新发展提供具体行动路线和解决方案。商务外语专业应在《国标》和《指南》的指导下，坚持内涵式发展、多元化发展和创新发展，培养时代需要、国家期待的外语专业人才。鉴于此，本书将围绕《国标》提出的商务外语人才的五大能力要求，开展能力指标体系的研究，即语言应用能力量表、跨文化交际能力量表、自主学习能力量表、批判性思维能力量表和商务实践能力量表。本书共参考了22个国际量表。这些量表由欧洲、加拿大、美国、澳大利亚、日本的一些机构和个人开发。经过5年的研究，本书共设计了1 133条能力描述语。

语言应用能力指开展商务活动所需的英语语言知识与技能，包含英语组织能力、英语应用能力和学习策略能力，本书将从听、说、读、写、译等多方面的交际语言能力来评估学习者的商务英语应用能力。在综合研究《"CAN DO"语言能力量表》（欧洲语言测试者协会，2022）、《加拿大语言等级标准——基本技能比较框架》（加拿大语言等级标准中心，2012）、《职业英语学习目标全球规范》（培生集团，2018）和《欧洲语言共同参考框架：学习、教学、评估》（欧洲理事会）等量表的基础上，《商务外语语言应用能力量表》设计了4级指标体系，分为 6 个等级，共 250 条描述语。

跨文化交际能力是商务外语学习者应具备的基本能力之一，也是外语教学的主要任务和目标。本书中的跨文化交际能力主要包括基本跨文化交际知识、态度、认知、技巧和行为五大能力。本书的跨文化交际能力量表通过对一系列真实的跨文化交际能力和跨文化交际任务的描述，来评估商务外语学习者的跨文化交际能力。在综合研究《跨文化知识和能力价值量表》（美国学院和大学协会，2017）、《工作角色和熟练水平能力量表》（美国 Workitect，2012）、《全球能力量表》（美国 the Metiri Group & NCREL，2009）、《人才能力框架》（日本 Kozai 公司，2010）、《文化智力简短量表》（加拿大 David C. Thomas，2015）、《跨文化敏感性量表》（美国 LINKs Inc，2001）等量表的基础上，《商务外语跨文化交际能力量表》设计了 4 级指标体系，分为初级、中级、较高级、高级 4 个等级，共 235 条描述语。

自主学习能力是一切能力的基础，它是一种自主学习新知识的能力。商务外语学习者应该具备较强的自主学习能力。本书设计的《商务外语自主学习能力量表》主要从认知能力、元认知能力、动机能力、学习技巧四个维度评估商务外语学习者的自主学习能力。在综合研究《跨文化知识和能力价值量表》（美国学院和大学协会，2017）、《有效终身学习量表》（英国布里斯托大学教授 Glaxton 等，2004）、《个人胜任力——培养学生学习能力的框架》（美国学习创新中心，2014）、《自我导向学习量表》（美国 Guglielmino，1991）等量表的基础上，《商务外语自主学习能力量表》设计了 4 级指标体系，分为初级、中级、较高级、高级 4 个等级，共 149 条描述语。

批判性思维能力是一种通用能力。对于商务外语学习者而言，批判性思维能力的培养同样重要。本书设计的《商务外语批判性思维能力量表》主要由认知技能、认知倾向和认知动机三大指标组成，可以综合评估商务外语学习者的批判性思维能力。在综合研究《跨文化知识和能力价值量表》（美国学院和大学协会，2017）、《批判性思维动机量表》（西班牙 Jorge Valenzuela Carreño，2011）、《整体批判性思维评分量表》（美国 Peter A. Facione and Norren C. Facione，2011）、《HEIghten 批判性思维测试》（美国 ETS，2016）、《批判性思维能力评价标准》（美国批判性思维协会，2005）、《加利福尼亚批判性思维倾向量表》（美国 Giancarlo & Facione，2000）等量表的基础上，《商务外语批判性思维能力量表》设计了 4 级指标体系，分为初级、中级、较高级、高级 4 个等级，共 194 条描述语。

商务实践能力是商务外语学习者的基础能力，它包括认知领域、情感领域和动作技能领域三个维度的能力。本书设计的《商务实践能力量表》可以综合评价商务外语学习者在认知领域、情感领域和动作技能领域所体现出的综合品格和实践能力。在综合研究《商务（通用）管理能力量表》（澳大利亚亚太国际学院，2011）、《领导能力等级量表》（美国人事管理局）、《工作角色和熟练水平能力量表》（美国 Workitect，2012）、《特许全球管理会计师能力框架》（美国注册会计师协会和英国皇家特许管理会计师公会，2014）等量表的基础上，《商务实践能力量表》设计了 4 级指标体系，分为初级、中级、较高级、高级 4 个等级，共305 条描述语。

本书坚持多元化和理论与实践相结合的原则，将五大能力的理论框架、能力模型建构、量表设计、指标设计、描述语选取等紧密地融合在一起。本书主要采用文献研究及统计分析的方法，在参考多个国际通用的能力量表的基础上收集描述语，并根据相应的理论框架和收集的描述语语料库设计商务外语人才能力标准指标体系。

本书的主要贡献为：第一，依照《普通高等学校本科专业类教学质量国家标准（外国语言文学类）》和《普通高等学校本科外国语言文学类专业教学指南》界定了商务外语人才应该具备的五大能力；第二，搭建了商务外语专业五大能力标准的理论框架；第三，构建了商务外语专业五种能力的模型；第四，设计了商务外语专业五大能力的指标体系；第五，在比较分析国内外权威描述语的基础上，首创性地编制出我国的商务外语人才能力量表。

本书旨在抛砖引玉，以期可以为新时代、新文科、大外语背景下的我国商务外语人才培养、学科建设、评估评价等提供一定的参考。

感谢在此书撰写过程中提出宝贵修改意见的专家、学者和同仁们，感谢符吉祥等同学在资料搜集整理过程中给予的帮助。

张蔚磊

2024 年 5 月 1 日

上海

目　录

第 1 章

商务外语人才能力标准的重要性

党的二十大报告强调"教育、科技、人才是全面建设社会主义现代化国家的基础性、战略性支撑",提出要深入实施科教兴国战略、人才强国战略、创新驱动发展战略,开辟发展新领域新赛道,不断塑造发展新动能新优势。这充分体现了以习近平同志为核心的党中央对教育、科技、人才的高度重视,也对高校人才培养提出了新任务、新要求。当下,中国正在从地区性大国向全球性大国迈进,逐步走进世界舞台的中央。作为国际社会的重要一员,我国积极参与全球活动,与许多国家保持经贸往来。商务人才在各个行业中发挥的作用也越来越大。因此,我国需要不断培养高质量的商务人才。近年来,商务外语逐渐成为高校中的热门专业,截至 2024 年,我国开设商务英语专业的高校达到 400 多所。这些高校培养的商务外语人才,在国际合作、商贸往来、经济发展中发挥着重要作用。因此,我们不得不深入思考,培养什么样的商务外语人才? 如何培养商务外语人才? 培养商务外语人才需要遵循什么标准?

俗话说,没有规矩,不成方圆。人才培养需要遵循一定的规律,人才培养方案的设计、知识体系的架构、课程体系的设计、教材的开发等都需要参照人才培养产出的最终的能力要求。《国标》和《指南》指出了我国商务外语人才培养的大致方向,但是缺少可具体操作的、可落实的、可细化的对标量表。因此,我们有必要研制一套具体的、可操作的、科学的、国际化的商务外语人才能力标准。

1.1　商务外语人才能力标准开发的背景

商务英语作为特定用途英语的一个分支，是在经济全球化和国际贸易快速增长的背景下设立的一个学科（Ellis & Johnson，1994），以英语作为开展各种跨文化商业活动的工具。随着国际贸易活动的频繁开展，许多企业将英语技能视为员工的重要竞争力。商务英语学习者需要具备多项能力，才能提升个人竞争力。因此，为了对商务英语学习者的能力进行科学评估，构建科学、健全、适用性强的能力量表体系至关重要。目前，大多数负责招聘的人员、职能经理和人力资源团队成员也认为他们缺乏一个客观评估员工商务英语技能的工具。

能力标准，又称能力量表、能力基准，是对学习者的能力从低到高的一系列描述（Bachman，1990）。每个能力量表从低到高划分为不同等级，它是对学习者行为表现（Galloway，1985）的等级划分，或对不同阶段学习者期望的代表性行为的描述（Trim，1978）。商务外语人才能力标准可以描述学习者不同阶段的某一特定能力的等级水平。能力量表对教学目标的确定、评价结果、教学大纲的构成以及学习者学习结果的判断具有重要作用。为了给商务英语学习者提供科学的衡量能力的工具，给教师、商务英语专业相关领导和政策制定者提供参考工具，本书将基于商务英语本科教学标准设计科学的能力量表体系。

自20世纪90年代以来，语言学家受到经济和社会改革的重大影响，其研究重点从语言使用规则转移到在不同场合的各种语言应用，因此，专门用途英语的研究日益受到重视。专门用途英语是服务于特殊学术或职业目的的语言教学思路（Hutchinson & Waters，1987）。

1.1.1　我国商务外语研究的现状

中国作为国际社会的重要一员，积极参与全球经济、政治、文化等交流，尤其跨国的经贸合作异常活跃，因此，对国际商务外语人才的需求越来越大。在市场需求的推动下，商务外语在中国的发展非常迅速，2007年3月，教育部正式批准开设商务英语本科专业。此后，商务外语教学和研究得到了极大的发展，各高校为国家培养了大量商务外语人才。

2021 年，笔者通过对 2010—2020 年以来收录于中国知网（CNKI）的论文进行定量分析发现，国内的商务英语研究主要集中于以下几方面：（1）商务英语知识和能力的研究；（2）高职院校商务英语人才培养；（3）商务英语教学模式；（4）商务英语课程设置；（5）商务英语应用；（6）商务英语翻译。未来，商务英语领域的研究将更加关注商务英语能力量表体系的研制；VR 虚拟现实技术与商务英语教学体系的融合；利用大数据和语料库技术，研究企业和区域贸易英语；根据国际市场人才需求，研究商务英语人才培养模式等。其中，商务英语能力量表体系的研制尤为重要。虽然商务英语知识和能力对商务英语人才培养和学科建设是非常重要的，但目前我国并没有专门评估商务英语学习者具备的能力的等级量表。2018 年 4 月，教育部、国家语言文字工作委员会发布《中国英语能力等级量表》。而商务英语作为专门用途英语的一个重要分支，编制相应的能力量表势在必行，这对于指导商务英语的课程设置、教师的课堂教学、学生的自主学习，为商务英语评价体系提供一个度量标准具有重要作用。商务英语的研究可以细化为：开发商务英语能力量表；研究商务英语能力测评工具；研究商务英语测试的信度和效度；建立商务英语教师的专业能力培养和评价机制；开发对应新量表的商务英语课程体系与课程标准；建立商务英语学生自主学习标准等。

当前，商务外语的发展进入了一个新的阶段。但相关研究并不局限于对理论和学科发展的探索，学者们对如何满足目前市场对商务外语人才的需求、如何规范商务外语人才评估和测试等实用性研究给予了同等的重视。

商务外语是一个应用型交叉学科，涉及语言学、心理学、社会学、经济学、管理学、法学、教育学、计算机科学等（对外经济贸易大学商务英语理论研究小组，2006）。商务外语的学科交叉性使商务英语的人才培养更加复杂。学者应掌握外国语言文学、应用经济学、工商管理、法学（国际商法）等多个学科（王立非等，2015）的知识和技能，并提升运用知识和技能完成复杂学习任务和沟通任务的能力。图 1-1 是笔者设计的商务外语研究的知识图谱。

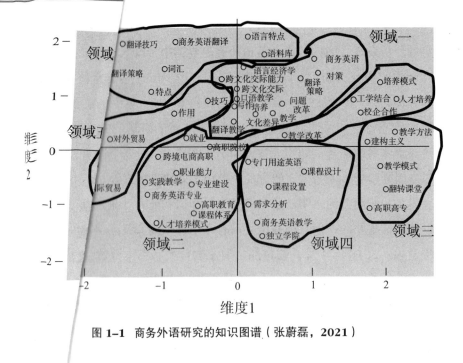

图 1-1　商务外语研究的知识图谱（张蔚磊，2021）

1.1.2 我国商务外语人才培养的现有政策

标准人才培养的基本准则，也是宏观管理的重要依据。应把促进人的全面发展和应社会需要作为衡量人才培养水平的根本标准，建立健全具有中国特色、世界平的本科人才培养质量标准体系（刘贵芹，2013）。《高等学校商务英语专业本科教学质量国家标准》对全国高校的商务英语专业建设具有重要指导意义（王非等，2015）。

2014 年，教育部组织编制了《高等学校商务英语专业本科教学质量国家标准》《高等学校商务英语专业本科教学质量国家标准》对商务英语学科发展和人才培养具有里程碑式的意义（孙毅，2016）。2018 年，教育部高等学校教学指导委员会发布了《普通高等学校本科专业类教学质量国家标准（外国语言文学类）》（以简称《国标》），《国标》是商务英语本科专业准入、建设和评价的依据。各高等校可根据本标准、相关行业标准和人才需求，制定本校的商务英语专业培养方案。

《国标》指明了培养目标：商务英语专业旨在培养英语基本功扎实，具有国际视野和人文素养，掌握语言学、经济学、管理学、法学（国际商法）等相关基础理论与知识，熟悉国际商务的通行规则和惯例，具备英语应用能力、商务实践能力、跨文化交际能力、思辨与创新能力、自主学习能力，能从事国际商务工作的复合型、应用型人才。《国标》对商务英语专业的培养规格作出了清晰的界定，明确了能力要求：商务英语学习者应该掌握英语应用能力、跨文化交际能力、商务实践能力、思辨与创新能力和自主学习能力五大能力（见图 1-2）。

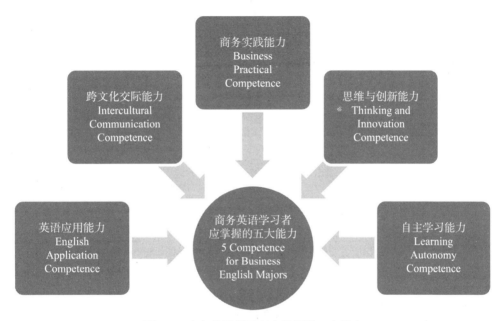

图 1-2　商务英语学习者应掌握的五大能力

2020 年，教育部高等学校外国语言文学类专业教学指导委员会正式发布《普通高等学校本科外国语言文学类专业教学指南》（以下简称《指南》）。《指南》是继 2018 年《国标》之后的又一纲领性文件。《指南》明确指出商务英语专业的人才培养目标是：培养具有扎实的英语语言基本功和相关商务专业知识，拥有良好的人文素养、中国情怀与国际视野，熟悉文学、经济学、管理学和法学等相关理论知识，掌握国际商务的基础理论与实务，具备较强的跨文化交际能力、商务沟通能力与创新创业能力，能适应国家与地方经济社会发展、对外交流与合作需要，能熟练使用英语从事国际商务、国际贸易、国际会计、国际金融、跨境电子商务等涉外领域工作的国际化复合型人才。在培养规格中对能力要求也作出了明确指示：本专业学生应具有良好的商务英语运用能力和跨文化商务沟通能力；具有思辨能力、量化思维能力、数字化信息素养；具有基本的商务分析、决策和实践能力；具有良好的团队合作能力，较强的领导、管理、协调和沟通能力；具有终身学习能力；具有良好的汉语表达能力和基本的第二外语运用能力。

《国标》提出了外语类专业准入、建设和评估的基本原则与总体要求，《指南》则为各专业创新发展提供具体行动路线和解决方案。商务外语专业应在《国标》和《指南》的指导下，坚持内涵式发展、多元化发展和创新发展，培养时代需要、国家期待的外语专业人才。鉴于此，本书将围绕《国标》提出的商务外语人才的英语应用能力、跨文化交际能力、思辨与创新能力、自主学习能力和商务实践能力等五大能力（见表1-1）展开研究。

表1-1　商务英语本科专业能力要求

能力模块	能力构成	能力要求
英语应用能力	语言组织能力	语音语调识读能力、词汇拼读能力、造句能力、谋篇能力等
	语言应用能力	听、说、读、写、译技能及语用能力、纠错能力等
	学习策略能力	调控能力、学习策略、社交策略等
跨文化交际能力	基本跨文化交际能力	跨文化思维能力、跨文化适应能力、跨文化沟通能力
	跨文化商务交际能力	商务沟通能力、商业实务能力、跨文化能力
商务实践能力	通用商务技能	办公文秘技能、信息调研技能、公共演讲技能、商务礼仪等
	专业商务技能	商务谈判技能、贸易实务技能、电子商务技能、市场营销技能、人力资源管理技能、财务管理技能等
思辨与创新能力	认知能力	理解、推理、评价、分析、解释、自我调控、精确性、相关性、逻辑性、深刻性、灵活性等
	情感调适能力	好奇、开放、自信、建议、开朗、公正、诚实、谦虚、好学、包容等
自主学习能力	学科自学能力	自我规划能力、自我决策能力、自我监控能力、自我评价能力

（来源于《普通高等学校本科专业类教学质量国家标准（外国语言文学类）》）

《高等学校商务英语专业本科教学质量国家标准》对商务英语本科专业教学和评价提出了明确和具体的要求，涉及学生、教师和教学环节（王立非等，2015）。

英语应用能力指开展商务活动所需的英语语言知识与技能（陈准民，2009），包括语言组织能力、语言应用能力和学习策略能力，本书将通过听、说、读、写、译等综合交际语言能力来评估使用者的商务英语应用能力。

商务英语的跨文化交际能力指具备全球意识，通晓国际惯例和中外文化与礼仪，按照国际惯例从事各种国际商务活动，处理各种关系，用英语沟通和完成工作的能力（陈准民，2009）。跨文化交际能力主要包括基本跨文化交际能力和跨文化商务交际能力，涵盖了商务英语学习者跨文化交际中需要的知识和技能。跨文化交际能力是商务英语学习者应该具备的基本能力之一，是外语教学的主要任务（毕际万，2005）。

商务实践能力也是商务英语学习者能力培养的基本任务。商务知识与技能指普通和专业商务知识与学科思维和创新能力（陈准民，2009）。商务英语学习者需要掌握相关的通用商务技能和专业商务技能才能开展国际业务。技术和网络的发展对商务英语学习者的商务实践能力提出了更高的要求，因此，学习者要重视商务实践能力的培养。

思辨与创新能力是通用能力，对于所有学习者而言，培养思辨和创新能力非常重要。《普通高等学校本科专业类教学质量国家标准（外国语言文学类）》规定，思辨与创新能力主要包括认知能力和情感调适能力。本书将聚焦批判性思维能力来评估商务英语学习者的思辨与创新能力，如分析能力、问题解决能力、情感调适能力等。

自主学习能力是一切能力的基础，是学会学习的能力。在充满变化、日新月异的国际大环境中，为了增强竞争力，积极应对各种变化和挑战，商务英语学习者需要具备较强的自主学习能力。因此，《普通高等学校本科专业类教学质量国家标准（外国语言文学类）》规定，自主学习能力也是商务英语学习者应该具备的重要能力。

《普通高等学校本科专业类教学质量国家标准（外国语言文学类）》为所有高校商务英语的人才培养提供了指导方针。它规定商务英语教学的终极目标是培养能够专业、自信地参与国际商业活动的人才。要实现商务英语人才的培养目标，学习者和教师必须具备培养这五大能力的意识。然而，除了英语应用能力外，商务实践能力、跨文化交际能力、思辨与创新能力和自主学习能力这四项能力的培养在某种程度上被忽视。无疑，英语应用能力是商务英语学习者应该培养的核心能力，但其他四种能力也至关重要。

1.1.3　我国商务外语五大能力量表的现有研究

在我国商务外语课堂上，五大能力的培养没有得到足够的重视。这个问题的原因很复杂，其中一个主要原因是对五大能力没有严谨和系统的科学定义，因而对五大能力的判定有一定的难度。另外，我国目前缺少有效的能力量表来衡量和评估商务外语学习者的五大能力。这些都不利于对商务外语五大能力的培养和评估。

近年来，我国语言能力量表的发展取得了一定的进展。2018年6月正式实施的《中国英语能力等级量表》，标志着中国在英语能力等级量表方面取得了突破性进展。中国有了第一个具有中国特色的语言能力的参考标准（中华人民共和国教育部，2018）。该量表对商务外语语言应用能力量表的设计和发展具有一定的借鉴意义。目前，部分学者已经认识到开发商务外语能力量表的重要性（杨惠中，桂诗春，2007；赵雯等，2015），并且探讨了制定语言能力量表的方法与原则（方旭军等，2011），有的学者还尝试开发了《商务英语口语能力等级量表》（王淙等，2016）、《商务英语翻译能力量表》（王淙等，2015）、《商务英语写作能力量表》（方明，2010）、《商务英语阅读能力量表》（王淑花，2012；王淙，张国建，2020）。这些研究指出了开发商务英语语言能力量表的重要性和可行性，对本书商务外语人才能力量表的构建有一定的启示意义。但目前我国对于跨文化交际能力、商务实践能力、思辨与创新能力和自主学习能力四项能力的相关研究不多，对这四项能力相关评估量表的开发和验证更为少见。能力评估工具的缺乏会导致商务外语学习者和教师不重视能力的培养，因此，开发科学、实用的商务外语能力量表势在必行。

1.2　商务外语人才能力标准的目标设定

笔者旨在以《普通高等学校本科专业类教学质量国家标准（外国语言文学类）》提出的商务英语专业人才培养规格中的能力要求为框架，构建商务外语能力评价体系，为此将会回答以下问题：（1）商务外语学习者需要具备哪些能力？（2）每项能力指标体系的理论框架和操作模型是什么？如何构建？（3）商务外语学习者能力指标体系是什么？如何构建？

朱正才（2015）将能力量表的设计和发展分为五个阶段：构念阶段、量表架构的设计阶段、描述语数据的建设阶段、描述语的量表化阶段和量表的效度验证阶段。由于时间和精力有限，笔者只对能力量表设计的前三个阶段进行初步研究。

笔者写作本书的目的是唤起商务外语学习者对需具备的五大能力培养的重视，设计衡量五大能力的科学评价工具。笔者总结他人对五大能力的定义和语言能力量表设计的经验，对商务外语五大能力进行了清晰的界定，构建五大能力的理论框架，并据此建构操作模型、设计指标体系、收集描述语、设计量表，为商务外语能力测试提供科学的评价工具。

1.3　商务外语人才能力标准的研制方法

笔者运用定量与定性相结合的方法，对商务外语人才能力标准进行深入研究。基于其他人对五大能力的研究成果，确定商务外语能力的概念构造和设计框架，给出具有重大影响力的国际通用的能力量表中的相关描述语。这些能力量表来自大学、公司、组织等不同机构，可增强笔者设计的能力量表的广泛应用性、有效性、可操作性、国际性。

在《商务外语语言应用能力量表》的设计中，笔者主要从以下量表中收集描述语：欧洲语言测试者协会开发的《"CAN DO"语言能力量表》（*Can Do Project*）、加拿大语言等级标准中心开发的《加拿大语言等级标准——基本技能比较框架》（*Canadian Language Benchmarks—Essential Skills Comparative Framework*）、培生集团开发的《职业英语学习目标全球规范》（*Global Scale of English Learning Objectives for Professional English*）和欧洲理事会开发的《欧洲语言共同参考框架：学习、教学、评估》（*Common European Framework of Reference Language：Learning，Teaching，Assessment*）。

在《商务外语跨文化交际能力量表》的设计中，笔者收集了来自大学、国家语言政策制定机构、国家语言能力测试机构等开发的重要的语言交际能力量表作为描述语来源，如美国学院和大学协会开发的《跨文化知识和能力价值量表》（*Intercultural Knowledge and Competence Value Rubrics*）、著名能力测试机构 Workitect 开发的《工作角色和熟练水平能力量表》（*Competence by Job Role and Proficiency Level*）、Metiri 集团和北中地区教育实验室开发的《全球能力量表》（*Global Competence Inventory*）、David C. Thomas 的《文化智力简短量表》（*Short Form Measure of Cultural Intelligence*）和 Links Inc 的《跨文化敏感性量表》（*Intercultural Sensitivity Scale*）。

在《商务外语自主学习能力量表》的设计中，笔者主要从以下四个重要的自主学习能力量表中收集描述语：《跨文化知识和能力价值量表》《有效终身学习量表》（*The Effective Lifelong Learning Inventory*）、《个人胜任力——培养学生学习能力的框架》（*Personal Competency—A Framework for Building Students' Capacity to Learn*）和《自我导向学习量表》（*Self-directed Learning Readiness Scale*）。

在《商务外语批判性思维能力量表》的设计中，笔者收集了批判性思维能力量表中最具代表性和权威性的量表，分别是：《跨文化知识和能力价值量表》《批判性思维动机量表》（*Critical Thinking Motivational Scale*）、《整体批判性思维评分量表》（*Holistic Critical Thinking Scoring Rubric*）、美国教育考试服务中心（ETS）开发的《HEIghten 批评性思维测试》（HEIghten ® Critical Thinking Assessment）以及《加利福尼亚批判性思维倾向量表》等。

在《商务实践能力量表》的设计中，笔者收集了《商务（通用）管理能力量表》[*Business（General）Management Chart of Competency*]、《领导能力等级量表》（*Proficiency Levels for Leadership Competencies*）、《工作角色和熟练水平能力量表》、《特许全球管理会计师能力框架》（*The Chartered Global Management Accountant Competency Framework*）4 个具有国际权威性的商务实践能力量表。

这些国际通用的量表对本书量表的设计意义重大，对笔者科学地设计能力量表、收集相关描述语具有重要的参考价值。

1.4　商务外语人才能力标准的开发意义

商务外语人才能力标准的开发意义可分为实践意义和理论意义。理论上，笔者将在他人研究的基础上整合并完善商务外语五大能力的理论基础和理论模型，从而为能力量表的设计奠定理论基础。实践中，商务外语五大能力量表的设计可以为商务外语学习者、教师、测试人员和相关政策制定者提供重要的能力衡量标准。对商务外语学习者的能力量表的相关研究目前在我国尚不多见，国外也无现成的量表可用，希望笔者的研究能为商务外语能力量表的构建添砖加瓦。

商务外语专业能力不是商务知识和外语听、说、读、写、译等能力的简单叠加，必须对语言、商务、交际、教育和文化等进行多元化、多层次考察，才能得出科学的结论。希望笔者设计的商务外语能力量表能够为商务外语学习者、教师和其他使用者提供实用的应用型能力评价工具。

本书共分为 6 章。在第 1 章，笔者明确了商务外语人才能力标准开发的背景、目标设定、研制方法、意义。之后几章，笔者介绍了商务外语学习者根据《国标》需要掌握的语言应用能力、跨文化交际能力、商务实践能力、批判性思维能力和自主学习能力这五大能力。每章的内容可以分为四大部分（见图 1–3）：国内外相关研究与概念界定、理论框架、模型构建、量表设计。笔者通过梳理和完善其他学者对这五大能力的定义，构建了系统的操作框架，从而为五个能力量表的设计奠定了科学的理论基础。此外，笔者广泛收集了通用的相关领域的国际能力量表，从中仔细选择并修订描述语，以建立能力尺度的描述语数据库。之后，笔者根据之前建立的指标体系和收集并修订的描述语，设计一个适用于商务外语学习者能力评估的科学的能力量表，最后总结全书的主要成果，即设计的商务英语量表及其意义，指出量表的局限性以及今后的研究方向。

图 1–3　商务外语能力量表的研究思路

第 **2** 章

商务外语语言应用能力量表

语言应用能力是《国标》规定的商务外语学习者应该具备的基本能力，是其他四种能力的基础。但是，语言应用能力是不是等同于语言能力？在商务外语中，语言的应用主要体现在哪些方面？如何通过语言应用能力量表来评估商务外语学习者的语言应用能力？

国际贸易的本质是货物与服务的国际交换，是为达成特定的商业目的以交际为核心的跨文化活动。因此，对于商务外语学习者而言，语言应用能力是在各种交际场合，尤其是商务交际场合使用语言来满足现实生活中各种交际需求的能力（蔡基刚，2018）。

商务外语学习者仅仅具备一定的语言知识并不能完成工作中的各种交际任务，学习者的语法能力并不能很好地体现语言能力（Tucker，1974），语言的本质功能是交际（Hymes，1972），交际是语言使用的根本目的（Munby，1981）。因此，语言交际能力可综合评估商务外语学习者的语言应用能力。

2.1 国内外语言应用能力的相关研究

如前文所述"语言交际能力可综合评估商务外语学习者的语言应用能力"，所以本部分的综述所选用的关键词为"语言交际能力"。

2.1.1 国外语言应用能力的相关研究

目前，国外对语言应用能力的研究主要有基本语言交际能力理论研究、社会语言学语言交际能力研究和综合语言交际能力理论研究（见图 2–1）。

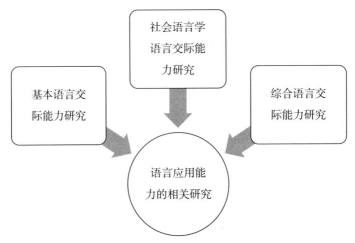

图 2–1 语言应用能力的相关研究

基本语言交际能力理论关注语言交际技能，主要描述学习者在外语交际情境中最常见的所需沟通的技能（Schulz，1977）。然而，基本语言交际能力研究忽视了交际能力的一些要素，例如，话语在社会政治背景下的适当性或话语知识（Rivers，1972），而且，这类研究并不强调语法的准确性，而是强调意思理解（Palmer，1978）。另外，基本语言交际能力理论并没有明确定义学习者完成交际任务的最低技能水平，这是它的一个不足。

在基本语言交际能力理论的基础上，一些研究者从社会语言学角度出发，对语言交际能力理论予以进一步完善，形成了社会语言学语言交际能力理论（Halliday，1978）。Hymes 模型将语言使用规则定义为交际能力的一个关键组成部分，这是语言交际能力理论发展的一个进步。事实上，任何一种语言都存在一定的社会意义的外延，说母语的人在特定语境中的话语可能会产生不同的意义。因此，学习者对第二语言的社会语言知识的理解和运用非常重要（Morrow，1977；Oller，1979）。虽然 Hymes 提出的语言交际能力框架促进了语言交际能力理论的发展，但一些基本问题仍有待澄清：例如，社会语境和语法形式如何相互作用，从而对语言理解和使用产生影响。尽管如此，社会语言学语言交际能力理论作为交际能力理论中一个至关重要的构成部分，可以帮助人们从社会语言学的角度来观察语言交际能力，探讨社会语境、语法对语言使用的影响。

综合语言交际能力理论是语言交际能力理论体系的一个重要组成部分（Allen，1978；Stern，1983；Widdowson，1975），它整合其他交际能力理论的研究成果，从话语层面考量个人语言交际能力。语言交际能力主要包括社会语言学知识、语言知识和基于话语规则的社会语义知识。然而，语言交际能力过分强调语言功能，而缺乏对语法复杂性的重视。

从以上语言交际能力的研究来看，语言知识或语言规则是语言交际能力的基础。学习者在运用相关的语法知识进行交流的过程中，应考虑语法复杂性等因素。另外，相关研究并不太关注说话者的交际策略。

2.1.2　国内语言应用能力的相关研究

语言交际能力理论传入中国后，相关研究在中国成为一个重要的课题，在外语教学中越来越受到重视。束定芳在他人的研究基础上提出交际能力是一个人运用各种可能的语言和非语言（如身体语言、面部表情等）手段来达到某种交际目的的能力，这种能力实际上体现了一个人的整体素质。它涉及以下几个方面的因素。

（1）语言知识，即组词成句、连句成段的能力。

（2）认识能力，即一个人对事物的认识、智力水平、反应能力和有关世界的知识等。

（3）文化知识，指一个人关于文化观念和习俗的知识。

（4）文体知识，指一个人根据交际对象和交际目的，选用不同风格的语词和句篇等进行交际的能力。

（5）其他知识，包括副语言知识，如身体语言、面部表情等。

（6）情感因素，一个人对他人及事物的社会态度及其交际动机、个人品质、性格和习惯等对交际能力也有影响。

束定芳在研究中强调语言理解能力对语言交际能力的重要性。语言交际是一个信息交流的互动过程，不仅包括表达部分，即发出信息，还包括理解部分，即接受信息。语言的表达和理解就像一张纸的两面，两者不可分割。语言理解能力从某种意义上讲比表达能力更为重要。

我国有关语言交际能力的研究落后于国外。吉哲民指出，中国的语言交际能力研究存在忽视书面语交际能力和忽视理解能力的现象。我国语言交际能力的研究集中于对交际能力具体内容的研究和在语言教学中如何有效获得交际能力的探索。由于研究领域的拓宽，交际水平理论涉及越来越多的语言内容，但相关的综合研究却几乎是空白。

语言交际能力是一个复杂的概念，它涉及语言、修辞、社会、文化、心理等诸多方面的因素。在中国，对商务外语学习者交际能力的研究还不够，还需要我们不断探索。当然，前人有关交际能力的研究对商务英语学习者交际能力的培养还是有一定借鉴意义的。笔者以交际能力理论框架和商务英语测评、博思职业外语水平测试、托业[①]等商务外语相关测试为基础，设计了商务外语语言应用能力量表，为使用者提供科学的测量工具。

2.1.3　语言应用能力的概念界定

提高语言应用能力是语言教育的根本目标，它并不是指学习者能在多大程度上了解语法规则并运用这些规则，更多的是评估学习者根据不同的语言应用场景完成交际目的的能力（**Widdowson**，1989）。

语言应用能力对每个人都至关重要，因为它能衡量个人完成复杂沟通任务的能力，对每个人的生活、教育、职业发展等方面都有重要影响（**Calculator**，2009；**Lund & Light**，2007）。商务外语学习者不仅要了解目标语言的准确表达方式，还要学习如何在商务交际场景中和特定的社会情境中使用这些语言表达方式，传达适当、连贯和有效的意义，完成交际目的。

[①] 针对在国际工作环境中使用英文交流的人而指定的英语能力测试考试，由美国教育考试服务中心主办。

2.2　语言应用能力的理论基础

语言应用能力的理论基础是语言交际能力理论。语言交际能力理论是 20 世纪 70 年代初由美国人类学教授、社会语言学家 Hymes 首先提出的。在 80 年代初加拿大学者 Canale 和 Swain 对其进行了补充，在 80 年代末 90 年代初又由美国学者 Bachman 作了进一步发展。这些学者对交际能力或语言交际能力的研究，代表了语言应用能力研究的三个发展阶段。

2.2.1　Hymes 的语言交际能力理论

"交际能力"一词源于 Hymes 对 Chomsky 关于社会语言学角度的"语言学能力"概念的挑战。Chomsky 将语言能力定义为母语使用者的语言（或语法）系统。从 Chomsky 的视角来看，语言能力理论等同于语法理论，即能够生成和描述语言的规则。Hymes 指出，Chomsky 的定义忽视了最重要的语言能力构成因素，即交际目的，他认为一个人应该不仅能按本族语的习惯说出合乎语法的句子，而且应该能在一定的场合和情境中使用最恰当的语言形式，这就是人们所应具有的交际能力。

（1）懂得哪些句子是合乎语法的。

（2）懂得哪些句子是可以被人们接受的。

（3）懂得哪些话是恰当的。

（4）懂得哪些话是常用的。

Hymes 认为交际能力包括以下几个方面的参数：（1）语法性；（2）可接受性；（3）得体性；（4）有效性（见图 2-2）。Hymes 提出的语言交际能力理论为语言交际能力理论的研究打下了坚实的基础。但应该指出的是，尽管 Hymes 提出的交际能力理论试图使交际能力与一定的语境、对象、目的联系起来，但它仍和 Chomsky 提出的语言交际能力一样，是一个绝对的、静态的、抽象的和理想化的概念（薛荣，2008）。交际能力应该是一个相对的、动态的、具体的、可比的概念。尽管如此，Hymes 对语言交际能力的研究大大推动了语言交际能力理论的发展，使后人能在其理论基础上不断丰富、完善语言交际能力理论体系。

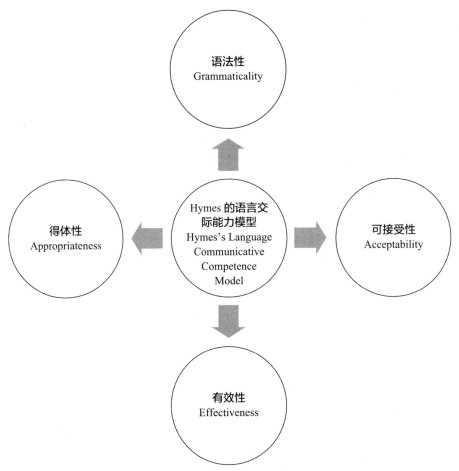

图 2-2　Hymes 的语言交际能力模型

2.2.2　Canale 和 Swain 的语言交际能力理论

20 世纪 80 年代，Canale 和 Swain 提出了一个有影响力的语言交际能力模型（见图 2-3），该模型在应用语言学界影响很大，为外语测试提供了比较科学的理论基础。在 Canale 和 Swain 的模型中，交际能力由四种能力组成：语法能力、社会语言能力、语篇能力和策略能力。

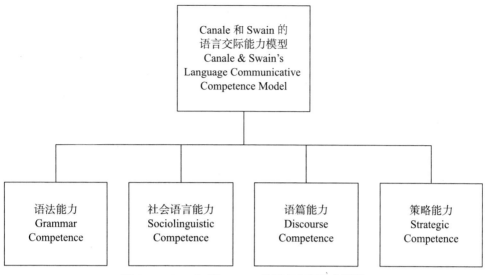

图 2-3　Canale 和 Swain 的语言交际能力模型

语法能力是指学习者能够使用语法上正确的话语的能力，学习者需要掌握词汇学、句法学、语义学和语音学等知识。语法能力是交际理论的一个重要关注点，可以为学习者提供如何确定和表达话语字面含义的知识。尽管目前对语法能力的重视程度不似以往，但我们不能否认语法能力对于语言交际能力的重要性。

社会语言能力是产生适当的社会话语的能力，学习者应该掌握与谁、何时、何地和以何种方式交流（**Hymes，1972**）。它涉及语言使用的社会规则以及对语言使用中社会背景的理解，主要包括社会语言技能和社会关系技能。社会语言技能主要指交际的语用能力，社会关系技能主要指建立有效关系基础的人际沟通技能。

语篇能力是产生连贯且一致的话语的能力。连贯是一个联系的概念，它涉及如何在文本中结构化地组织文字并阐释文字的意义。一致性与话语的交际价值（或上下文意义）之间的关系有关（**Widdowson，1978**）。

策略能力是解决沟通问题的能力，是指在真实的交际情景下应对和保持沟通畅通的能力。正确的策略可以用来弥补对规则的不了解或者其他因素的干扰，如交际疲劳、注意力不集中和外界干扰等。

2.2.3 Bachman 的语言交际能力理论

20 世纪 90 年代，美国著名应用语言学家 Bachman 借鉴和发展了 Halliday、Hymes 等人的研究成果，提出了新的交际能力理论模式，被认为是"语言测试史上的里程碑"。Bachman 对语言交际能力进行了十分详细和严格的定义。他认为语言交际能力包括语言能力（Language Competence）、策略能力（Strategic Competence）和心理生理机制（Psychophysiological Mechanism）三部分（见图 2–4）。

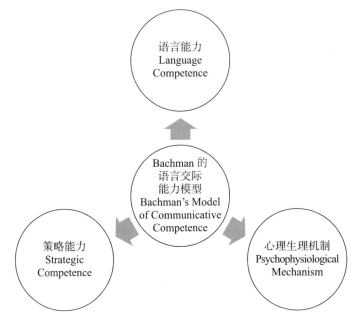

图 2–4　Bachman 的语言交际能力模型

（1）语言能力

在 Bachman 看来，语言能力包括语法规则知识和如何使用语言达到特定交际目的的知识，他认为语言能力包括两部分：语言组织能力和语用能力，其中每种能力又可以分成更小的范畴（见表 2–1）。

1）语言组织能力

语言组织能力包括控制语言形式结构的能力、能够生成和辨认语法正确的句子及理解命题内容并把句子按顺序排列成语篇的能力。语言组织能力又可以进一

表 2-1　语言能力分类

语言能力	组织能力	语法能力	词汇
			语法
			句法
			语音
		语篇能力	衔接
			修辞手段
	语用能力	言外能力	表意功能
			操作（控制）功能
			启发功能
			想象功能
		社会语言能力	对语言变体的敏感性
			对语域的敏感性
			对地道语言的敏感性
			对文化所指和修辞语的敏感性

步分为语法能力和语篇能力。语法能力由几个彼此相关而又独立的成分组成，包括词汇、语法、句法和语音等方面的知识。语篇能力指根据衔接和修辞手段的规则，把两个或两个以上的话语或句子连接成语篇的能力。

2）语用能力

使用交际语言时必然会涉及语言使用者和交际语境的关系，因此，在 Bachman 的语言交际能力模型中，语用能力是语言能力的一个重要组成部分。语用能力由言外能力和社会语言能力组成。言外能力具有表意、操作、启发和想象的功能，这四个功能是同时在语言交际行为中起作用的。社会语言能力指人们对语言惯用准则的敏感性或控制能力，它取决于特定语言使用环境中的特征，涉及对语言变体、语域的敏感性，对地道语言的敏感性及对文化所指和修辞语的敏感性。

（2）**策略能力**

策略能力是指在具体情景下运用语言知识进行交际的心理能力，它是语言使用中的一个重要部分，是一种综合运用已掌握的知识解决问题的能力，语言使用者的策略能力使其能将语言能力与知识结构和交际情境的特征联系起来。例如，当语言使用者的语言能力出现障碍时，他的策略能力会起到某种补偿作用，以保证交际的顺利进行。

（3）心理生理机制

心理生理机制是语言交际时的一种神经和生理过程，如在接收语言过程中使用的是视听技能，而在产生语言的过程中使用的是神经肌肉技能。心理生理机制涉及信息输入和信息产出的生理、心理过程，由于该机制对研究手段和工具要求很高，其具体操作过程还有待深入研究。

Bachman 的语言交际理论的一个重要意义在于，他认为语言使用是一个动态过程，语言能力的各成分之间互相作用。Bachman 认为语言交际能力的构成及其成分有内在关系（见图 2–5）。

图 2–5 中的知识结构指语言使用者的社会文化知识及关于现实世界的知识。语言使用环境包括交际双方、环境、话题和目的等。Bachman 强调语言在具体环境、社会文化背景下的使用，认为语言能力不仅是对语言知识的掌握，更重要的是运用所掌握的知识进行有效交际。

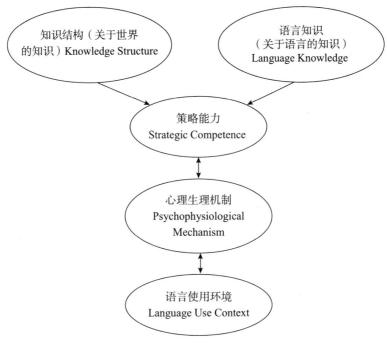

图 2–5　Bachman 的语言交际能力架构

Bachman 的语言交际能力理论是迄今为止我们所能见到的语言能力理论中最全面、最完整的（徐强，苏晓军，2000）。本书将在 Bachman 的语言交际能力理论的基础上构建商务外语语言应用能力的操作模型。

2.3　商务外语语言应用能力模型的构建

Bachman 的语言交际能力模型包括学习者对第二语言的了解以及如何使用第二语言，在有意义的语言情境中能够实际展示其知识的能力。它是交际能力的综合理论，包括综合的语法知识、语言在社会语境中的应用知识以及如何执行交际功能的知识。本书的《商务外语语言应用能力量表》是建立在 Bachman 的语言交际能力理论基础上的，通过综合衡量商务外语语言能力、商务外语策略能力、心理生理机制，对学习者完成语言任务的应用能力进行评价（见图 2–6）。商务外语语言应用能力不仅仅是语言与商务知识的融合，它是在一定的语境下，尤其是商务语境下，借助语言知识，产生互动增值效应的能力。

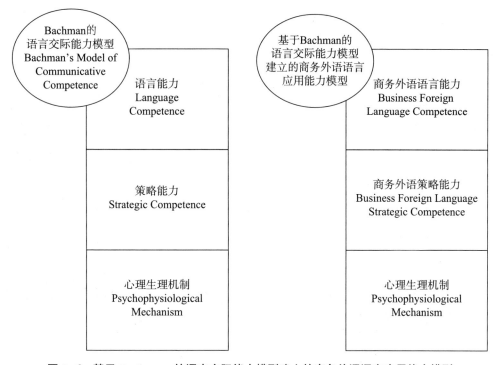

图 2–6　基于 Bachman 的语言交际能力模型建立的商务外语语言应用能力模型

2.3.1 商务外语语言能力

在商务外语领域，商务外语语言能力要从沟通、文化、组织、商业、信息传播、职业行为等多视角来研究（严明，2012）。商务外语语言能力包括语法规则知识和如何使用商务语言达到特定商务交际目的的能力，是基于体裁和情境的商务外语话语能力。连贯性和一致性是评估商务外语语言能力的两个最重要的指标。连贯性是与话语能力最密切相关的一个语言能力（Halliday，1976），它涉及有助于生成文本的自下而上的元素，如说明代词、指示词、文章其他标记语在书面和口头话语中的使用。一致性与话语的宏观结构有关，重点是自上而下一致地表述内容和目的。语言使用者应该在特定的语言环境中使用适合的语言。在商务环境下，语言的使用应遵循礼貌原则、委婉原则，但它是服务于交际目的的，商务外语语言能力也指学习者通过语言功能完成商务交际任务的能力。

2.3.2 商务外语策略能力

商务外语策略能力指沟通并解决问题的能力。在真实的商务交际情境下，商务外语学习者应具备良好的沟通能力和使用适当的社会话语的能力。商务外语策略能力包括社会语言技能和社会关系语言技能。社会语言技能是指交际的语用能力，即话语技巧（例如话语轮次、发起和终止交际、维持和发展交际）和表达交际目的的技能（例如引起关注、请求信息、提供信息、确认信息）。社会关系语言技能是指建立有效关系基础的人际沟通技能。社会语言技能，涉及语言使用的社会规则以及对语言使用中社会背景的理解。参与者在交际中的作用、社会地位、共享的信息以及交际的目的等因素都影响着交际。同时，社会背景是指嵌入某一特定文化环境中的道德规范、价值观、信仰和行为模式等。

2.3.3 心理生理机制

前文说过，交际语言能力的心理生理机制是一个非常复杂的研究课题，对其进行测量有一定的难度，虽然心理生理机制是商务外语交际语言能力理论框架的一个组成部分，但是此项能力在本书中不作过多说明。

2.4　《商务外语语言应用能力量表》的设计

　　语言能力、策略能力和心理生理机制是衡量商务外语学习者语言应用能力的重要因素，笔者将基于这三大能力，结合听、说、读、写、译等交际任务来设计《商务外语语言应用能力量表》，综合评估商务外语学习者的语言应用能力。

2.4.1　商务外语语言应用能力指标体系

　　结合 Bachman 的语言交际能力理论和商务外语的学科特征，笔者建立了商务外语语言应用能力模型。基于此模型，笔者又建立了商务外语语言应用能力指标体系（见图 2–7），以期尽量全面、科学地评估学习者的语言能力。

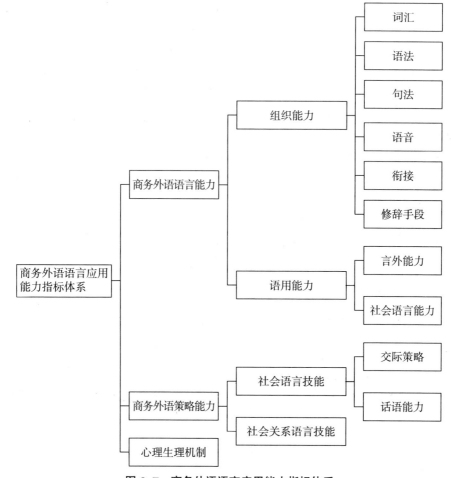

图 2–7　商务外语语言应用能力指标体系

2.4.2　描述语的来源

笔者主要收集了四个国际上应用最广泛的语言应用能力量表,《商务外语语言应用能力量表》主要从这四个语言应用能力量表中选取描述语（见表2-2）。这四个语言应用能力量表是：欧洲语言测试者协会的《"CAN DO"语言能力量表》《加拿大语言等级标准——基本技能比较框架》《职业英语学习目标全球规范》《欧洲语言共同参考框架：学习、教学、评估》。

表2-2　《商务外语语言应用能力量表》的描述语来源

量表	开发者	时间（年）
《"CAN DO"语言能力量表》(Can Do Project)	欧洲语言测试者协会 (Association of Language Tester in Europe)	2002
《加拿大语言等级标准——基本技能比较框架》(Canadian Language Benchmarks—Essential Skills Comparative Framework)	加拿大语言等级标准中心 (Center for Canadian Language Benchmarks)	2012
《职业英语学习目标全球规范》(Global Scale of English Learning Objectives for Professional English)	培生集团 (Pearson Group)	2018
《欧洲语言共同参考框架：学习、教学、评估》(Common European Framework of Reference Language: Learning, Teaching, Assessment)	欧洲理事会 (European Council)	2001

2.4.2.1　欧洲语言测试者协会的《"CAN DO"语言能力量表》

《"CAN DO"语言能力量表》由欧洲语言测试者协会发布，该协会建立了语言表现的"关键水平"框架，旨在开发和验证一组与语言表现相关的量表，描述学习者在外语学习中实际可以做什么。《"CAN DO"语言能力量表》有400条左右描述语，描述语主要包括三部分：（1）社会；（2）旅游；（3）工作和学习。笔者针对商务外语的交际语言能力框架，主要收集了有关工作和学习的描述语。欧洲语言测试者协会将语言能力共分为入门级、等级1、等级2、等级3、等级4、等级5，共6个等级，结合听说、阅读和写作三大语言任务，采用"CAN DO"的描述形式，可以详细评估使用者的语言交际能力（见图2-8）。

ALTE study statements summary

ALTE Level	Listening/Speaking	Reading	Writing
ALTE Level 5	CAN understand jokes, colloquial asides and cultural allusions.	CAN access all sources of information quickly and reliably.	CAN make accurate and complete notes during the course of a lecture, seminar or tutorial.
ALTE Level 4	CAN follow abstract argumentation, for example the balancing of alternatives and the drawing of a conclusion.	CAN read quickly enough to cope with the demands of an academic course.	CAN write an essay which shows ability to communicate, giving few difficulties for the reader.
ALTE Level 3	CAN give a clear presentation on a familiar topic, and answer predictable or factual questions.	CAN scan texts for relevant information and grasp the main point of the text.	CAN make simple notes that will be of reasonable use for essay or revision purposes.
ALTE Level 2	CAN understand instructions on classes and assignments given by a teacher or lecturer.	CAN understand basic instructions and messages, for example, computer library catalogues, with some help.	CAN write down some information at a lecture, if this is more or less dictated.
ALTE Level 1	CAN express simple opinions using expressions such as "I don't agree."	CAN understand the general meaning of a simplified text book or article, reading very slowly.	CAN write a very short simple narrative or description, such as "my last holiday."
ALTE Break-through Level	CAN understand basic instructions on class times, dates and room numbers, and on assignments to be carried out.	CAN read basic notices and instructions.	CAN copy times, dates and places from notices on classroom board or notice board.

图 2-8 欧洲语言测试者协会《"CAN DO"语言能力量表》节选

2.4.2.2 《加拿大语言等级标准——基本技能比较框架》

第二个重要的可供参考的语言交际能力量表是《加拿大语言等级标准——基本技能比较框架》。其最初旨在发展和衡量在加拿大就业的移民的语言水平。该语言等级标准结合工作中需要的口头交流、文本阅读、资料使用、写作等核心技能，评估学习者听、说、读、写等综合语言交际能力。《加拿大语言等级标准——基本技能比较框架》将语言能力分为六个等级，包含数百条描述语。由于该量表的设计主要是为了满足把英语作为第二语言的移民的需求，评估其在工作场所的语言交际能力，因此，该量表对于《商务外语语言应用能力量表》的设计有借鉴意义。图 2-9 是《加拿大语言等级标准——基本技能比较框架》的四个基本维度及基本技能要求；图 2-10 是该量表的描述语节选。

Canadian Language Benchmarks	Essential Skills
Listening	Oral Communication
Speaking	Oral Communication
Reading	Reading Text
Reading	Document Use
Writing	Writing
	Numeracy
	Thinking Skills
	Working with Others
	Computer Use
	Continuous Learning

图 2-9 《加拿大语言等级标准——基本技能比较框架》的基本维度及基本技能要求

Listening - CLB 12			ES - Oral Communication			
Associated ES Skills & Levels:	Oral Communication		Pre-ES	ES 1	ES 2	ES 3	ES 4

CLB Profile of Ability

The listener can:

Understand an extensive range of complex, abstract formal and informal communication on most general and specialized topics.

When the communication is:	Demonstrating these strengths and limitations:
Spoken clearly at a normal to fast rate	Identifies, analyzes and critically evaluates communication
Face-to-face, on the phone or via digital media (with individuals, small or larger groups)	Understands a wide range of concrete, abstract and technical language appropriate for the content and purpose
Related to unfamiliar, abstract, conceptual or technical matters	Uses knowledge of complex grammar and syntax to interpret nuances in meaning
Lengthy	Infers meaning from almost all unstated information
In demanding contexts	Recognizes the nuances in different styles, registers and language varieties
	Has almost no difficulty interpreting verbal humour, ow-frequency idioms, irony, sarcasm, cultural references and figurative, symbolic and idiomatic language

图 2-10 《加拿大语言等级标准——基本技能框架》描述语节选——听力五级

结合商务外语语言交际能力模型，笔者选取了《加拿大语言等级标准——基本技能框架》中与商务场景相关的描述语和交际语言，因此，该量表对《商务外语语言应用能力量表》的设计意义重大。

2.4.2.3 《职业英语学习目标全球规范》

第三个重要的国际语言交际能力量表是《职业英语学习目标全球规范》，它旨在准确定义学习者的英语能力标准，描述其英语能力的特定"水平"。《职业英语学习目标全球规范》将语言能力分为六个等级，描述语主要包括四部分：公共生活、个人领域、教育领域和职业领域，从不同方面评估学习者完成听、说、读、写的语言任务的能力。图 2-11 是《职业英语学习目标全球规范》在教育和职业领域的部分描述语。

2.4.3 《商务外语语言应用能力量表》的研制

2.4.3.1 《商务外语语言应用能力量表》

笔者以商务外语的语言应用能力理论为基础，收集国际上三大重要的应用语言能力量表，通过考察学习者在工作场中听、说、读、写、译等交际任务的完成情况，综合评估其语言交际能力水平。笔者构建的《商务外语语言应用能力量表》篇幅较长，具体量表请参见附录1。

Writing

GSE 10–21/Below A1: Writing

10	Can write the letters of the alphabet in upper and lower case. (P)
	Can write their name, address and nationality. (C$_A$)
12	Can write cardinal numbers from 1 to 20 as words. (CSE$_A$)
18	Can copy familiar words and short phrases about everyday objects and set phrases. (C$_A$)
20	Can write consistently with joined-up letters. (P)

GSE 22–29/A1: Writing

23	Can complete simple forms with basic personal details. (C$_A$)
24	Can copy short sentences on everyday subjects (e.g. directions how to get somewhere). (C)
25	Can write simple sentences about things that they and other people have. (P)
26	Can use basic punctuation (e.g. commas, full stops, question marks). (P)
27	Can write simple sentences about personal interests. (P)
	Can spell a range of common names. (P)
	Can write simple sentences about their family and where they live. (C$_A$)
	Can complete a simple form requiring travel information (e.g. landing card, customs declaration). (P)
28	Can write dates using both digits and words. (P)
	Can spell a range of common greetings. (P)
	Can spell a range of common jobs. (P)
	Can write simple sentences about someone's life and routines. (P)
	Can write short, simple notes, emails and postings to friends. (N2000$_A$)

图 2–11　《职业英语学习目标全球规范》描述语节选

经过收集、筛选、修订、整理，《商务外语语言应用能力量表》共包含 250 条 "CAN DO" 描述语，涉及个人活动和社会活动的多项语言任务，下面是该量表的描述语节选（见表 2–3）。学习者可根据完成本量表中的语言任务的情况，评估自己的语言应用能力水平。

表 2–3　《商务外语语言应用能力量表》描述语节选

A1	10	CAN provide personal information, such as name and address, and spell some of the words orally.
A1	11	CAN follow a short simple instruction.
A1	12	CAN identify price, tax and total on a receipt for supplies.

（续表）

A1	13	CAN choose words from a list to match illustrations of common familiar objects.
A1	14	CAN copy information from an invoice to complete a cheque.
A1	15	CAN address an envelope for mailing by following a model.
A1	16	CAN understand a short goodwill expression from a co-worker.
A1	17	CAN read a simple two-step instruction for a work task.
A1	18	CAN locate a specific short piece of information on a simple invoice.
A1	19	CAN read a simple customer comment and identify whether it is positive or negative.
A1	20	CAN fill out a simple form with date, first and last name, address, postal code, phone number, date of birth, age.
A2	21	CAN state simple requirements within my own job area.
A2	22	CAN understand most short reports or manuals of a predictable nature within his/her own area of expertise, provided that enough time is given.
A2	23	CAN write a short, comprehensible note of request to a colleague or a known contact in another company.
A2	24	CAN understand a simple work schedule.

2.4.3.2　对《商务外语语言应用能力量表》的分析

在《商务外语语言应用能力量表》中，学习者的语言应用能力被分为六个等级（A1、A2、B1、B2、C1、C2）见（表2-4）。在前两个等级（A1和A2）中，要求学习者可以理解有限的常见句型，使用一些常见、熟悉的单词和公式化的表达来回答与眼前需求有关的简单问题，完成简单的交际任务。中间水平的两个层次（B1和B2），要求学习者通过努力可以理解适度复杂、具体的语言形式，完成与日常生活和经验相关的交际任务，基本达到特定的交际目的。专业水平的两个等级（C1和C2），要求学习者可以理解和完成各种专业的、复杂的正式交流和非正式交流，完成一系列交际目的和任务，如自信地沟通非日常工作、教育和社会情况及介绍有关复杂、抽象的信息。

表 2-4　《商务外语语言应用能力量表》的等级

语言应用能力等级	
合格（A1-A2）	理解有限的、常规的语言公式，使用常见、熟悉的语言表达，完成简单的交际任务
良好（B1-B2）	理解适度复杂、具体的语言表达，在日常的社会情境中完成交际任务，基本达到交际目的
优秀（C1-C2）	理解和完成各种专业的、复杂的正式交流和非正式交流，完成一系列交际任务

（1）真实性

人们在社会生活中面临的交际任务纷繁复杂，选择什么样的任务进行测试能有效评估学习者的商务外语能力是测试应用者、组织者和开发者必须考虑的问题。《商务外语语言应用能力量表》强调"任务"与目标任务的一致性，即量表中的描述语与现实生活中语言使用任务的一致性，体现了该量表的真实性。

以"任务"为手段进行商务外语测试，目的在于通过测试结果推断学习者的商务外语能力，即预测学习者在目标语境中应用英语完成商务活动的能力。由于能力测试本身要受到时间、空间和测试项目容量等多方面的限制，因此，所应用的任务必须具有代表性，从而使测试结果具有可推断性，能够反映学习者的商务外语能力，如第 1 条 "CAN understand short reports or product descriptions on familiar matters, if these are expressed in simple language and the contents are predictable."，通过阅读短篇报告或者产品描述这个真实的任务，来评估学习者的语言能力。

学习者可通过《商务外语语言应用能力量表》测量他们对语言实际使用的熟练程度，因为量表中的语言任务，如制作或阅读简历、报告工作等是真实的。

（2）实用性

《商务外语语言应用能力量表》的另一个特点是实用性，其描述语都使用"可以做（CAN DO）"的表达方式，可以评估学习者在不同场合的语言交际表现。在特定情况和特定场景下，通过学习者完成的有意义的任务的语言表现或语言绩效来判定其语言应用能力，这是本量表衡量学习者语言应用能力的依据。首先，学习者通过与描述语进行对照，根据语言表现和能完成的语言任务评估自己的商务外语语言应用能力，由于操作简便，学习者能有效地进行自我评估和自我检测。其次，本量表的描述语简单易懂，通过对语言交际任务的明确描述为学习者提供衡量语言应用能力的指标。此外，本量表并不分别衡量每个语言应用能力的子能力，而是衡量学习者完成听、说、读、写等具体交际任务的综合能力，这样更能体现出语言能力评估的科学性和综合性。

第 **3** 章

商务外语跨文化交际能力量表

近年来，随着全球化进程的加快，跨文化交际能力习得的研究成为热门课题（Kuada，2004）。跨文化交际能力是国际化发展的必然需求。让学生更有效、更成功地生活、沟通和工作被认为是高等教育的核心目标之一（Cole，1994）。在中国，跨文化交际能力的培养也越来越重要，受到许多大专院校的重视。跨文化交际能力在包括商务外语在内的许多专业的国家教学大纲中已经被规定为学习者必须具备的核心能力。

毫无疑问，因为生活和工作在跨文化环境中，商务外语学习者必须发展自己的跨文化交际能力。尽管大家对跨文化交际能力的重要性有广泛的共识，但目前对学习者跨文化交际能力的评估仍然缺乏科学、系统的工具。虽然有关跨文化交际能力的理论研究很多，但学者们对如何评估跨文化交际能力，尤其是如何评估商务外语学习者的跨文化交际能力，仍缺乏共识。

作为商务外语能力量表中的一个关键量表，跨文化交际能力量表的研制必须引起足够的重视。通过科学的评估工具，学习者可以提升跨文化交际能力，找出他们的技能或知识差距。

3.1 国内外跨文化交际能力的相关研究

3.1.1 国外跨文化交际能力的相关研究

国外有关跨文化交际能力的研究比较多，成果也比较丰富，有关的量表和测试也很多。早在 1986 年，Bennett 等就进行了交际行为能力与跨文化适应性的研究，是较早运用测试的方法来评价和预测跨文化交际能力的学者。此后，许多学者都对此进行了相关研究，不断丰富跨文化交际能力理论。比较典型的是 Richard L. Griffith 等在 "Assessing Intercultural Competence in Higher Education：Existing Research and Future Directions" 一文中做的跨文化交际能力理论综述（见表 3–1）。

表 3–1　跨文化交际能力理论综述

Source(s)	Construct(s)/Dimensions	Description	Model Type
Bennett (1986)	Intercultural Sensitivity	"The way people construe cultural difference and ... the varying kinds of experience that accompany these constructions." Development of intercultural sensitivity through six stages: denial, defense/reversal, minimization, acceptance, adaptation, and integration	Developmental
Gallois, et al. (1988)	Intercultural Communicative Accommodation	Interacting individuals adjust their communication styles to match the other individual's style. Competence is judged both within and between groups	Adaptational
J.W. Berry, et al. (1989)	Acculturation	Views toward adapting to a foreign culture and retaining one's cultural identity can be both orthogonal and dichotomous	Adaptational
Imahori and Lanigan (1989)	Intercultural Competence	Relationship subfactors index, competent intercultural interaction between a sojourner and a host-national	Casual

（续表）

Source(s)	Construct(s)/ Dimensions	Description	Model Type
Y. Y. Kim (2000)	Host Communication Competence	One's adaptive capacity to suspend/ modify old cultural ways, learn/ accommodate to new cultural ways, and creatively manage dynamics of cultural difference/unfamiliarity and accompanying stress	Adaptational
Paige (1993)	Intercultural Learning	Ability to effectively function in an intercultural situation abroad overtime	Co-orientational
Gudykunst et al. (1994)	Global Competence	Motivation, knowledge, and skills make up global competence	Co-orientational
Lambert (1994)	Global Competence	World knowledge, foreign language proficiency, cultural empathy, approval of foreign people and cultures, ability to practice one's profession in an international setting	Compositional
Fantini (1995)	Intercultural Communicative Competence	1) The ability to develop and maintain relationships, 2) the ability to communicate effectively and appropriately with minimal loss or distortion, and 3) the ability to attain compliance and obtain cooperation with others	Co-orientational
Chen and Starosta (1996)	Intercultural Communication Competence	Ability to effectively and appropriately execute communication behaviors in a culturally diverse environment	Compositional
Byram (1997)	Communicative Competence (CC)	Knowledge of others; knowledge of self; skills to interpret and relate; skills to discover and/or to interact; valuing others' values, beliefs, and behaviors; and relativizing one's self. Linguistic competence plays a key role	Co-orientational

（续表）

Source(s)	Construct(s)/ Dimensions	Description	Model Type
Fennes and Hapgood (1997)	Intercultural Learning	The expand ability, flexibility, and adaptability of one's frame of reference/filter	Compositional
Howard-Hamilton, Richardson, and Shuford (1998)	ICC	Competence components consist of knowledge, attitudes, and skills across three levels: awareness, understanding, and appreciation of another culture	Compositional
Hammer, et al. (1998)	ICC	Satisfying intercultural interactions are mediated by conditions, strategies, and saliencies that lead to greater attribution confidence and reduction of uncertainty (anxiety)	Casual
Ting-Toomey and Kurogi (1998)	ICC	Cognitive and behavioral abilities are predicted to increase the likelihood of positive (appropriate, effective, mutually satisfying, and mutually adaptive) intercultural interactions	Compositional
Ting-Toomey (1999)	ICC	The ability to manage changes in the self and the environment brought about by individual, interpersonal, and systemic influences during intercultural encounters	Casual
D. A. Griffith and Harvey (2001)	Intercultural Communication Competence	A component in a network of intercultural constructs that can be collectively judged by the criterion of relationship quality; cultural understanding and intercultural communication competence directly predict relationship quality	Casual
Olebe and Koester (1989)	Intercultural Communication Effectiveness	Behaviors that a nonexpert, nonnative English speaker can reliably assess as effective or not in a cross-cultural setting	Compositional

（续表）

Source(s)	Construct(s)/ Dimensions	Description	Model Type
Lustig and Koester (2003)	ICC	Not comprised of individual traits or characteristics but rather the characteristic of the association between individuals. Dependent on the relationships and situations within which the interaction occurs. No prescriptive set of characteristics guarantees competence in all intercultural situations: "social judgment that people make about others."	Co-orientational
Deardorff (2004, 2006)	ICC	The ability to communicate effectively and appropriately in intercultural situations based on one's intercultural knowledge, skills, and attitudes	Compositional/ Causal
P. M. King and Baxter Magolda (2005)	Intercultural Maturity	Through ongoing study, observation, and interaction with individuals from another culture, one can develop greater intercultural awareness and sensitivity	Developmental
Navas, et al. (2005)	Relative Adaptation	Extent of competence depends on the alignment between the strategies actually used by one group and the preferences of the other group	Adaptational
W. D. Hunter, et al. (2006)	Global Competencies Model	A person should attempt to understand his or her own cultural box before stepping unto someone else's	Compositional
Rathje (2007)	ICC	Transformation of intercultural interaction into culture itself; the coproduction of culture, not just the reflection of common cultural identities	Co-orientational

（续表）

Source(s)	Construct(s)/ Dimensions	Description	Model Type
Arasaratnam (2009)	Intercultural Communication Competence	Intercultural communication competence is a direct function of cultural empathy. Motivation for competent communication is influenced by experience, interaction involvement, and one's global attitude, as well as prior experience with intercultural communication	Casual
Kupka (2008)	ICC	Impression management that allows members of different cultural systems to be aware of their cultural identity and cultural differences, and to interact effectively and appropriately with each other in diverse contexts by agreeing on the meaning of diverse symbol systems with the result of mutually satisfying relationships	Co-orientational

从表 3-1 中可以看出，国外众多学者从不同角度对跨文化交际能力进行了深入研究。此外，Lustig 和 Koester（1996，2003）认为成功的跨文化交际是在一定的情境之中发生的得体、有效的行为，学习者需要具备丰富的知识、合理的动机和有技巧的行动。Spitzberg（1989）指出，对成功的跨文化交际行为的判定是认定某一行为在给定环境下得体、有效，他认为交际环境是判定跨文化交际能力的一个重要因素。不难发现，上述定义中都提及了两个要素："特定环境"和"得体、有效"。

能力指的是一系列才能或者有技巧的行为。然而，对能力的判定会随着标准的不同而不断改变。在一种环境中被认为是有能力的行为完全有可能在另一种环境中被认为是无能的表现。对任何能力都不能孤立地判断，应该将其放在一定的环境中进行判断，因此，跨文化交际能力必须在特定环境中来考察。

有能力的跨文化交际者能与其他文化背景的成员进行得体、有效的交际。所谓得体，是指交际行为合理、适当，符合特定文化、特定交际情境，交际者之间的特定关系对交际的预期有效是指交际行为得到了预期的结果（Lusting & Koester 1996）。

除了"特定环境"与"得体、有效"，Wiseman 在对跨文化交际能力的定义中还提到了进行跨文化交际能力所必须具备的知识、意识和技能。知识指一个优秀的跨文化交际者，必须对交际所在地的文化有一定的了解，包括有关交际规则的知识或者有关文化禁忌的知识等。意识指的是在跨文化交际中的情感、意愿等主观感受。技能是指在交际中选择得体、有效行为的能力。

3.1.2　国内跨文化交际能力的相关研究

我国的跨文化交际能力研究虽然开始得比较晚，但是自 20 世纪 90 年代初至今取得了令人瞩目的成果。陈国明将跨文化交际能力定义为"在特定环境中有效、得体地完成交际行为以获得预期回应的能力"。这个定义表明具备跨文化交际能力的交际者不但要得体、有效地进行交际，而且还要通过这些能力获得预期的回应，达到自己的交际目的。

我国在跨文化交际的实证性研究方面成果不多，胡文仲是较早进行研究的学者之一。他在 1986 年和 1990 年分别做了两项关于文化差异的调查，引起了国内外语教学界对文化差异与语言学习关系的关注。胡文仲指出，中国文化与西方文化的差异是显而易见的，然而，在外语教学中我们过分重视语言的训练，却忽视了文化的习得。要改变这种情况，必须在教学中增加语用规则的讲解和文化信息的输入。王振亚的《社会文化测试分析》是国内较早涉及文化测试的研究。王振亚指出"语言能力和社会文化能力之间不存在相关关系，需要分别对待，单独培养"。刘建达也指出语言能力的提高不一定会导致语用能力的提高，教师应该在教学中增加语用知识的输入。这些研究成果也支持了"语言能力与跨文化交际能力不是同一种能力"的观点。

国内外对跨文化交际能力的研究构建了科学的跨文化交际能力体系，这对笔者有关跨文化交际能力的定义和研究帮助很大，尽管学者们在文化交际方面进行了大量的学术研究，但对商务活动中跨文化交际能力的研究还有待深入。商务外语中的跨文化研究交际能力的概念在较传统的跨文化研究方法中较难看到。鉴于跨文化交际能力对在国际环境中工作和生活的学习者的重要性，我们需要在国际商务背景下对跨文化交际能力进行定义。笔者对跨文化交际能力的定义将侧重于商务外语领域，《商务外语跨文化交际能力量表》也是针对商务外语专业设计的。

3.1.3　商务外语跨文化交际能力的概念界定

跨文化交际能力的研究目前是一个热门的学术问题，尤其是在语言研究中。尽管国内外对这一问题的理论研究很多，但对于商务外语中的跨文化交际能力，仍缺乏一个系统、科学、公正的评价量表。要为商务外语学习者设计一个实用的跨文化交际能力量表，需要考虑以下几个问题：这个专业需要什么样的跨文化交际技能和知识？学习者如何获得这些跨文化技能和知识？学习者需要掌握哪些新的知识、技能？需要具有什么样的学习态度？

要编制跨文化交际能力量表，就必须明确其基本概念。什么是跨文化交际能力？跨文化交际能力包括哪些要素？在学术研究中，"跨文化交际能力"一词很常见，因为它不受任何特定文化的制约（Bradford，2000）。

跨文化交际能力指在不同环境下与不同文化背景的人交际的能力，主要包括跨文化交际知识、跨文化交际态度和跨文化交际能力。

跨文化交际能力的研究相对复杂，学者们对跨文化交际能力的术语并没有达成共识（Deardorff，2006）。跨文化交际能力的术语因学科而异（Fantini，2009），其中包括跨文化敏感性、文化智力、国际沟通能力、跨文化沟通能力等。虽然这一概念在不同语境下的术语不同，但其主要研究内容和研究方法是相似的。

对于商务外语学习者来说，他们不仅面临着文化价值观的差异，而且要面对不同的经济、政治、法律、技术和社会制度。在国际商务交流中，他们要建立信誉、给予和接受反馈、获取信息、评估、建立全球合作团队等，因此，商务外语学习者面对的是一个相当复杂的跨文化交际环境（Gundling，2003）。简单来说，跨文化交际能力是"可以从有效的信息交流中建立和维持人际关系"。具体来说，商务外语的跨文化交际能力指在商务环境下，有效、得体地从事跨文化活动的能力。为了与国内外不同民族和文化背景的人有效地合作和沟通，商务外语学习者需要具有相应的跨文化交际知识、跨文化交际技能和跨文化交际意识，能综合调用各种资源，如知识、实际技能、运作计划、社会表现、价值观和态度等。

3.2　跨文化交际能力理论的框架

3.2.1　跨文化交际能力理论的五种模型

许多学者对跨文化交际能力理论模型有不同的理解，大体而言，可以分为五大类（见图 3-1）：组合式模型（e.g., Deardorff, 2006; Hunter, 2006）、双向互动模型（e.g., Kupka, 2003; Rathje, 2007）、发展性模型（e.g., Bennett, 1986; King, 2005）、适应性模型（e.g., Kim, 1988; Gallois 等, 1988）和因果过程模型（e.g., Arasaratnam, 2009; Griffith, 2001）。

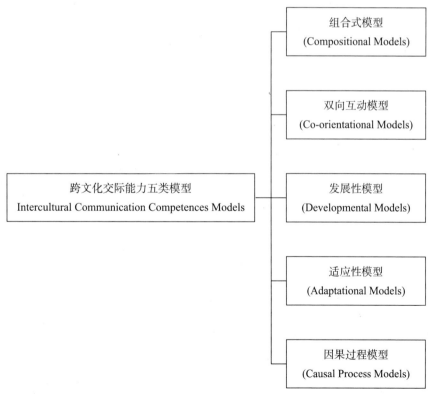

图 3-1　跨文化交际能力理论的五类模型

跨文化交际能力的五种模型是相辅相成的。组合式模型描述跨文化交际能力的特征（知识、技能和态度），例如，Deardorff（2006）认为跨文化交际能力是由跨文化敏感性、跨文化意识和语言/非语言技能等元素组成的。这是根据跨文化交际能力的组成部分下的定义。

双向互动模型倾向于描述成功的跨文化交流的要素或过程，如 Fantini（2001）认为跨文化交际能力由三项子能力组成：建立和保持关系的能力、以最少的损失进行有效和适当沟通的能力以及获得承诺和与他人合作的能力。

发展性模型从个体发展的角度来描述跨文化交际能力。例如，Bennett（1993）将跨文化交际能力定义为一种发展模式，学习者朝着"成功获得国际视角"的目标不断前进。该模型指出，这一过程包括克服种族中心主义、异文化移情的能力、跨文化沟通能力以及跨文化合作能力。发展模型的最大优点是，将跨文化交际能力的发展视为一个与外国文化互动或学习的过程，但很难准确地界定学习者处于哪个阶段，因为跨文化交际能力的培养是一个持续的过程，很难将其明确地划分为几个阶段，每个阶段的特点也很难描述，例如，不同阶段学习者的心理和认知情况是多变且灵活的。

适应性模型借鉴了发展模型的研究，将跨文化交际能力置于与外国文化互动和适应的环境中。这意味着跨文化交际能力的发展伴随着文化适应。适应模型强调跨文化交流适应（Gallois，1988），认为跨文化交际能力水平取决于一个群体实际使用的战略与其他群体的偏好之间的一致性。

因果过程模型整合了成分模型的特征和相互作用的变量。Griffith（2001）认为跨文化交际能力就是一个人运用跨文化知识技能和态度有效和适当地沟通的能力。在该模型中，跨文化交际能力要素之间的关系与跨文化交际能力的发展密切相关。

3.2.2　跨文化交际能力的重要理论

跨文化交际能力模型界定了跨文化交际能力和其组成要素，可以帮助教育工作者和学习者确定具体的跨文化交际能力的特征并将其转化为明确的学习目标。为构建完整的跨文化交际能力的理论框架，笔者基于 Arasaratnam 的模型及 Deardorff 的模型提出了新的跨文化交际能力模型。

（1）Arasaratnam 的跨文化交际能力模型

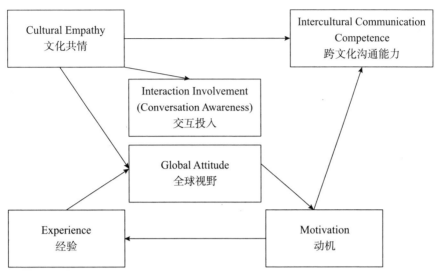

图 3-2　Arasaratnam 的跨文化交际能力模型

共情既能直接影响跨文化交际能力，也能通过交互投入和全球视野间接影响跨文化交际能力；全球视野受到跨文化沟通能力和互动经验的影响；动机影响跨文化沟通和互动经验，也直接影响跨文化交际能力。

（2）Deardorff 的跨文化交际能力模型

除了 Arasaratnam 的跨文化交际能力模型之外，Deardorff 的跨文化交际能力模型也是非常有影响力的。该模型包括五个关键要素：1）期望的外部结果；2）期望的内部结果；3）知识和理解；4）技能；5）必要的态度（见图 3-3）。

图 3-3　Deardorff 的跨文化交际能力模型

1）态度

尊重、开放和好奇是三个关键态度。尊重体现对不同文化背景的人的重视；开放和好奇则促使人们走出舒适区，积极探索不同文化，这是获取跨文化交际知识和技能的基础。

2）知识

包括文化自我意识、特定文化知识、深层文化知识（对其他世界观的理解）和社会语言意识。即了解自己的文化，掌握不同文化的具体特点和差异，理解不同文化的世界观以及对语言在社会交往中的运用等。

3）技能

观察、倾听、评估、分析、解释和关联等技能是处理知识所必需的。在与不同文化背景的人互动时，需要运用这些技能来理解和处理信息。

4）内部结果

由态度、知识和技能共同作用产生的内部结果，包括灵活性、适应性和同理心。具备这些能力的个体在一定程度上实现了跨文化交际能力，能够从他人视角看问题，并以他人期望的方式回应。

5）外部结果

个体基于态度、知识、技能和内部结果所展现出的行为和沟通技巧，即有效且恰当的行为和沟通，是跨文化交际能力的外在可见表现。

3.2.3　跨文化交际能力的要素

学者们从不同的角度对跨文化交际能力模型进行了研究，从他们的研究中可以得出一个结论，即跨文化交际能力包括知识、情感或认知、行动、态度和技能五个层面的能力。

从知识层面而言，要完成跨文化交际，学习者必须学习一般文化知识。学习者的跨文化交际能力在所有跨文化交际情况下都应保持恒定（Kim，1992）。本书应用"深层文化知识"或"文化常识"来描述学习者的跨文化交际能力。深层文化知识是指对文化和知识的全面、情景式的理解，并用以解释、处理和适应跨文化交际。它是了解个人背景、价值观和信仰如何影响跨文化能力的框架（Brenneman，2016）。学习者只有具有深厚的文化知识，才有能力与来自不同文化背景的人互动，或接受和适应陌生的文化。

在情感或认知层面，跨文化交际能力包括对文化差异的敏感性、对异文化的包容性、对本族文化的理解以及对其他文化的尊重等。作为跨文化交际能力的一个关键要素，文化适应能力意味着学习者必须知道在不同的情况中应用不同的行为和技能（Spitzberg，1984）。培养跨文化思维技能比实际获得知识更重要（Bok，2006）。

就行动层面而言，跨文化交际能力意味着交际者为进行顺畅的跨文化交际而采取的行动，如心理调节和环境适应等。

除了上述三个关键要素，还有两个要素可用于评估跨文化交际能力。一是态度，也属于情感或者认知层面。学习者对外国文化的态度会影响他们的跨文化交际能力。二是学习者运用技能或策略成功地进行跨文化交流。因此，跨文化交际能力包含五个要素（见图3-4），它们相互联系、相互影响。在跨文化交际能力中，跨文化交际知识处于核心地位，会影响学习者跨文化交际的认知和态度，而跨文化交际的认知和态度也会对跨文化交际知识产生一定的影响。积极正面的认知和态度有助于跨文化知识的积累。跨文化交际技能和行动基于跨文化交际知识的积累，同时通过跨文化交际技能和行动，跨文化交际知识也会不断丰富（见图3-5）。

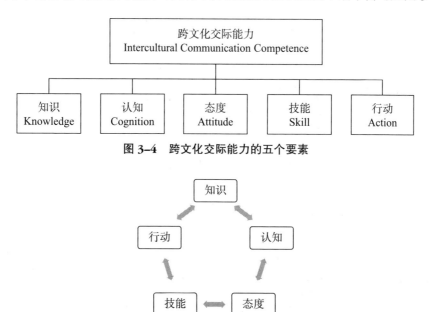

图 3-4　跨文化交际能力的五个要素

图 3-5　跨文化交际能力五要素关系图

3.3　商务外语跨文化交际能力模型的构建

笔者建立的商务外语跨文化交际能力模型主要包括五个要素，即跨文化交际知识、跨文化交际认知、跨文化交际行动、跨文化交际技能和跨文化交际态度（见图 3-6）。该模型涵盖了跨文化交际的整个核心心理过程，包括对沟通问题的认知、信息分析、完成交际任务的资源分配以及对交际过程的监测和评估。

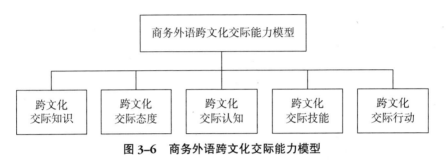

图 3-6　商务外语跨文化交际能力模型

3.3.1　跨文化交际知识

跨文化交际知识是本书中商务外语跨文化交际能力模型的一个要素。丰富的文化知识可以减少文化误解。在商务环境下，跨文化交际知识会极大地影响跨文化交际的效果。在本书中，跨文化交际知识指交际文化知识、商务文化知识和对文化差异性的认知。在跨文化交际研究领域，有学者对"知识文化"与"交际文化"作了区分：知识文化对跨文化交际不会产生直接的影响，而交际文化对跨文化交际则会产生直接的影响（林大津，2005）。张占一曾指出，所谓交际文化，指的是两个文化背景不同的人进行交际时，直接影响信息准确传递的语言和非语言的文化因素。因此，从跨文化交际的需要出发，应当强调交际文化知识的传授，而不是教授某一国别的文化知识。外语教学中的交际文化知识教学可概括为价值观、社会习俗、历史与宗教四个方面，其中，价值观是文化知识的核心，直接影响着人们的生活和行为方式。

由于不同文化对于贸易的认知存在差异，因此，商务外语学习者应该了解不同国家的商务文化知识，提高对文化差异性的敏感度，在交际过程中积极寻求和使用文化信息，从而在跨文化环境中提高有效工作的能力。

3.3.2　跨文化交际态度

跨文化交际是商务外语学习者学习、工作、生活的重要内容，学习应该对跨文化交际秉持着积极的态度。跨文化交际态度是衡量学习者跨文化交际能力的基本要素之一，它包括积极的文化取向、对模糊性的容忍度和自我效能。

积极的文化取向是一个总括性术语，包括世界观（Beechler，2007；Levy，2007）、开放性（Terrell，2013）、求知欲（Black，2005）、好奇心和对其他文化的尊重等。

对模糊性的容忍度也是跨文化交际能力的重要组成部分，因为跨文化交际就是与来自不同文化背景的人自然的交际过程，这个过程中必然会出现文化差异甚至文化冲突，因此，学习者应该提高对模糊性的包容度。

自我效能作为跨文化交际态度的重要组成部分，会极大地影响个人跨文化交际的自信。一个对跨文化交际持积极乐观态度的人在交际中获得成功的可能性更大。具备自我效能的学习者更有信心面对跨文化交际挑战，这有利于实现交际目标，在跨文化交际中更好地调整自己的行为，完成复杂商务环境中的跨文化交际活动。

3.3.3　跨文化交际认知

跨文化交际认知主要包括跨文化意识和跨文化思维。跨文化意识也称作文化知觉能力，它是人们对自身、本族文化和异族文化的感知。跨文化思维是对文化现象进行分析、综合、比较和概括的能力（杨盈，2007），包括文化理解能力和文化分析能力。文化理解能力指理解不同文化背景下人们交际行为的差异，并寻求产生差异的文化根源的能力；文化分析能力则是对本族文化和异族文化进行比较、归纳异同的能力。培养跨文化思维能力有利于学习者在交际中理解文化差异、解决文化冲突、实现有效交际。

3.3.4　跨文化交际技能

跨文化交际技巧包括非语言交际策略和语言交际技巧。非语言交际策略包括灵活应变能力、情绪调节能力、移情能力、交际驾驭能力、关系行为能力（杜瑞清，1998）等。跨文化交际能力框架下的灵活应变能力不仅仅是对语言上的要求，它还要求交际者灵活运用交际文化知识、跨文化思维以及交际策略等各方面的能力，以应对跨文化语境下的各种交际场合。情绪调节能力指控制情绪、调节情绪、表达情绪的能力（Gross，1998）。移情能力又称为文化认可度，指平等、开放地对待不同的文化，像尊重自己的文化一样尊重其他的文化。交际驾驭能力和关系行为能力指在跨文化交际过程中，保持顺畅地沟通，实现跨文化交际目的的能力。

语言交际策略包括语言能力和社会语言能力。语言能力主要是指语用能力、语篇能力和语言知识及技巧，来自不同文化的人们常常会有不同的有时甚至是截然相反的语言构建方式。社会语言能力是指能够依据各种语境因素恰当地运用与理解适合于不同社交场合和环境的言语。社会语言能力是语言运用的文化，习得一种社会语言能力实际上就是习得一种文化能力。

3.3.5 跨文化交际行动

跨文化交际行动涵盖语言交际能力、非语言交际能力和文化调适能力，要求学习者通过对语言、非语言、交际文化等各种知识的综合、灵活运用，从而在实际工作中完成交际任务，解决实际问题。

在跨文化交际实践中，参与者要注意谈话双方的社会地位、性别以及各自对对方的态度等因素对跨文化交际可能产生的影响，还要意识到文化对交际言语行为的时间、地点以及所谈的话题的影响。特定文化中的环境因素会在很大程度上决定交流信息的形式以及语言的声调、语体、词汇、结构的恰当与否。

当遇到文化冲突和矛盾时，参与者要适时地进行文化调适。文化调适能力是学习者在跨文化环境中根据文化特征调节自身行为的能力。它建立在对一定文化的理解基础上，与个人心理素质密切相关，直接影响到跨文化交际效果。心理调适能力和灵活应变能力是文化调适能力的两个要素。心理调适能力主要指在文化冲突中能适时调整心理状态、减少不确定性、减轻压力，达到自我放松状态的能力。

总之，跨文化交际知识、态度、认知、技巧和行动五项能力共同构成商务外语学习者的跨文化交际能力，它们相互交织、缺一不可。其中任何一项能力的不足都会影响跨文化交际活动的顺利进行。同时，它们之间存在层次关系（见图3-7）：跨文化交际知识是跨文化交际能力中最为基础的能力。不具备跨文化交际知识，就谈不上跨文化交际能力。跨文化交际态度和认知处于跨文化交际能力的第二层，积极的跨文化交际态度和认知会促进学习者在跨文化交际中逐步实现文化适应，有利于跨文化交际活动的有效完成。跨文化交际技巧和行动是跨文化交际能力的最高层次，是前三大能力培养的目标。基于以上五个维度，笔者对跨文化交际能力量表的理论框架进行了精心设计。

图 3-7　商务外语跨文化交际五项能力层级关系图

3.4　商务外语跨文化交际能力量表的设计

　　跨文化交际能力应该成为外语教学培养的最终目的，而语言综合应用能力的提高是外语教学的一个主要任务，是实现跨文化交际能力的途径和依托，跨文化交际能力最终还是要通过有效沟通、完成特定交际目的来体现（杨盈，2007）。因此，为了建立一个切实可行的跨文化交际能力量表，前面我们构建了由跨文化交际知识、跨文化交际态度、跨文化交际认知、跨文化交际技巧、跨文化交际行动五大能力系统组成的商务外语跨文化交际能力模型，以期有助于科学评估商务外语学习者的跨文化交际能力。

3.4.1　商务外语跨文化交际能力指标体系

　　基于商务外语跨文化交际能力理论模型建立的跨文化交际能力指标体系也主要有五大指标：跨文化交际知识、跨文化交际态度、跨文化交际认知、跨文化交际技巧、跨文化交际行动（见图 3-8）。这五大指标体系可从知识、心理（态度和认知）和实践（技巧和行动）三个层面系统地评估商务外语学习者的跨文化交际能力。跨文化交际知识包括交际文化知识和商务文化知识两大指标。跨文化交际态度分为积极的文化取向、对模糊性的容忍度和自我效能三大指标，其中积极的文化取向又细分为世界观、开放性、求知欲、好奇心和对其他文化的尊重五

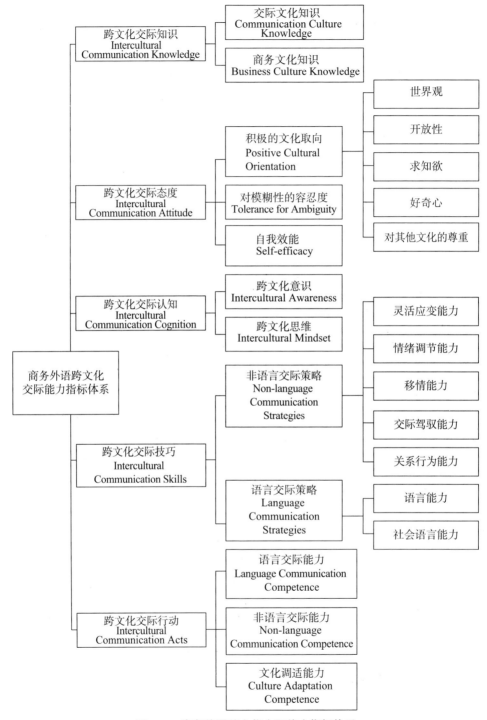

图 3-8　商务外语跨文化交际能力指标体系

大能力。跨文化交际认知分为跨文化意识和跨文化思维。跨文化交际技巧分为非语言交际策略和语言交际策略，其中非语言交际策略包括灵活应变能力、情绪调节能力、移情能力、交际驾驭能力、关系行为能力五大能力；语言交际策略包括语言能力和社会语言能力。跨文化交际行动分为语言交际能力、非语言交际能力和文化调适能力。基于此指标体系，笔者收集了多条描述语，以准确评估商务外语学习者的跨文化交际能力。

3.4.2　描述语的来源

为了制定符合我国国情的科学的跨文化交际能力量表，笔者收集了国际上许多重要的跨文化交际能力量表，因此，《商务外语跨文化交际能力量表》的描述语来源于仍在跨文化交际能力评估方面发挥着重要作用的国际跨文化交际能力量表，这些量表包括《跨文化知识和能力价值量表》《工作角色和熟练水平能力量表》《人才能力框架》《全球能力量表》《文化智力简短量表》《跨文化敏感性量表》等（见表 3–2）。由于笔者从《人才能力框架》《文化智力简短量表》《跨文化敏感性量表》三个量表中收集的描述语较少，下文将不展开介绍这三个量表，但会对《跨文化知识和能力价值量表》、《工作角色和熟练水平能力量表》和《全球能力量表》进行详细介绍。

表 3–2　《商务外语跨文化交际能力量表》的描述语来源

量表名称	开发者	时间	国别
《跨文化知识和能力价值量表》(Intercultural Knowledge and Competence VALUE Rubrics)	美国学院和大学协会 (The Association of American Colleges and Universities)	2017	美国
《工作角色和熟练水平能力量表》(Competence by Job Role and Proficiency Level)	Workitect	2012	美国
《人才能力框架》(Talent Competence Framework)	the Metiri Group & NCREL	2009	美国
《全球能力量表》(Global Competence Inventory)	Kozai 公司	2009	日本
《文化智力简短量表》(Short Form Measure of Cultural Intelligence)	David C. Thomas	2015	加拿大
《跨文化敏感性量表》(Intercultural Sensitivity Scale)	Chen and Starosta	2000	美国

3.4.2.1 《跨文化知识和能力价值量表》

《跨文化知识和能力价值量表》是由美国各地学院和大学的教师、专家组成的团队基于大学现有的人才培养标准开发出来的，主要描述美国大学生的学习成果。《跨文化知识和能力价值量表》阐释了每个维度学习结果的基本标准，并给出了对各个维度上学习结果的更高水平的描述。跨文化知识和能力价值标准包括好奇心和分析、批判性思维、创造性思维、书面沟通、口头沟通、定量分析、信息素养、阅读、团队合作、解决问题、公民知识和参与度、跨文化知识和能力、道德推理与行动能力、全球学习、终身学习以及整合性学习能力。《跨文化知识和能力价值量表》基于这几大能力制定了多个独立的子量表，每个子量表将能力分为四个等级，如图 3–9 的《跨文化知识和能力价值量表》中将跨文化知识和能力细分为知识、技能和态度三大能力，并给出相应的跨文化交际能力描述语。该量表中与跨文化交际能力相关的描述语符合本书的商务外语跨文化交际能力的内容，鉴于该量表在美国教育和测试中的广泛应用及取得的良好反响，因此笔者设计的《商务外语跨文化交际能力量表》选取了该量表中的部分描述语。

3.4.2.2 《工作角色和熟练水平能力量表》

《工作角色和熟练水平能力量表》是由国际著名咨询和培训公司 Workitect 开发的，它是基于能力的人力资源国际通用的重要管理工具。该量表根据不同工作种类和能力等级水平而设计，为人才衡量和能力发展提供了重要框架。这个量表包括与人交际能力、处理业务能力、自我管理能力三大部分（见图 3–10），并从中细分出多项能力，是工作场所中国际通用的能力量表。笔者在《商务外语跨文化交际能力量表》的设计中重点关注《工作角色和熟练水平能力量表》中多样性促进、建立合作关系和全球视角等能力评估，因此，该量表中有关三大能力的描述语可以为《商务外语跨文化交际能力量表》的设计提供借鉴。图 3–11 节选了该量表的部分描述语。

Association of American Colleges and Universities

INTERCULTURAL KNOWLEDGE AND COMPETENCE VALUE RUBRIC

for more information, please contact value@aacu.org

Definition

Intercultural Knowledge and Competence is "a set of cognitive, affective, and behavioral skills and characteristics that support effective and appropriate interaction in a variety of cultural contexts." (Bennett, J. M. 2008 Transformative training: Designing programs for culture learning. In *Contemporary leadership and intercultural competence: Understanding and utilizing cultural diversity to build successful organizations*, ed. M. A. Moodian, 95-110. Thousand Oaks, CA: Sage.)

Evaluators are encouraged to assign a zero to any work sample or collection of work that does not meet benchmark (cell one) level performance.

	Capstone 4	Milestones 3	Milestones 2	Benchmark 1
Knowledge *Cultural self-awareness*	Articulates insights into own cultural rules and biases (e.g. seeking complexity; aware of how her/his experiences have shaped these rules, and how to recognize and respond to cultural biases, resulting in a shift in self-description.)	Recognizes new perspectives about own cultural rules and biases (e.g. not looking for sameness; comfortable with the complexities that new perspectives offer.)	Identifies own cultural rules and biases (e.g. with a strong preference for those rules shared with own cultural group and seeks the same in others.)	Shows minimal awareness of own cultural rules and biases (even those shared with own cultural group(s)) (e.g. uncomfortable with identifying possible cultural differences with others.)
Knowledge *Knowledge of cultural worldview frameworks*	Demonstrates sophisticated understanding of the complexity of elements important to members of another culture in relation to its history, values, politics, communication styles, economy, or beliefs and practices.	Demonstrates adequate understanding of the complexity of elements important to members of another culture in relation to its history, values, politics, communication styles, economy, or beliefs and practices.	Demonstrates partial understanding of the complexity of elements important to members of another culture in relation to its history, values, politics, communication styles, economy, or beliefs and practices.	Demonstrates surface understanding of the complexity of elements important to members of another culture in relation to its history, values, politics, communication styles, economy, or beliefs and practices.
Skills *Empathy*	Interprets intercultural experience from the perspectives of own and more than one worldview and demonstrates ability to act in a supportive manner that recognizes the feelings of another cultural group.	Recognizes intellectual and emotional dimensions of more than one worldview and sometimes uses more than one worldview in interactions.	Identifies components of other cultural perspectives but responds in all situations with own worldview.	Views the experience of others but does so through own cultural worldview.
Skills *Verbal and nonverbal communication*	Articulates a complex understanding of cultural differences in verbal and nonverbal communication (e.g. demonstrates understanding of the degree to which people use physical contact while communicating in different cultures or use direct/indirect and explicit/implicit meanings) and is able to skillfully negotiate a shared understanding based on those differences.	Recognizes and participates in cultural differences in verbal and nonverbal communication and begins to negotiate a shared understanding based on those differences.	Identifies some cultural differences in verbal and nonverbal communication and is aware that misunderstandings can occur based on those differences but is still unable to negotiate a shared understanding.	Has a minimal level of understanding of cultural differences in verbal and nonverbal communication; is unable to negotiate a shared understanding.
Attitudes *Curiosity*	Asks complex questions about other cultures, seeks out and articulates answers to these questions that reflect multiple cultural perspectives.	Asks deeper questions about other cultures and seeks out answers to these questions.	Asks simple or surface questions about other cultures.	States minimal interest in learning more about other cultures.
Attitudes *Openness*	Initiates and develops interactions with culturally different others. Suspends judgment in valuing her/his interactions with culturally different others.	Begins to initiate and develop interactions with culturally different others. Begins to suspend judgment in valuing her/his interactions with culturally different others.	Expresses openness to most, if not all, interactions with culturally different others. Has difficulty suspending any judgment in her/his interactions with culturally different others, and is aware of own judgment and expresses a willingness to change.	Receptive to interacting with culturally different others. Has difficulty suspending any judgment in her/his interactions with culturally different others, but is unaware of own judgment.

图 3-9　《跨文化知识和能力价值量表》描述语节选

COMPETENCIES DEALING WITH PEOPLE

COMPETENCIES DEALING WITH BUSINESS

SELF MANAGEMENT COMPETENCIES

图 3-10 《工作角色和熟练水平能力量表》架构图

	BASIC	PROFICIENT	ADVANCED
Professional/ Specialist	*Not Applicable*	*Not Applicable*	*Not Applicable*

	BASIC	PROFICIENT	ADVANCED
Supervisor/ Manager	• Acts to align own unit's goals with the business • Communicates the business's mission to people in the unit • Communicates the unit's mission to the people • Develops goals that relate to the business's mission	• Acts to align own unit's goals with the strategic direction of the business • Ensures that people in the unit understand how their work relates to the business's mission • Ensures that everyone understands and identifies with the unit's mission • Ensures that the unit develops goals and a plan to help fulfill the business's mission	• Clearly and distinctly aligns own unit's goals with the mission and strategic direction of the business • Ensures that people in the unit understand and see how their individual goals and work specifically relate to the business's mission • Ensures that everyone understands, identifies with, and "buys into" the unit's mission • Ensures all individuals in the unit develop goals and specific plans to help fulfill the business's mission

	BASIC	PROFICIENT	ADVANCED
Director/ Executive	• Acts to align own unit's goals with the direction of the business • Ensures that people in the unit understand how their work relates to the business's mission • Ensures that everyone understands and identifies with the unit's mission • Ensures that the unit develops goals and a plan to help fulfill the business's mission	• Clearly and distinctly aligns own unit's goals with the mission and strategic direction of the business • Ensures that people in the unit understand and see how their individual goals and work specifically relate to the business's mission • Ensures that everyone understands, identifies with, and "buys into" the unit's mission • Ensures all individuals in the unit develop goals and specific plans to help fulfill the business's mission	• Is a role model for clearly and distinctly aligning own unit's goals with the mission and strategic direction of the business; helps others leaders to do the same • Creates a culture that ensures that people in the organization understand and see how their individual goals and work specifically relates to the business's mission • Ensures that leaders in the organization understand, identify with, and "buy into" the business's mission • Has a long track record of always ensuring that the organization develops goals and a specific plans to help fulfill the business's mission

图 3-11　《工作角色和熟练水平能力量表》描述语节选

3.4.2.3　《全球能力量表》

　　《全球能力量表》旨在评估与有不同的文化规范和行为的人交往的能力，同时这个量表也能评估与不同种族、性别、世代、阶级、宗教信仰、政治哲学等的人进行跨文化交际的能力。该量表主要从观念管理、关系管理和自我管理三个层面评价跨文化交际能力（见图 3-12）。观念管理由非主观判断、好奇心、歧义容忍度、全球观、兴趣五个维度组成。关系管理由利益相关、交际投入、情绪敏感性、自我意识和社交灵活性五个维度组成。自我管理由乐观、自信、自我认同、情绪韧性、减压能力和压力管理六个维度组成。这 16 个维度可以综合评估学习者的跨文化交际能力，对笔者设计的《商务外语跨文化交际能力量表》有重要的参考意义。

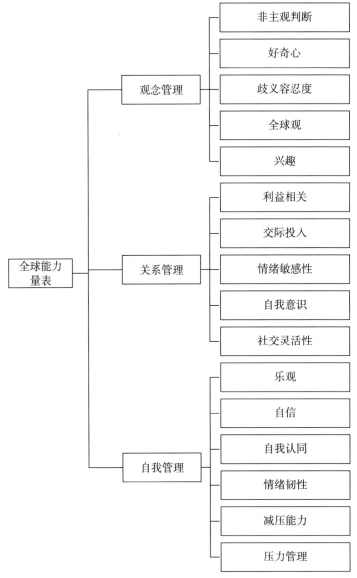

图 3-12 《全球能力量表》的框架

3.4.3 《商务外语跨文化交际能力量表》的研制

3.4.3.1 《商务外语跨文化交际能力量表》

笔者设计的《商务外语跨文化交际能力量表》旨在衡量商务外语学习者的跨文化交际能力，根据学习者的跨文化交际知识、态度、认知、技巧和行动，

评估其跨文化交际能力。该量表能为商务外语学习者提供一个实用的工具来自
己进行跨文化交际能力评估。表 3-3 是《商务外语跨文化交际能力量表》的
节选。

表 3-3　《商务外语跨文化交际能力量表》节选

Capstone 4	210	actively uses a variety of stress reduction strategies and technique on a regular and daily basis.
Capstone 4	211	has an excellent understanding of the ways in which culture impacts decision-making of specific nations/groups (This understanding is fair and takes into account multiple cultural perspectives).
Capstone 4	212	has specific and well-developed knowledge of ways in which access to technology/information is impacted by culture and political ideology.
Capstone 4	213	is able to transfer this knowledge when learning about similar issues with which he/she is unfamiliar.
Capstone 4	214	seeks to understand the global impact of personal actions (e.g., consumerism based on company policies, consumption of energy, or recycling), and acts accordingly.
Capstone 4	215	is aware of the levels and stages of intercultural development of those he/she works with (students, program participants, colleagues, etc.).
Capstone 4	216	is aware of factors which help and hinder his/her own intercultural development and ways to overcome them.
Capstone 4	217	is aware he/she perceive himself/herself as a communicator, facilitator, mediator in intercultural/multicultural situations.
Capstone 4	218	is aware how he/she is perceived by others as a communicator, facilitator, mediator in intercultural/multicultural situations.
Capstone 4	219	is aware of the multiple perspectives, complexities, and implications of choices in intercultural and multicultural contexts.
Capstone 4	220	exhibits appreciation for and interest in individuals and groups in particular cultural contexts.
Capstone 4	221	is flexible in communicating and interacting with those who are linguistically and culturally different (and with limited knowledge of his/her own language and culture).
Capstone 4	222	suspends judgment and appreciates the complexities and subtleties of intercultural and multicultural communication and interaction.
Capstone 4	223	extends a sense of empathy to those oppressed because of their sociocultural status.

3.4.3.2 对《商务外语跨文化交际能力量表》的分析

《商务外语跨文化交际能力量表》共有 235 条描述语，将跨文化交际能力分为四个级别。跨文化交际能力等级越高，学习者的跨文化交际能力越强。本书的量表主要是对跨文化交际知识、态度、认知、行动和技巧的测评，如第 11 条 "describes the experiences of others historically or in contemporary contexts primarily through one cultural perspective, demonstrating some openness to varied cultures and worldviews" 评估学习者对历史等文化知识的了解；第 7 条 "uncomfortable with identifying possible cultural differences with others" 评估学习者对歧义的包容度，这是跨文化交际态度的重要组成部分，初级的跨文化交际者对歧义的包容度较低，对文化差异性具有一定的排斥性；第 10 条 "identifies multiple perspectives while maintaining a value preference for own positioning（such as cultural, disciplinary, and ethical）" 从文化、纪律和道德方面来评估对跨文化交际的认知，初级的跨文化交际者可能具有一定的文化、价值偏向性，很难平等地对待所有文化；第 210 条 "actively use a variety of stress reduction strategies and techniques on a regular and daily basis." 评估学习者跨文化交际能力中的压力管理策略和技巧；第 154 条 "engages with others and tries to understand differences in his/her behavior, values, and attitude" 和第 155 条 "interacts in a variety of ways, some quite different from those to which he/she is accustomed" 都是评估学习者的跨文化交际行为。

《商务外语跨文化交际能力量表》的所有描述语都统一使用"动词＋名词短语"的格式，从而使量表更加简单易懂，如 "tolerates ambiguity and uncertainty well and even welcomes it in almost all situations"。《商务外语跨文化交际能力量表》中的描述语可以分为两大类：（1）有关跨文化交际能力的描述语，如描述语 "has extensive global experience: clearly considers problems and opportunities from a global perspective" 就是描述学习者的全球意识；（2）有关跨文化交际任务的描述语，如描述语 "can discuss models for understanding learning styles and strategies, and describe prevailing styles in his/her own culture and another culture and their implications" 是评估学习者的跨文化交际能力的直接指标。

商务外语自主学习能力量表

《普通高等学校本科专业类教学质量国家标准（外国语言文学类）》中商务英语专业的能力要求的第三条是自主学习能力。随着以学习者为中心的教学模式的发展，自主学习已成为一种重要的学习方式（Benson，2011）。自主学习，又称自主性或自我导向学习（Long，1989），意味着个人学习者有权对与学习有关的各种决定承担越来越多的责任（Little，1994）。

自主学习可以极大地激发学生的学习兴趣。在自主学习中，学生成为个人发展和自我完善的主人，自主决定学习什么内容和采取何种学习策略，而老师不再是唯一的决策者。最有效率的自主学习者知道如何通过灵活应用完成新的学习任务，丰富他们的知识（Little，1994）。自主学习不仅对学习者的学习生活很重要，而且对其整个生活也很重要。在当今的知识社会和信息时代，学习者面临着许多挑战：不断提高的专业化程度、新技术、市场变化、跨文化交流等。面对这些挑战，学习者必须掌握越来越多的新技能，而有些新技能并不能立即从学校学来，所以学习者必须掌握学习新技能的能力。

尽管我国对自主学习的相关研究起步较晚，但自主学习的重要性已经得到了学者们的广泛认同。在国家商务英语教学质量标准中，自主学习能力是学习者需要具备的重要能力之一。这说明自主学习能力对商务英语学习者的学习、生活和工作都是至关重要的。虽然自主学习的重要性已为学者们所公认，但对自主学习能力量表的学术研究较少，为商务外语学习者设计的自主学习能力量表更是尚不多见。因此，商务外语学习者非常需要一个科学的、易于使用的能力量表来评估他们的自主学习能力。要设计自主学习能力量表，首先要构建自主学习的理论框架，因为理论框架是能力量表的指导。目前，学者和学习者对自主学习能力的理论框架仍缺乏共识。因此，首先要对自主学习理论、自主学习的各种定义和构成要素进行综述和剖析，为量表的设计打下坚实的理论基础，进而才能进行相关量表的设计和研究。

4.1 国内外自主学习能力的相关研究

4.1.1 国外自主学习能力的相关研究

国外许多学者对自主学习能力的概念作了界定。Holec 将自主学习能力定义为学生自主掌握学习。他的定义指出了自主学习的本质，那就是一个人对自己的学习的控制。他进一步解释说，自主学习是"掌握自己的学习并对和学习有关的所有决定承担责任"。Holec 的定义对人们关于自主学习的认识有很大影响。随着以学习者为中心个性化教学的发展，越来越多的学者对自主学习能力进行了深入探讨。Little、Kenny、Gardner、Benson 等从"学习者自主学习的心理关系""学习者控制自己学习的能力""承认学习者在教育系统内的权利""学习者对与学习相关的所有决定完全负责"等不同角度探讨了自主学习能力。这些定义为自主学习能力理论框架的构建奠定了坚实的基础。

Little 对于自主学习能力的定义是非常重要的。根据 Little 的研究，自主学习能力可界定为三种能力：进行客观的评判性反思的能力、作出决策的能力和采取独立行动的能力。Little 把自主学习能力看作学习者与学习过程的心理关系。他将三种能力纳入自主学习中，因为学习者的这些行为能力可以被观察到，从而使自主学习能力更加直观。然而，他对自主学习的定义过于简单化，侧重于战略层面，而不是行动层面。

后来，Benson 和 Voller 对自主学习能力给出了更详细的定义，他们认为自主学习能力是控制自己学习的能力，强调学习者在完全自主学习的情况下有权作出相关决定的能力，包括具备在自主学习环境下的相关能力与技能，不受教育制度制约的能力。Benson 最重要的贡献之一是，他认为自主学习能力包括技能和能力。能力指与天赋有关的各项能力，技能指学习者随着自主学习的进展得到加强和发展的各项能力。这意味着自主学习能力的培养是一个持续的过程。

4.1.2　国内自主学习能力的相关研究

国内对自主学习能力的研究始于 20 世纪 90 年代初，不少学者致力于这一领域的研究，并取得了一些进展（郑敏，2000）。国内学者主要从过程、策略、环境三个角度界定和解释外语自主学习的本质。

（1）过程观的自主学习。李红美认为从学习的维度看，自主学习实际上是指学习者主动对学习的各维度作出选择、控制和调节的一种学习方式；从学习的过程来看，自主学习实际上是学习者自觉主动地确定学习目标、营造学习环境、选择学习方法、监控学习过程、评价学习结果的过程。范捷平对外语自主学习的本质也持"过程观"的观点，认为外语自主学习是学习者有意识地计划、监控、实行和测试反思的学习过程。外语学习者需要根据各自不同的需求、学习动机和学习目标，积极、主动、独立决定自己的学习内容、学习方法、学习过程和学习形式。

（2）策略观的自主学习。董奇认为自主学习可分为三方面：一是能事先安排、计划自己的学习活动；二是能对自己的学习活动进行监督、评价和反思；三是对自己的学习活动进行调节、修正和控制。这个定义实际上把自主学习简单等同于语言学习者的策略了，显然不能反映外语自主学习的所有本质属性。

（3）环境观的自主学习。张殿玉对外语自主学习的概念作了如下论述："自主学习是学习者外部环境和内部环境协调统一的结果。外部环境由教师、教学设施和语料构成，对内部环境有促进作用，是实现自主学习的前提条件和物质基础。内部环境则蕴藏着学习者的态度和能力。"

4.1.3　自主学习能力的概念界定

有些学者将自主学习定义为一种能力，有些学者认为自主学习是一种学习过程，还有些学者认为自主学习是一种教学实践，尽管学者们对自主学习能力的定义不尽相同，但大家普遍认为：自主学习的本质是学习者的学习能力或责任。笔者认为，自主学习能力是一种可以在人的一生中发展起来的能力，可以用量表来衡量。设计科学的自主学习能力量表，必须有明确和合理的操作定义。国内外学者的定义和解释对笔者自主学习能力理论框架的设计有着重要的借鉴意义，下面会对自主学习能力的实现和评价作出详细、具体的界定。

自主学习能力被认为是 21 世纪学习者必备能力之一。商务外语学习者的自主学习能力不仅是商务外语教育发展的强大推动力，还是值得探索的重要课题。

在对国内外学者"自主学习能力"定义进行批判性分析的基础上，笔者将自主学习能力定义为：自主学习是一种持续的过程，学习者能够控制自己的全部学习过程，例如决定学习目标、学习内容；创设学习环境，选择学习方法；采用哪种学习形式和学习策略；监控学习过程和评估学习效果。自主学习能力也包括学习者从一个学习情境转移到另一个学习情境的能力。

笔者的定义包含以下几个要素：第一，自主学习是终身发展的过程；第二，自主学习强调学习者的学习自主性，也就是其对学习的掌控；第三，自主学习可以采取任何形式，在正式或非正式场景下，学习者可以单独学习，也可以与他人合作学习；第四，学习者必须能应用他们自主学习的能力；第五，学习者必须知道在不同的情况下怎么更有效率地学习。以上要素涵盖了自主学习能力发展过程中的关键指标。

4.2　自主学习能力的理论框架

20 世纪 90 年代，学者们提出了自主学习能力的诸多模型，这些模型可以为本书自主学习能力理论框架的构建提供指导，下面将讨论三种最具代表性的自主学习能力模型。

4.2.1　McCombs 的自主学习能力模型

McCombs 是最早提出自主学习能力模型的学者之一。他认为，自主学习是个人发展和自我概念发展的结果。自我存在感和自我价值感对自主学习能力的培养起着重要作用。在他的模型中，自主学习的过程可以分为三个阶段（见图 4-1），包括目标设定、学习规划与策略选择、改进与评价。首先，学习者必须分析学习任务，评估个人能力与学习效果，确定学习目标；其次，学习者需要制定学习规划，选择合适的学习策略；最后，学习者需要对自己的学习进行自我评价。虽然 McCombs 的模型是具备逻辑性的，但忽略了学习者自身和外部因素对自主学习的影响。

图 4-1　McCombs 模型中自主学习过程的三个阶段

4.2.2　Winne 与 Butler 的自主学习能力模型

Winne 和 Butler 是认知学派的代表人物。基于其他学者的自主学习能力模型，他们设计了一个更详细、更系统的描述自主学习过程的模型。他们将自主学习分为四个阶段（见图 4-2）：（1）任务界定阶段；（2）目标设计和计划阶段；（3）策略执行阶段；（4）元认知调节阶段。首先，学习者根据原有的知识和认知解释新的学习任务的特点，并对学习任务进行拆解和分析，选择适合的策略进行学习。该模型的特点是它将"老"知识与"新"知识紧密结合，这意味着自主学习者必须懂得如何进行新老知识的传递。Winne 和 Butler 认为学习者的自主性是最基本的。学习者的目标决定了学习策略的运用和最终的学习效果。

图 4-2　Winne 与 Butler 的模型中自主学习过程的四个阶段

与 McCombs 的模型相比，Winne 和 Butler 的模型清晰地划分了任务界定、目标设计和计划、策略执行、元认知调节四个阶段，构成了一个完整的学习周期。该模型特别重视元认知调节，使学习者在学习过程中可以不断反思自己的学习策略是否有效，学习目标是否合理，这有助于提高学习者的学习能力和自我管理能力。当然，Winne 和 Butler 的模型也有不足之处，其忽视了自我评价和外部因素影响的重要性。

4.2.3 Zimmerman 的自主学习能力模型

Zimmerman 是世界上最具影响力的自主学习研究领域的学者之一，他的自主学习能力模型对自主学习能力理论研究具有很大的影响。他的模型指出了个体、行为和环境之间的相互作用（见图 4–3）。

个体因素包括自我效能感、目标设定、学习动机等，这些内在因素影响着个体的学习态度和意愿。

行为因素涵盖了自我观察、自我判断和自我反应等。例如，学习者对自己的学习过程进行监控和评估，根据结果调整学习策略。

环境因素则包含家庭、学校和社会等方面的支持或限制。良好的学习环境能激发学习积极性，反之则可能产生阻碍。

这三个方面相互影响，个体因素驱动特定的学习行为，而环境又对个体和行为产生促进或制约作用。同时，行为的改变也会反作用于个体因素和所处环境。在这个动态的过程中，个体不断调整和优化自己的自主学习能力。

自主学习者不仅可以控制和调节内部学习过程，而且他们可以自主调整外部学习环境。自主学习者必须知道如何最大限度地利用外部资源。**Zimmerman**在模型中论证了教师在学习者自主学习中的重要性，这得到了许多学者的认同。**Little** 认为自主学习并不意味着不需要教师，不能简单地认为自主学习是没有教师指导的学习。自主学习不是独立学习或孤立学习，不意味着自主学习者学习时需要与他人隔离。现有研究也证明自主学习能力较弱的教师可能会对学生的自主学习能力产生负面影响（Burkert，2008）。通过课堂指导和互动，教师可以帮助学生学会自主学习。在学生自主学习过程中，老师可以扮演积极角色，如帮助者、促进者、指导者、参与者或者顾问等，帮助学生提高学习效率。

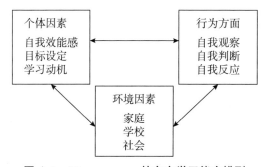

图 4–3　Zimmerman 的自主学习能力模型

4.3　商务外语自主学习能力模型的构建

　　基于国内外学者的自主学习能力的一些重要模型，笔者设计了针对商务外语学习者的自主学习能力模型，为自主学习能力量表的设计奠定了基础。商务外语学习者应具备将知识和技能应用到新的商务场景并且获得新商务知识的能力。

　　自主学习是一种个体渐进的、永无止境的学习（Candy，1991），自主学习能力不是结果，而是过程（Nunan，1997）。在笔者构建的模型中，自主学习分为不同的阶段，自主学习能力也分为不同的层次。作为一种必须不断培养的能力，自主学习能力不是与生俱来的，学习者可以通过运用自主学习技巧和形成自主学习思维来提高自主学习能力。

　　自主学习是循序渐进的过程，包括多个阶段或者步骤。自主学习大体可分为以下几个阶段（见图4–4）:确定学习需求、设定目标、规划学习、选择学习资源、选择学习策略、实践、监测进度、评估和修订。这是一个不间断的循环过程，确定学习需求是第一步。

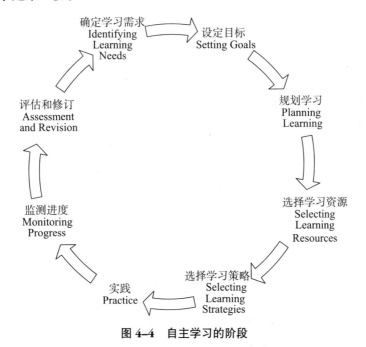

图 4–4　自主学习的阶段

　　学习需求是学习者对学习实际和学习的理想状态之间的差异的认知。许多学习者对自己的学习需求知之甚少。自主学习者必须了解自己的优势和劣势，然后根据不同的情况确定学习需求。在了解自己的优势和劣势并确定学习需求后，学习者需要设定学习目标，这可以帮助他们明确想获得的学习结果。当学习者设定了学习目标并创造机会学习时，他们已经具备了一定的自主学习能力（Nunan，1999）。学习规划与目标设定是分不开的，学习目标是学习者努力的方向。学习规划包括制定切实可行的学习任务，并为每个学习任务分配适当的时间和资源。学习资源对自主学习非常重要，借助合适的、有用的学习材料和工具，学习者可以大大提高学习效率。学习者还要选择正确的学习策略，具备根据自主学习任务采用正确的学习策略的能力，这些策略包括认知策略、元认知策略和社会认知策略。通过在学习中的实践，学习者可以利用所学到的知识获得更多的新知识。当然，学习者还需要对学习过程进行监测、评估和修订。

在商务外语的自主学习能力模型中，学习者自主学习能力的发展不是线性的，而是螺旋式上升的，自主学习能力的提升不是静态的，而是动态的。在全球化时代，商务外语学习者需要不断发展自主学习能力，提高学习新技能的能力。

4.4 《商务外语自主学习能力量表》的设计

在理论框架建立之后，笔者将设计一个评估商务外语学习者自主学习能力的量表。自主学习能力量表可从多个维度评估学习者设定学习目标、选择学习材料、监测和评估自主学习过程的能力，以及评估和检查学习结果、学习反馈的能力。

4.4.1 商务外语自主学习能力指标体系

学者们的大量研究确定了下列对个人自主学习能力和动机有影响的变量，如自尊、自控能力、学习倾向、目标倾向、学习风格和学习动机（Deci，1985；Alsaker，1989；Katzell，1990）。Sam Redding 2014 年在 "Personal Competency: A Framework for Building Students' Capacity to Learn" 一文中指出，这些变量可以分为认知能力、元认知能力、动机能力和社会/情感能力四个维度，自主学习能力也由这四大维度的变量组成。

基于自主学习能力的四大维度的相关研究及前文介绍的自主学习能力模型，本书给出了商务外语自主学习能力的四大指标体系：认知能力、元认知能力、动机能力和社会/情感能力（如图 4-5）。这四项能力还可以继续细分，每项能力可

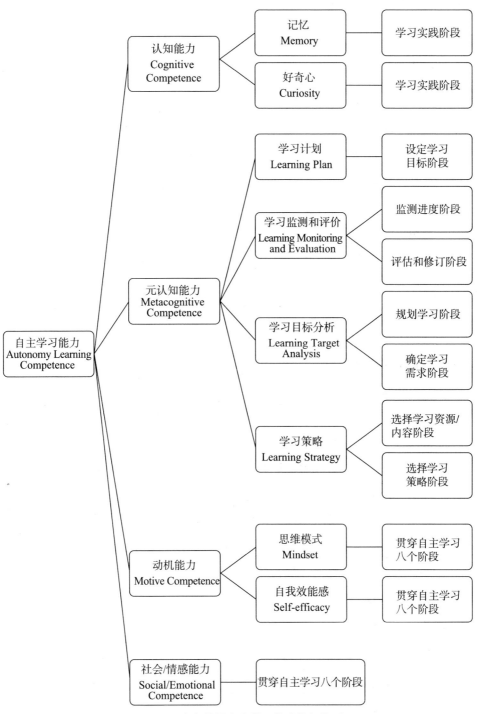

图 4-5　商务外语自主学习能力指标体系

分为多个子能力，认知能力包括记忆和好奇心；元认知能力包括学习计划、学习监测和评价、学习目标分析；动机能力包括思维模式和自我效能感，这些能力同时也贯穿在自主学习者确定学习需求、设定目标、规划学习、选择学习资源、选择学习策略、实践、监测进度、评估和修订八个阶段中。

（1）认知能力

认知能力是学习者现有认知的库存，它能帮助学习者建构知识网络和联系，从而有效地获得新的知识。

认知能力有两个关键因素：一是记忆；二是好奇心。学习者可以通过各种记忆技巧来增强记忆能力，把长期记忆作为学习资源。借助原有知识，自主学习者可以把新知识融入已有的知识网络中，促进对新知识的学习。好奇心指一个人寻求新的信息和新的知识的心理（Litman，2005）。好奇心是动机的组成部分，属于认知能力的范畴。它涉及认知和动机的混合（Loewenstein，1994）。好奇心始于自我认知。

（2）元认知能力

在自主学习中，学习者需要具备一定的学习技能，如任务分析、目标设定、自我监控等。这些技能可以包含在元认知能力中。元认知能力是"关于思考的思考"，是问题分析和解决的思维过程，即如何更好地掌握一项学习任务。它是一个认知过程，个人可以有意识地控制学习，包括自我评价和自我管理（Hacker，1998）。自我评价是学习者对自身学习能力、学习过程和学习结果的评估，自我管理是学习者选择恰当的学习策略来解决学习问题和掌握新知识。元认知策略包括学习计划、学习监测和评价（Ellis，1994）、学习目标分析以及学习策略。

（3）动机能力

自主学习的动机跟个人行为的内在和外在因素有关（Dweck，1999；Grant，2001），例如，内在的对学习任务的追求、外在的奖励激励都会影响学习者自主学习的动机（Walberg，2011）。本书主要关注学习者自主学习动机的内在因素。思维模式和自我效能感是自主学习能力动机的重要组成部分。

思维模式指一个人对待事情的态度和思考方式，即学习者的学习价值观，它是影响学习者自主学习动机的内在因素（Dweck，2000）。随着学习者的自主学习能力越来越强，学习的动机也越来越重要，学习者应该树立正面的学习价值观，培养对新知识和新技能的兴趣，保持学习的动力。面对问题和困难，学习者应该积极进行自主学习和保持"取得成功"的期望（Wigfield，1994）。

Bandura 认为，自我效能感也是影响学习者动机的一个重要因素，强调知识与行动的相互作用。自我效能感是指一个人对完成特定行为或目标的信心或信念，它能够影响人们对自己行为的选择：人们通常会避免做他们认为无法完成的事情，或者满怀信心地完成他们觉得能够完成的事情。自我效能感会影响学习者的努力程度，对学习者的思维模式和情绪反应模式产生影响：自我效能感低的学习者在面对潜在的学习挑战时容易产生心理压力，并且他们更倾向于将注意力集中在潜在的不好的学习结果上，而自我效能感高的学习者则更愿意迎接挑战，产生更大的学习动力。

（4）社会 / 情感能力

社会 / 情感能力与学业成功有关（Durlak，2011；Zins，2004）。自主学习可能在教师和学习伙伴的课堂上产生。在自主学习中，学习者不是知识填充的容器，不再被动地接受教师的观念和知识。教师更像是中介者，促进学习者的自主学习（Benson，2000；Hardré 等，2006）。自主学习者必须与教师和学习伙伴打交道。学习，特别是学校学习，既是一种个人活动，也是一种社会活动。温暖而富有挑战性的课堂和学校环境（Elias，2006）对学生自主学习能力的培养是有利的。学生的社交能力和情感能力会对自主学习能力产生很大影响，对学习者实现学习目标、处理学习挫败感、高效进行小组学习等帮助很大。

自主学习能力的四项子能力在确定学习需求、设定目标、规划学习、选择学习资源、选择学习策略、实践、监测进度、评估和修订自主的八大阶段都非常重要。在动态的自主学习过程中，学习者需要灵活应用这四大能力，保持对自主学习的热情，及时调整学习策略，促进新旧知识的融会贯通，形成完整系统的知识体系。

总之，笔者结合自主学习动态过程的能力模型建立的商务外语自主学习能力评估的指标体系，有助于商务外语学习者增强对自主学习能力的过程和自主学习能力量表的理解。该量表可以有效评估自主学习动态过程中学习者展现的自主学习认知能力、元认知能力、动机能力和社会 / 情感能力，并给出了对学习者自主学习态度、能力和行为的描述语。

4.4.2 描述语的来源

对于自主学习能力的测量，国际上有很多重要的测试和能力量表。经筛选，笔者主要收集了四个重要的自主学习能力量表（见表 4–1），分别是：《跨文化知识和能力价值量表》《有效终身学习量表》《个人胜任力——培养学生学习能力的框架》《自我导向学习量表》。《跨文化知识和价值能力量表》已在前文介绍过。笔者会从以下四个量表中筛选、编辑、修订与自主学习能力相关的描述语加入《商务外语自主学习能力量表》的描述语中。

表 4–1 《商务外语自主学习能力量表》的描述语来源

文件名	开发者	时间	国别
《跨文化知识和能力价值量表》 (*Intercultural Knowledge and Competence VALUE Rubrics*)	美国学院和大学协会 The American Association of Colleges and Universities	2017	美国
《有效终身学习量表》 (*The Effective Lifelong Learning Inventory*)	Glaxton 教授等	2002	英国
《个人胜任力——培养学生学习能力的框架》 (*Personal Competency—A Framework for Building Students' Capacity to Learn*)	学习创新中心 Center on Innovations in Learning	2014	美国
《自我导向学习量表》 (*Self-directed Learning Readiness Scale*)	Lucy M. Guglielmino	1991	美国

4.4.2.1 《有效终身学习量表》

《有效终身学习量表》是由英国布里斯托大学教授 Glaxton 等人经过 15 年的研究，通过总结成功学习者的特质，研发的用于测量终身学习能力的量表，多达数十万人参与了本量表的测试。该量表的可靠性和实用性使其成为学校、公司常用的对学习能力进行测量的工具。《有效终身学习量表》主要从以下七个方面测量学习能力（见图 4–6）：学习意识、批判性好奇心、关联能力、创造性、互助能力、策略意识和学习韧性。学习意识是在任何情况下都保持学习热情的意识；

批判性好奇心指挖掘知识本质的能力；关联能力是将所学知识联系实际创造价值
的能力；创造性包括承担风险、发现学习乐趣和培养想象力和自觉性；互助能力
是培养小组学习和协作学习的能力；策略意识指在学习过程中学习者保持自我意
识和自我管理行为；学习韧性指学习者面对学习问题和困难的信心和方法。《有
效终身学习量表》的七大维度可以有效评估学习者的自主学习能力，笔者会有选
择地把它融入《商务外语自主学习能力量表》的设计中。表 4-2 是该量表的描述
语节选。

Dimension	Description
Changing and learning	A sense of myself as someone who learns and changes over time.
Critical curiosity	An orientation to want to "get beneath the surface."
Meaning making	Making connections and seeing that learning "matters to me."
Creativity	Risk-taking, playfulness, imagination and intuition.
Interdependence	Learning with and from others and also able to manage without them.
Strategic awareness	Being aware of my thoughts, feelings and actions as a learner, and able to use that awareness to manage learning processes.
Resilience	The readiness to persevere in the development of my own learning power.

图 4-6 《有效终身学习量表》的七大维度

表 4-2 《有效终身学习量表》描述语节选

Benchmark 1	25	wants to learn new information	ELLI	motivational
Benchmark 1	27	tends to get upset when he/she has trouble learning something	ELLI	social/emotional
Benchmark 1	28	struggles to learn something because he/she is not very bright	ELLI	social/emotional
Benchmark 1	29	has difficulty in dealing with new learning tasks	ELLI	social/emotional
Benchmark 1	30	gives up all too easily when the going gets tough	ELLI	social/emotional
Benchmark 1	31	can find at least one person who is an important guide for him/her in learning	ELLI	social/emotional
Benchmark 2	48	can prioritize his/her work	ELLI	metacognitive
Benchmark 2	49	is able to focus on a problem	ELLI	metacognitive
Benchmark 2	50	tries to know himself/herself better	ELLI	metacognitive
Benchmark 2	59	likes to question the things he/she is learning	ELLI	motivational
Benchmark 2	60	likes to learn about things that really matter to him/her	ELLI	motivational

（续表）

Benchmark 2	61	likes learning new things that make sense	ELLI	motivational
Benchmark 2	62	needs to know why	ELLI	motivational
Benchmark 2	63	is open to new learning opportunities	ELLI	motivational
Benchmark 2	64	is open to new ideas	ELLI	motivational
Benchmark 2	65	enjoy challenges	ELLI	motivational
Benchmark 2	66	is willing to take risks	ELLI	motivational
Benchmark 2	70	treats the role of the teacher is to act as a resource person	ELLI	social/emotional
Benchmark 2	71	is willing to accept advice from others	ELLI	social/emotional
Benchmark 2	73	goes on learning for a long time	ELLI	learning habit
Benchmark 2	74	prefers to solve problems on his/her own	ELLI	learning habit
Benchmark 2	75	prefers to plan his/her own learning	ELLI	learning habit
Benchmark 2	76	can set specific times for his/her study	ELLI	learning habit
Benchmark 2	77	seeks answers and asks questions of his/her data positively	ELLI	learning habit
Benchmark 3	81	learns from his/her mistakes	ELLI	cognitive
Benchmark 3	87	is confident in his/her ability to search out information	ELLI	cognitive
Benchmark 3	88	regards that getting to the bottom of things is more important than getting a good mark	ELLI	cognitive
Benchmark 3	89	is able to improve the way he/she do things	ELLI	metacognitive
Benchmark 3	90	solves problems using a plan	ELLI	metacognitive

4.4.2.2 《个人胜任力——培养学生学习能力的框架》

《个人胜任力——培养学生学习能力的框架》是由美国国家学习创新中心开发的学习创新能力评估量表，已经在美国多所学校广泛应用，是学习成绩和教育成果的重要评估工具。《个人胜任力——培养学生学习能力的框架》将自主学习能力主要分为五个部分：个人能力、学习习惯、对学习的掌控、能力的提升、能力的强化和环境。其中个人能力是量表的主体部分，分为认知能力、元认知能力、动机能力和社会 / 情感能力（见图 4-7 和图 4-8）。鉴于该表在学习能力评估中的重要地位和广泛应用，其对笔者设计的《商务外语自主学习能力量表》具有重要的参考意义。

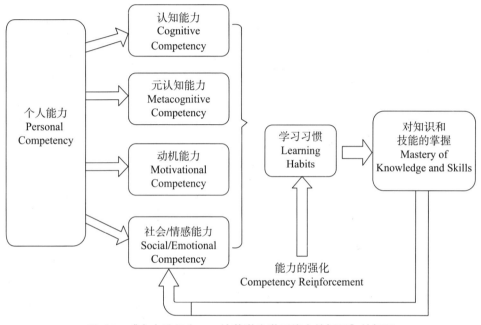

图 4-7 《个人胜任力——培养学生学习能力的框架》的框架

4.2.2.3 《自我导向学习量表》

《自我导向学习量表》是衡量自主学习能力广泛使用的量表，它的效度和信度已经被多位学者认可（Delahaye & Smith，1995；Durr，1992）。《自我导向学习量表》涵盖了自我导向学习中个人展示的态度、能力和品质（Wiley，1983）。

图 4-9 是《自我导向学习量表》的描述语节选，该量表的描述语简单易懂，使用者将自主学习能力行为与量表描述语进行对照和反省，可以评估个人的自主学习能力，如第 1 条 "I solve problems using a plan" 就是评估使用者使用自主学习策略的能力。

《自我导向学习量表》为自主学习能力的测量提供了客观可靠的测评工具，因此，笔者甄选了此量表的部分自主学习能力的相关描述语作为《商务外语自主学习能力量表》的描述语。

Context: School Community

Table 1: Cognitive Competency in the School Community

Theory of Action	When the entire school community works together to enhance students' cognitive competency, every student's reservoir of knowledge is expanded and their new learning is facilitated.
Goal	All members of the school community (families, students, administrators, teachers, other school personnel, and volunteers) will understand and support the importance of building each student's reservoir of knowledge through a standards-aligned curriculum, rich reading, writing, memorization, and vocabulary development.

Logic Model

Indicator/Objective/Evidence	Strategy	Resources, Technology
Indicator: The School Community Council ensures that all parents understand the purpose of a standards-aligned curriculum, their own children's progress, and their role in supporting learning at home. **Objective**: The School Community Council will ensure that all parents understand the purpose of a standards-aligned curriculum, their own children's progress, and their role in supporting learning at home. **Evidence**: Documentation of initiatives. Surveys administered to parents confirm their understanding of cognitive competency, their own children's progress, and their role in supporting learning at home. Pre- and post-questionnaires from professional development workshops.	Communication: Provide information for parents on the school community's goal for building cognitive competency, the purpose of a standards-aligned curriculum, and how parents support learning at home. Include parent-provided examples.	Resources: Newsletter, community "town hall" discussion Technology-aided Resources: School website section for parents; parent feedback via website; ongoing social media campaign; streaming and archived video of "town hall" meetings; online library of digital videos of student, parents, graduates, and educators on the importance of cognitive competency
	Education: Provide workshops for parents on the purpose of a standards-aligned curriculum and home strategies to encourage rich reading, writing, memorization, and vocabulary development.	Resources: Curricula and protocol for workshops and workshop leaders for face-to-face and for synchronous and asynchronous online delivery Technology-aided Resources: Webinars; interactive learning modules; e-workbooks; in-situ and post workshop online surveys of relevance, utility, and application; "recommended" lists of cognitive enrichment software and apps for use at home
	Connection: Include a discussion of cognitive competency and the parents' role in supporting their children's cognitive development at home at the open house and in parent–teacher–student conferences.	Resources: Agendas for open houses and parent–teacher–student conferences; guiding questions Technology-aided Resources: Online resource library of related digital articles, and video samples of parent/child interactions and parent/educator discussions for modeling and review

Personal Competencies

Table 1: Cognitive Competency in the School Community

Indicator: The School Community Council ensures that all school personnel and volunteers understand cognitive competency and their roles relative to its enhancement in students. **Objective**: The School Community Council will ensure that all school personnel and volunteers understand cognitive competency and their roles relative to its enhancement in students. **Evidence**: Copies of job descriptions and descriptions of role of volunteers. Surveys of personnel and volunteers. Pre- and post-questionnaires from professional development.	Goals and Roles: Include in job descriptions and description of role of volunteers ways to enhance students' cognitive competency.	Resources: Job descriptions and description of role of volunteers, job aides to support practices in action Technology-aided Resources: Online resource library of related articles and digital video samples of volunteers enhancing cognitive competency; "recommended" lists of cognitive enrichment software and apps for use within the school day
	Education: Provide professional development for all school personnel and volunteers on cognitive competency.	Resources: Curricula and protocol for professional development leaders for face-to-face and for synchronous and asynchronous online delivery Technology-aided Resources: Webinars; interactive learning modules; e-workbooks; in-situ and post workshop online surveys of relevance, utility, and application; "recommended" lists of cognitive enrichment and other related software and tools

图 4-8 《个人胜任力——培养学生学习能力的框架》描述语节选

I solve problems using a plan
I prioritize my work
I like to solve (answer) puzzles/questions
I manage my time well
I have good management skills
I set strict time frames
I prefer to plan my own learning
I prefer to direct my own learning
I believe the role of the teacher is to act as a resource person
I am systematic in my learning
I am able to focus on a problem
I often review the way nursing practices are conducted
I need to know why
I critically evaluate new ideas
I prefer to set my own learning goals
I am willing to change my ideas
I will ask for help in my learning when necessary
I am willing to accept advice from others
I learn from my mistakes

图 4-9　《自我导向学习量表》描述语节选

4.4.3　《商务外语自主学习能力量表》的研制

4.4.3.1　《商务外语自主学习能力量表》

笔者设计的《商务外语自主学习能力量表》可以为学习者提供一个自我评估的工具，鼓励学习者进行批判性思考，提升自己的学习能力。自我评估是培养学习者自主学习能力的重要步骤，学习者需要根据自身的学习成果进行自我评估并不断发展自己新的能力（Nunan，1999；Benson，2001；Egel，2003）。《商务外语自主学习能力量表》也有利于商务外语教学，教师可以根据对学生自主学习能力的评估来决定教学内容和教学计划的安排。表 4-3 是《商务外语自主学习能力量表》的节选。

表 4-3　《商务外语自主学习能力量表》节选

Benchmark 1	9	applies knowledge and skills to demonstrate comprehension and performance in novel situations
Benchmark 1	10	has difficulty defining the scope of the research question or thesis
Benchmark 1	11	has difficulty determining key concepts
Benchmark 1	12	presents examples, facts, or theories from one field of study or perspective

（续表）

Benchmark 1	13	completes required work
Benchmark 1	14	is not very familiar with useful information resourees or websites
Benchmark 1	15	cannot find target information effectively
Benchmark 1	16	has limited capacity in search of the information
Benchmark 1	17	uses no strategies in information search
Benchmark 1	18	describes one's own performances with general descriptors of success and failure
Benchmark 1	19	can list a learning plan
Benchmark 1	20	begins to show interest in pursuing knowledge independently

4.4.3.2 对《商务外语自主学习能力量表》的分析

自主学习能力作为一种不断发展的动态能力，是可以监控和测评的。根据美国心理学家、自主学习专家 Zimmerman 和 Schunk 建立的自主学习能力评价体系，笔者设计的量表将商务外语自主学习能力分为四个等级（见表4-4）：第一等级要具备自主学习观察能力，学习者只能观察好的学习案例，但无法将新的信息和技能整合到自己的信息和技能中。第二等级是自主学习模仿层次，在这个层次，学习者正在发展向优秀学习者学习的能力，他们可以通过模仿好的学习案例来制定自己的学习策略和方法。第三等级是自主学习自我控制，学习者有能力调整学习策略以适应各种学习情境。第四等级是完全自主学习，学习者可以在新的学习环境中独立、灵活地运用所学的技能，并补充必要的策略和技能来完成新的学习任务。

表4-4　商务外语自主学习能力四大等级

第一等级	自主学习观察能力	学习者具备观察好的学习案例的能力，但无法将新的信息和技能整合到自己的信息和技能中。
第二等级	自主学习模仿层次	学习者具备模仿好的学习案例来制定自己的学习策略和方法的能力。
第三等级	自主学习自我控制	学习者有能力调整学习策略以适应各种学习情境，有效地完成学习任务。
第四等级	完全自主学习	学习者具备在新的学习环境中独立、灵活地运用所学的技能，并补充必要的策略和技能来完成新的学习任务的能力。

　　《商务外语自主学习能力量表》共有 149 条描述语，综合评估学习者自主学习的认知能力、元认知能力、动机能力、社会 / 情感能力。例如，第 4 条 "reviews prior learning at a surface level" 就是考查学习者灵活利用已学知识的能力，具备第一等级"自主学习观察能力"的学习者只能从表面上掌握已学习的知识。第四等级的学习者能够利用已学知识促进新知识的学习，将新知识融入已有的知识网络中，提高自主学习的效率。第 59 条 "is open to new learning opportunities" 和第 60 条 "is open to new ideas" 描述了处于第二等级"自主学习模仿层次"的学习者的自主学习能力，这个层次的学习者对新的学习机会和新想法充满好奇心，愿意尝试去探索。第 91 条 "can list a systematical and effective learning plan"、第 86 条 "solves problems using a plan" 和第 80 条 "can recognize one's strengths and weaknesses" 评估学习者的元认知能力，这三条分别描述了学习者自主学习目标分析、自主学习策略选择和自主学习检测的能力。学习者的自主学习能力越强，就越有能力制定合理的学习目标，抓住一切学习机会，自觉监控学习过程，根据出现的问题及时调整学习策略，提高自主学习效率。第 97 条 "prefers to set his/her own learning goals" 和第 98 条 "has high beliefs in his/her abilities" 描述了学习者的自主学习动机，他们能够独立设定学习目标并且对学习能力充满信心，具备较强的自主学习自我效能感。第 108 条 "asks for help in his/her learning when necessary" 和第 109 条 "can control his/her feeling when learning" 主要评估学习者的社会 / 情感能力。自主学习并不意味着个体学习，自主学习能力强的学习者遇到困难时，有能力通过不同渠道寻找学习资料并具备整合、分析学习资源的能力。同时，他们具有很强的学习韧性，不断向自主学习过程中出现的困难发起挑战，找到高效的解决困难的方法。

　　笔者设计的《商务外语自主学习能力量表》的描述语易于理解，虽然描述语来源于一些具有国际影响力的自主学习能力量表，但并不是机械地从中提取出来的。每个描述语都经过精心筛选、修订和加工，使学习者更易于理解。例如，为了让意义更加明确，在不改变意思的情况下对一些冗长的句子进行了简化。量表中的描述语大多数格式统一，看起来更直观。

商务外语批判性思维能力量表

在 21 世纪，批判性思维被公认为人们生活中最重要和最必要的思维技能（Facione，1990；Friedman，2005）。信息时代的知识更新很快，如果学习者只学习书本中的知识，可能会发现自己学到的东西可能已经落后了。学校将批判性思维置于教育的中心，学生会终身受益（Boeckx，2010）。批判性思维应该是高等教育目标的核心要素，受过高等教育的人必须懂得如何从各个学科中汲取知识并作合理的判断（Giancarlo，2001）。批判性思维可以引导学习者深入学习，鼓励他们发现和处理信息，学会全方位思考，得出合理的结论；批判创新思维鼓励学习者在复杂问题上为自己的立场辩护，理解各种观点，分析和澄清问题、结论，检查和评估事实、猜想；批判性思维有利于学习者发展创新能力，通过自己的推理和判断得到创新性的合理方案。

现在，批判性思维已成为大学教学和政府政策中明文规定的核心学习目标（Facione，1995）。近年来，针对外语学习者批判性思维能力培养不力的批评越来越多。一些学者认为外语学习者批判性思维能力不如其他学科的学习者，甚至缺乏批判性思维（黄源深，1998；文秋芳，周燕，2006）。这些批评提醒商务外语学习者培养批判性思维能力的重要性和紧迫性。《普通高等学校本科专业类教学质量国家标准（外国语言文学类）》规定，创新能力是商务外语人才必须具备的几大能力之一。

培养批判性思维能力，教师和学习者需要一个科学合理的批判性思维能力量表来帮助其确定学习目标、评价学习成果，这是培养批判性思维能力的基础

（文秋芳等，2011）。为此，笔者会构建批判性思维能力的理论框架并设计一个衡量商务外语学习者批判性思维能力的量表，以评价商务外语学习者的批判性思维能力。

5.1 国内外批判性思维能力的相关研究

5.1.1 国外批判性思维能力的相关研究

20世纪30年代，哲学家John Dewey首次强调教师和教育者应把培养科学思维放在教学首位，加强人们对"反思在教育过程中重要性"的认识。尽管Dewey当时尚未提出"批判性思维"一词，但他对批判性思维的研究有着重要的影响。随后，一些认知心理学家和研究智力理论的学者又进一步深入研究批判性思维，并在批判性思维与反思判断、问题构建、高阶思维、逻辑思维、决策、问题解决与科学方法之间建立了概念联系（Kitchener，1990；Sternberg，1985）。在过去的二三十年间，西方学者在批判性思维领域进行了大量研究，如批判性思维的定义、子能力的缺位、批判性思维能力量表的设计与开发以及高等教育中培养批判性思维的教育方法（文秋芳等，2009）等。这些研究大致可以分为三个部分。

（1）界定批判性思维能力的分项能力。1987年，一些美国著名的哲学家经过探讨研究，完成了"德尔菲"项目，构建了思辨能力的双维结构模型。1995年，美国学者Richard Paul从教学需求出发，构建了思辨能力的三元结构模型。

（2）构建批判性思维能力的量具。国外文献报告有一定的科学依据的思维能力量具数量众多，有近30种。量具试题是客观性的选择题，包括思维人格倾向量具和批判性思维能力量具两种。例如，美国"德尔菲"项目组开发了两个量具：《加利福尼亚批判性思维技能测试量表（CCTST）》《加利福尼亚批判性思维倾向问卷（CCTDI）》，这两个量具经过了4年的信度和效度检验。牛津大学、剑桥大学、伦敦经济学院等将思维能力测试（TSA）列入本科录取进程，该考试于2001年开始在剑桥大学试用，参加测试的人数逐年增长。

（3）探索高等教育中批判性思维能力培养的途径及其有效性。研究者们围绕批判性思维能力是否应教、如何教等问题展开研究，不少研究者着力分析各学科特需的批判性思维能力。Pithers 和 Soden 总结了英国学者在该领域的研究状况，指出了高校教学在此方面存在的诸多问题（文秋芳，王建卿，赵彩然，等，2009）。

总之，国外有关批判性思维能力的研究已形成较为成熟的理论体系。思辨能力测量工具种类多样，都是在科学界定思辨能力及其分项技能的基础上经过反复研究编制而成的，且都进行过长时期、大规模检验，有良好的信度、效度，被广泛应用于学校和社会领域（文秋芳，王建卿，2011）。为评估批判性思维能力，国外学者对批判性思维能力量表的设计和开发作出了大量的努力，开发出了超过20 个具有影响力的能力量表。这些能力量表是笔者设计《商务外语批判性思维能力量表》的重要描述语资源。

5.1.2　国内批判性思维能力的相关研究

与国外的研究相比，我国对批判性思维能力的研究较少。20 世纪 90 年代，我国开始引入批判性思维的概念，主要在教育心理学和逻辑学方面开展研究（王瑞霞，2011）。2000 年以后，有关批判性思维的研究成果明显增加。国内对于大学生思维能力的研究大多是对思维定义、分类的讨论或是一些评述或综述性的研究（文秋芳，2008）。有关批判性思维方面的图书、介绍性论文主要有：武宏志、周建武的《批判性思维：论证逻辑视角》（修订版），谷振诣、刘壮虎的《批判性思维教程》，董毓的《批判性思维原理和方法——走向新的认知和实践（第二版）》等。其中，武宏志在研究批判性思维方面作出了很大贡献，2008 年在延安大学成立了 21 世纪新逻辑研究院。

在测量或评估批判性思维方面，目前国内主要探究了四种方法：第一种最为常见，即对国外量表进行汉化并使用，如 2001 年罗清旭、杨鑫辉基于 CCTDI修订的《加利福尼亚批判性思维倾向问卷》中文版、2015 年赵婷婷和杨翊基于美国教育考试服务中心的能力透视测试（ETS Proficiency Profile）设计的《EPP（中国）批判性思维能力测试》。第二种是在国外量表汉化的基础上，经过修改和本土化后形成适宜国内使用的批判性思维量表，如彭美慈、汪国成 2004 年针对护理专业学生制定的基于 CCTDI 的《批判性思维能力测量表》（《CTDI-CV》）。这两类量表存在试题翻译不准确、不符合中国国情等问题，无法反映中国学生思辨能力的真实情况。第三种是自主研发的量表，如沈红等在全国本科生能力测评中使用的加拿大籍华裔学者董毓领衔的团队开发的《全国本科生批判性思维测评》；汕头大学高教所自编的经四次修订的《大学生批判性思维测试量表》；文秋芳团队提出的以层级模型为理论框架的量具（文秋芳，刘艳萍，王海妹，等，2010）。这类量具质量参差不齐，有些量具缺乏可靠的信度和效度检验（文秋芳，2008）。第四种是用国外的模型对批判性思维能力进行编码并评估，如冷静、郭日发使用学者 Murphy 的批判性思维编码体系对在线话语的批判性思维水平进行分析。

值得一提的是文秋芳团队的研究成果。2008 年，文秋芳着手主持国家社科基金项目"我国外语类大学生思维能力现状研究"，构建符合中国国情的大学生思维能力量具。同年 5 月，文秋芳提出了以层级模型为理论框架的量具，该量具的理论框架与思路得到认可，但试题不够完善。2010 年，文秋芳团队继续修订该量具，对测试题进行整合，同时增加题量、缩短测试时间、加大难度。修订后的新量具具有较好的信度与效度，基本上可以用于测量我国文科专业大学生的思辨能力。当然，量具的完善是一个永无止境的过程，文秋芳团队仍在修订量具，今后学界应该关注的是如何进一步运用量具发现外语类大学生在思辨能力上的不足，探索提高思辨能力的途径（文秋芳，刘艳萍，王海妹，等，2010）。

在设计批判性思维能力量表之前，笔者将给出批判性思维能力的定义，再构建相关的理论框架。

5.1.3　商务外语批判性思维能力的概念界定

"Critical Thinking Skills"这一术语在西方被广泛使用，在我国，有的学者将其译为"批判性思维能力"，也有学者将其翻译为"高层次思维能力"和"思辨能力"（文秋芳等，2009）。本书采用"批判性思维能力"这个翻译。对批判性思维能力进行科学定义是批判性思维能力教学和评估的基本任务（Jones，1993；Kurfiss，1988；Norris & Ennis，1989）。学者们从不同的角度对批判性思维下了不同的定义。我国学者文秋芳认为批判性思维能力包括两个层次：元思辨能力和思辨能力。元思辨能力是指对自己的思辨进行计划、检查、调整与评估的技能；思辨能力包括与认知相关的技能和标准，以及与思辨品质相关的情感特质。批判性思维比较有代表性和影响力的概念是由美国批判性思维中心主任保罗提出的。保罗认为，"批判性思维就是通过一定的标准评价思维，进而改善思维，它是一种主动、持续和缜密地解析、应用、分析、综合、评估、支配信念和行为的过程"。简言之，批判性思维的核心要素是在解决问题之前进行思考并作出延迟判断（崔诣晨，刘青玉，李凡姝，2018）。

美国哲学协会有关批判性思维能力是理想批判者的描述是被广泛接受的批判性思维的定义："理想的批判性思维者通常是好奇的、见多识广的，相信推理，思想开放，灵活，能公正评估，诚实面对个人偏见，审慎判断，乐于深思熟虑，对问题有清晰认识，处理复杂问题时条理分明，用心搜寻相关信息，合理选择评价标准，专注探究，坚持寻求探究领域和环境所能允许的最为精确的结果。"

美国哲学协会对批判性思维者详细的描述明确了批判性思维者应该具备核心认知技能和批判性思维的子技能，这为笔者对批判性思维能力的定义具有一定的参考价值。

对于传统的批判性思维能力的评价，学者们一直把重点放在对批判性思维技能的测试上。然而，一些批判性思维学者认为批判性思维能力不应该只局限于思维技能上，还必须包括认知能力和思维态度（Ennis，1990；Halpern，1998；Paul，2001）。思维技能指学习者在批判性思维中运用的认知技能；认知能力和思维态度，是人们在解决问题、评价观点、作出决策时的思维倾向。批判性思维是一种深思熟虑的思维，学习者需要利用认知能力和思维倾向来自我激励，培养并保持批判性思维。基于此，笔者认为，批判性思维能力由认知技能、认知倾向和认知动机组成。动机是批判性思维能力的核心能力（Eccles，2002）。整合Ennis、Halpern、Paul 等学者的研究成果，笔者认为批判性思维能力的要素可以用图 5–1 表示。

由认知技能、认知倾向和认知动机组成的批判性思维能力模型是笔者设计的《商务外语批判性思维能力量表》的主要理论框架。这三个子能力相互关联。批判性思维认知倾向影响认知技能和认知动机（Lewin，1935），重视批判性思维认知倾向会促使人们掌握认知技能，强化培养批判性思维能力的动机。思维倾向

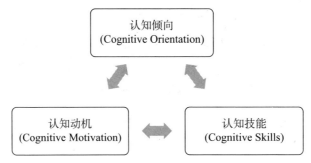

图 5–1　批判性思维能力要素关系图

可以视作固定的、始终如一的内部动机（Facione，2000）。认知倾向与认知技能的培养也是互相促进的。认知倾向有利于认知技能的发展，同时，认知技能的掌握也有利于认知倾向的形成。这三个子能力作为批判性思维的核心要素，是笔者设计的《商务外语批判性思维能力量表》的理论基础。

5.2　批判性思维能力的理论框架

批判性思维是人类有目的的反省式的认知过程（Giancarlo，2001）；批判性思维是一种自觉的具有目的的思维过程，也是深思熟虑的推理过程（Valenzuela，2011）。批判性思维能力主要由认知技能、认知倾向和认知动机三个子能力组成（见图 5–2）。

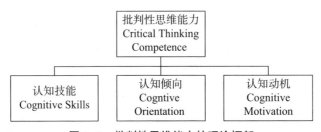

图 5–2　批判性思维能力的理论框架

5.2.1　Halpern 的认知技能理论

认知技能是批判性思维的认知能力，主要指在批判性思考时知道该做什么和如何去做（Valenzuela，2011）。批判性思维认知技能的培养对学习者在学校和整个人生中取得成功至关重要（Halpern，1998）。学习学科知识时，人们要掌握各种各样的认知技巧，学会批判性地思考。认知技能是重要的思维工具，学习者要取得理想的学习结果需要培养批判性思维技能。尽管大部分人具有一定的批判性思维能力，然而，能够思考是培养批判性思维能力的必要条件，而不是充分条件。批判性思维是一种较高级的思维，综合使用了多种不同的高级思维技能。要具备批判性思维能力，学习者需要发展自己的推理能力，不要被动接受信息，应该积极思考，提高思考的自主性。

5.2.2　Facione 的思维认知倾向理论

思维认知倾向指的是在认知过程中批判性地思考的内在倾向或趋势（Facione，1997）。有时批判性思维认知倾向被认为是批判思想家的品质（Sears，1991）或批判精神（Orr，1991）。态度、价值观和偏好是影响人的行为和批判性思维认知倾向的重要人格维度。对学习者批判性思维认知倾向的描述也可以看作对其智力性格的一系列描述（Tishman，1994）。具备批判性思维认知倾向的学习者更能在教学环境和非教学环境中应用各种批判性思维关键技能。

5.2.3　Valenzuela 的认知动机理论

认知动机是批判性思维的一个重要因素，它影响着认知过程中批判性思维的激活和保持。内在动机十分重要，如个人对知识的好奇心，能促使个人积极主动思考和质疑。外在动机也不可忽视，如获得奖励，可在一定程度上推动个体进行批判性思考。认知动机和认知倾向是相互联系的，具有积极的认知倾向的人更可能成为批判性的思想家，而认知动机是提升学习者批判性思维能力的重要因素。

5.3　商务外语批判性思维能力模型的构建

基于前文的批判性思维能力框架和其他人的研究，下面进一步将批判思维能力细化，以便全面评估商务外语学习者的批判性思维能力（如图 5–3）。笔者建立的模型主要整合了以下学者的研究成果：Facione、Halpern、Giancarlo 和

Valenzuela 等学者对批判性思维能力认知技能的研究；Facione、Giancarlo、Ennis 等学者对批判性思维认知倾向的研究；Wigfield、Eccles、Duncan、McKeachie、Valenzuela、Nieto、Saiz 等对批判性思维动机的研究。

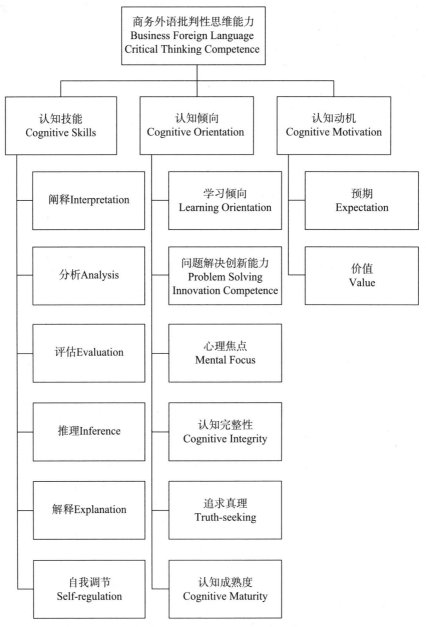

图 5-3　商务外语批判性思维能力模型

5.3.1　商务外语批判性思维认知技能

认知技能有很多种，不同学者对认知技能的分类也有所不同。例如，Ennis 认为认知技能具有五个子技能：（1）问题调查；（2）论点分析；（3）答案分析或提出问题；（4）信息来源的可信度判断；（5）观察和判断假设。Halpern 认为认知技能包括五大子能力：（1）检查假设；（2）口头推理；（3）不确定性和决策分析；（4）解决方案分类；（5）创造性激发。Swartz 和 Perkins 从更广泛的角度来定义认知技能，他们将认知技能分为以下几类：创造性思维、批判性思维、决策能力、日常问题决策和数学推理能力。Facione 对于认知技能的分类得到了大家的广泛认可，他认为认知技能包括六种技能：阐释、分析、评估、推理、解释和自我调节（见表 5–1）。这些技能的划分非常清晰并且合乎逻辑。虽然这六种技能并不能涵盖所有批判性思维技能，但它们是批判性思维的核心（Facione，1990）。因此，笔者基于 Facione 在 "Critical Thinking: A Statement of Expert Consensus for Purposes of Educational Assessment and Instruction" 一文中提出的批判性思维技能框架，构建了商务外语批判性思维能力模型，以评估商务外语学习者的批判性思维能力。

表 5–1　认知技能（Facione，1990）

批判性思维认知技能 Critical Thinking Cognitive Skills	阐释 Interpretation	分类 Categorization 意义解码 Decoding Significance 意义澄清 Clarifying Meaning
	分析 Analysis	观点探测 Examining Ideas 论证确认 Identifying Arguments 论证分析 Analyzing Arguments
	评估 Evaluation	判断评价 Assessing Claims 论证评价 Assessing Arguments
	推理 Inference	证据查证 Querying Evidence 设想多种可能性 Conjecturing Alternatives 导出结论 Drawing Conclusions
	解释 Explanation	说明结果 Stating Results 过程判断 Justifying Procedures 展示结论 Presenting Arguments
	自我调节 Self-regulation	自省 Self-examination 自我纠错 Self-correction

（1）阐释

阐释是对意义的理解，它包括分类、意义解码和意义澄清（Facione，1990）。为了在学习和思考过程中正确地阐释，首先，人们必须理解或恰当地表述类别、区别和描述日常经验、事件和信念的意义；其次，人们还必须从已知的场景中描述、检测信息和动机，比如在被询问问题时解读提问者的目的或者面对面交流时观察面部表情或手势的意义（Facione，1990）；最后，人们应该分析阐释的词语、观念、概念，对陈述的行为、事件等的语境意义作出明确的描述。

（2）分析

分析是一个重要的思维工具，包括探测观点、论证确认和论证分析论据。当分析观点时，学习者应该首先确定问题的专业术语和表达，然后比较关于某个问题的不同观点、概念，确定其他相关的概念之间的关系。意义分析是论证确认、论证分析的过程。论证确认和论证分析是分析的关键，需要得出分析的主要结论和观点的整体推理结构。

（3）评估

评估是根据认知、经验和推理得出观点和思维过程的可信度，主要包括评估论点和论据的逻辑性（Facione，1990）。所有思维过程都具有潜在的优势和劣势，学习者需要全面分析思维推理过程，对所有相关观点进行客观评价。

（4）推理

所有的思维过程都包含推理，通过合理的推理，人们会根据手头的信息确定就某一问题采取什么立场或意见。推理需要学习者根据已知的信息得出合理结论和猜想，从而对已知的数据、信息和情境赋予更多的意义。推导过程中需要考虑的因素不仅来自已知信息，还来自合理的假设。因此，学习者应寻找和收集更多的信息，得出更科学、更全面的结论。针对一个问题，学习者需要根据不同条件推导出问题的多个可能性，并制定多种备选方案。

（5）解释

解释是陈述推理结果，并证明推理过程是由恰当的证据、论证方法等所支持的。批判性思维者需要证明其推理过程是合理、符合逻辑且具有信服力的，其论据和论证过程能支持他的论点和结论。

（6）自我调节

批判性思维也需要自我调节，批判性思维者应该有意识地监控自己的认知活动和思维过程。自我调节的关键步骤是自省和自我纠错。自省是为了反省自身推理，以作出客观反思和自我评估。当发现错误或缺陷时，学习者应该进行自我纠错。通过自省和自我纠错，可以不断提高批判性思维认知能力。

上述六种思维认知技能作为重要的思维能力指标，已集成到笔者设计的《商务外语批判性思维能力量表》中。

5.3.2　商务外语批判性思维认知倾向

不同学者对批判性思维认知倾向的定义各不相同（Nieto，2009）。一些学者强调批判性思维认知倾向的动机，因为他们认为批判性思维认知倾向是激发技能的过程（Ennis，1996；Norris，1994；Jay，1996 等），而有的学者则认为批判性思维认知倾向更像是一种态度强化的智力习惯（Salomon，1994）。基于 Paul、Salomon、Siegel 等人的研究，笔者设计的《商务外语批判性思维能力量表》将批判性思维认知倾向定义为人的性格或智力特征，在 Peter A. Facione 和 Noreen C. Facione（1992）看来，批判性思维认知倾向包括学习倾向、问题解决创新能力、心理焦点、认知完整性、追求真理和认知成熟度（见图 5-4）。

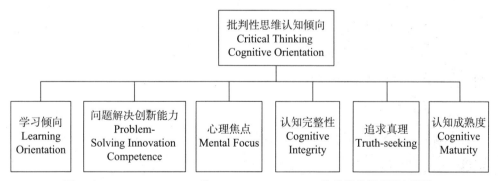

图 5-4　Peter A. Facione 和 Noreen C. Facione 的批判性思维认知倾向

（1）学习倾向

学习倾向是自觉提高人们的知识和技能基础的一种倾向。具有良好的学习倾向的学习者将学习过程作为解决问题的重要手段，乐于接受挑战，并把寻求有效信息作为重要策略。学习倾向主要包括两个因素：批判性思维自信和求知欲。

批判性思维自信可以衡量人们对自己推理过程的自我信任程度。它让人们相信自己有能力作出正确的推理判断，并能合理地解决问题。具有批判性思维自信的人更倾向于批判性思考，更有信心掌握批判性思维技能。

求知欲指学习者的智力好奇心和学习欲望，即使新知识在不久的将来并不是直接有用的，他们仍愿意学习新知识。求知欲是人们获得成功必不可少的因素。

具有高度批判性思维自信和求知欲的学习者，具有更强的学习倾向，反之亦然。笔者设计的《商务外语批判性思维能力量表》会通过批判性思维自信和求知欲衡量学习者的学习倾向。

（2）问题解决创新能力

问题解决创新能力是一种使用创新的想法来解决问题的能力，包括想象力、创造力、自主性、多元文化包容性。创新是指学生在学习中的探索精神与了解新事物和新方法的求知意志。在面对困难的问题时，人们需要富有想象力和创造力，并且找到创新性的问题解决方法。当人们渴望进入新奇而富有挑战性的情境时，就会倾向于成为一个创造性的问题解决者。创造性的问题解决者更倾向于自主学习、思考，进而取得新的突破。

要成为创造性的问题解决者，必须思想开放，对不同的观点持容忍态度，并对自己存偏见的可能性很敏感。在文化多元的社会中，人们要具备一定的包容心，尊重他人不同的信仰和生活方式。愿意接受新思想的人更加富有创造力，否则，人们容易被限制在自己的世界里。

（3）心理焦点

心理焦点是批判性思考时系统性的任务导向，是保持头脑清醒的心理聚焦。能进行批判性思考的人明白，所有的思考都应该指向某个目标。如果人们对自己的目标很清楚，那么更有可能实现目标（Paul，2005）。当人们有心理焦点时，会集中精力处理他们要完成的任务。系统性和分析性是心理焦点的两个重要指标。

系统性是指人们在思考问题时是有组织的、有序的、专注的并且坚持不懈的。无论人们面临什么问题，找到解决方法并最终解决问题是最重要的。

分析性是指人们运用推理和证据解决问题的能力。分析能力是探究性思维的核心倾向（Facione，1995）。分析能力强的人更倾向于通过逻辑推理来解决问题。

由于思维具有系统性和分析性，人们在思考时应该有一个更清晰的焦点，从而有利于养成批判性思维倾向。笔者也将系统性和分析性纳入了《商务外语批判性思维能力量表》。

（4）认知完整性

认知完整性指分析针对同一问题的不同观点后达成最佳决策的能力，包括观察力和客观公正性。具有批判性思维的学习者能观察到他人思想、语言和行为的不一致，他们需要承认有时自己也言行不一。学习者要公平客观地对待不同观点，减少或避免偏见，从而得出客观、全面、合理的结论。

（5）追求真理

追求真理是指学习者在特定的环境中寻求正确知识的倾向。学习者应该勇敢地提出问题，探求正确的答案，客观对待真理。为了寻求真理，学习者必须不断评估新的数据和证据，同时还要检查现有的信息和证据。追求真理的两个重要指标是反思能力和探索能力。

反思能力体现在个体对自身思考过程和得出结论的不断审视上。个体不能仅仅接受最初的想法或结论，要深入思考其合理性、逻辑性和可靠性。例如，在面对一个观点时，要反思自己得出支持或反对这一观点的依据是否充分，思考过程中是否存在偏见或漏洞。通过反思，个体能够发现错误、纠正偏差，从而更接近真理。

探索能力促使个体积极主动地寻求新的知识和信息，以拓展对事物的理解。具有较强探索能力的人不会满足于现有的解释和答案，他们会不断追问"为什么"和"还有什么"。比如，在研究一个科学问题时，不局限于已有的研究成果，而是努力挖掘尚未被发现的方面，尝试新的研究方法和途径。这种探索精神帮助个体突破既有认知的局限，发现更多关于真理的线索。

（6）认知成熟度

认知成熟度主要测试人们在决策过程中是否明智。认知成熟度高的学习者对问题、观点和决策等具有很强的敏感性。学习者即使面对一些习以为常的问题也应该保持批判性的思考态度，不能认为一切都是理所当然的。学习者必须仔细思考每一个认知决策，尤其是面对复杂的决策时，更加应该展示出认知成熟度，作出正确的决策。认知成熟度包括两个指标，即问题敏锐度和平衡多元利益相关者。

问题敏锐度是指个体能够迅速且精准地察觉问题的本质和关键所在。具有较高问题敏锐度的人，能够在复杂的情境中迅速识别出潜在的问题，不被表面现象所迷惑。他们善于捕捉细微的异常和矛盾，能够从不同的角度审视情况，从而准确界定问题的范围和性质。例如，在一个项目策划中，他们能够快速发现潜在的风险点或可能导致项目延误的关键因素。

个体在思考和决策过程中，要充分考虑到涉及的各方利益，并找到一个相对公平和有效的平衡方案。这需要个体具有全局观，理解不同利益相关者的需求、期望和限制，能够协调各方的矛盾和冲突，避免片面地追求某一方的利益而忽视其他方。比如在制定公共政策时，要兼顾企业、居民、环保组织等多方的利益诉求，以实现整体的最优效果。

5.3.3　商务外语批判性思维认知动机

许多研究人员致力于研究哪些因素会影响人们的批判性思维动机（Boekaerts，2001；Elliott，2007）。Wigfield 和 Eccles 提出的预期/价值模型以及 Valenzuela 等人的研究为笔者提出批判性思维能力的动机概念奠定了理论基础。Wigfield 和 Eccles 认为个体的选择会受到自觉和非意识因素的影响，尤其是动机的影响。他们的动机模型试图解释人们对任务的选择以及对这些任务的坚持，这说明，人们执行一项任务的动机取决于两个因素：预期和价值。

（1）预期

预期指对成功的期望，它能影响对一项任务的坚持和成就。但是预期不同于 Bandura 提出的自我效能感概念。预期是对完成一项任务后自己能够增长的能力的期待。预期不一定符合实际，但拥有恰当的或者较高的预期，学习者会产生更强的完成任务的动机。预期包含两个指标：判断力、积极性。

判断力指个体对自身在批判性思维过程中能否准确分析和评估信息、得出合理结论的预估能力。具有良好判断力的个体，能够较为准确地判断自己在面对问题时，是否具备足够的知识和技能去进行有效的批判性思考。他们能清晰地认识到自己的优势和不足，从而对思考的结果有一个相对合理的预期。

积极性反映在个体对于投入批判性思维活动的主动意愿和热情程度上。当个体对批判性思维的预期较为乐观时，会更积极地参与思考、讨论和分析。他们相信通过自己的努力和思考能够获得有价值的成果，这种积极的心态推动着他们主动运用批判性思维去解决问题。

（2）价值

价值指给任务分配的权重，主要包括四个部分：成就感、兴趣、实用性和成本（Wigfield，1992）。成就感与人们对任务完成的重要性认知密切相关，指一个人从完成某项任务中获得的自我价值实现感；兴趣指人们对完成某项任务的感觉喜好或关切的情绪（Wigfield，1994），当人们重视某一任务时，会产生积极的心理结果；实用性是指个人对任务的价值评估，通常人们会评估某项任务对他们未来计划和其他目标产生的影响（Wigfield，1994）；成本指对某项活动的开展在何种程度限制了其他活动开展的可能性（Valenzuela，2011）。成本包括完成该项任务的情感成本和资源成本（Wigfield，2000）。

本书中商务外语批判性思维能力由认知技能、认知倾向和认知动机三大能力组成，这三大能力又包含多个子能力。虽然这些能力并不能涵盖所有的批判性思维能力，但本书选择的考查批判性思维能力的多项子能力符合科学的思维认知过程，有助于评估商务外语学习者的批判性思维能力。

5.4　《商务外语批判性思维能力量表》的设计

在批判性思维理论框架和商务外语批判性思维能力模型建立之后，能力量表的设计与开发是接下来的一项重要任务。

5.4.1　商务外语批判性思维能力的指标体系

基于前文的商务外语批判性思维能力模型，笔者构建了商务外语批判性思维能力指标体系，该指标体系是构建《商务外语批判性思维能力量表》的基础。

批判性思维能力指标分为认知技能、认知倾向和认知动机三大能力群（二级指标）（见图 5-5）。每个二级指标又可分为若干个三级指标，如认知技能由阐释、分析、评估、推理、解释和自我调节六大指标构成；认知倾向由学习倾向、问题解决创新能力、心理焦点、认知完整性、追求真理、认知成熟度六大指标构成；认知动机由预期和价值两大指标构成。在二级指标的基础上，笔者结合他人的研究和自己的分析，又细化了三级指标（能力），例如，阐释可分为分类、意义解码和意义澄清三项能力；分析可分为观点探测、论证确认和论证分析三项能力；评估可分为判断评价和论证评价两项能力；推理可分为证据查证、设想多种可能性和导出结论三项能力；解释可以分为说明结果、过程判断和展示结论三项能力；自我调节可分为自省和自我纠错两项能力。笔者构建的商务外语批判性思维能力指标体系与批判性思维能力理论框架紧密联系，可以科学、全面地评估商务外语学习者的批判性思维能力。

5.4.2　描述语的来源

通过研究多个国际通用的批判性思维能力量表，笔者选取了几个最具代表性和权威性的量表（见表 5-2），分别是《跨文化知识和能力价值量表》《批判性思维动机量表》《整体批判性思维评分量表》《HEIghten 批判性思维测试》《批判性思维能力评价标准》《加利福尼亚批判性思维倾向量表》，并基于前文建立的批判性思维能力模型和指标体系对描述语进行了仔细筛选、修订和设计，形成了《商务外语批判性思维能力量表》描述语的来源。描述语来源的广泛性可以保证批判性思维能力量表的应用性和科学性。同时，笔者参考的批判性思维能力量表在批判性思维能力的测试方面具有很大影响并且仍在大范围使用，这在一定程度上说明了参考量表的有效性和可靠性，为《商务外语批判性思维能力及量表》的设计和描述语的选择奠定了扎实的基础。由于《批判性思维能力评价标准》没有进行分级，其描述语被收入《商务外语批判性思维能力量表》中的很少，在此就不做

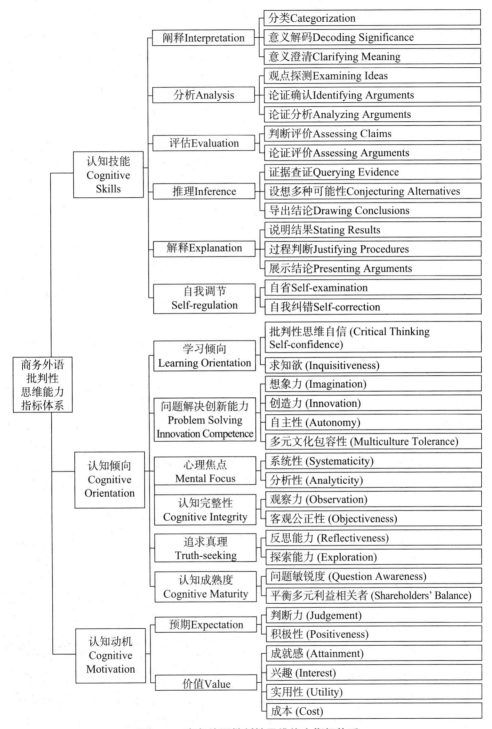

图 5-5　商务外语批判性思维能力指标体系

表 5-2 《商务外语批判性思维能力量表》的描述语来源

文件名	开发者	时间	国别
《跨文化知识和能力价值量表》(Intercultural Knowledge and Competence VALUE Rubrics)	美国学院和大学协会 (The American Association of Colleges and Universities)	2017	美国
《批判性思维动机量表》(Critical Thinking Motivational Scale: A Contribution to the Study of Relationship Between Critical Thinking and Motivation)	Jorge Valenzuela Carreño 等	2011	西班牙
《整体批判性思维评分量表》(Holistic Critical Thinking Scoring Rubric)	Peter A. Facione and Noreen C. Facione	1994	美国
《HEIghten 批判性思维测试》(HEIghten ® Critical Thinking Assessment)	美国教育考试服务中心 (Educational Testing Service)	2016	美国
《批判性思维能力评价标准》(Critical Thinking Competency Standards)	批判性思维协会 (Foundation for Critical Thinking)	2005	美国
《加利福尼亚批判性思维倾向量表》(California Critical Thinking Disposition Inventory)	Peter A. Facione and Noreen C. Facione	1992	美国

介绍了。《跨文化知识和能力价值量表》在前文中已经做过详细介绍，其在大学生综合能力评判中具有重要作用，笔者选择其中的批判性思维能力的部分描述语作为评判商务外语学习者批判性思维能力的重要指标。笔者将对《批判性思维动机量表》《整体批判性思维评分量表》《HEIghten 批判性思维测试》《加利福尼亚批判性思维倾向量表》四个量表进行详细介绍。

5.4.2.1 《批判性思维动机量表》

《批判性思维动机量表》是 Jorge Valenzuela Carreño 博士等研究开发的，通过深入了解学习者的批判性思维动机水平，探索哪些因素可能与批判性思维能力相关，从而对这些因素进行干预和测量。该量表通过评估使用者的批判性思维动机及其组成部分来确定他们的批判性思维能力，目前是国际上较为通用的批判性思维能力评估量表。《批判性思维动机量表》的理论框架是期望理论和任务价值理论（见图 5–6），即学习者给思维任务分配的期待和价值是他们批判性思维动机的决定因素，这两大理论也是本书中批判性思维动机重要的参考理论框架，在上文中已经详细论述过。因为动机是批判性思维能力及其量表的理论框架的组成部分，因此，该量表对《商务外语批判性思维能力量表》的设计具有重要的参考意义。

Expectancy
Concerning reasoning correctly, I am better than most of my peers.
I feel capable of understanding everything related to thinking in a rigorous way.
I am able to learn how to think in a rigorous way.
I am able to learn how to reason correctly better than most of my peers.

Task value
Attainment.
For me it is important to learn how to reason correctly.
For me it is important to be good at reasoning.
For me it is important to use my intellectual skills correctly.
For me it is important to be good at solving problems.
Utility value
Thinking critically will help me to become a good professional.
Thinking critically will be useful for my future.
Thinking critically is useful in everyday life.
Thinking critically is useful for other subjects and courses.
Intrinsic/interest value
I like to reason properly before deciding about something.
I like to learn things that will improve my way of thinking.
I like thinking critically.
I like to reason in a rigorous manner.
Cost
If I have a problem that requires me to reason in a critical way, I am disposed to sacrifice the time that I would otherwise have devoted to other things.
I am disposed to sacrifice quite a lot of time and effort in order to improve my way of reasoning.
It is worth investing time and efforts to acquire and use critical thinking.

图 5–6　《批判性思维动机量表》描述语节选

5.4.2.2　《整体批判性思维评分量表》

《整体批判性思维评分量表》是国际知名批判性思维能力测试机构 Insight Assessment 的评分标准，其为批判性思维能力提供了重要度量标准，通过评估演示文稿、报告、论文、项目、课堂讨论、小组演示等批判性思维任务考量学习者可被观察到的批判性思维能力，为评估学习者的批判性思维能力提供了实用的工具。该量表将批判性思维能力划分为四个等级（见图 5–7），目前在课堂和教学中得到较广泛的应用。该量表把学习者完成批判性思维任务的表现（参见图 5–8 的描述语节选）作为批判性思维能力的评判标准，使批判性思维能力的评判更具有直观性和可操作性，因此，笔者将此量表作为《商务外语批判性思维能力量表》描述语的来源。

Scoring Level	Interpretation	Analysis & Evaluation	Presentation
4 - Accomplished	Analyzes insightful questions Refutes bias Critiques content Examines inconsistencies Values information	Examines conclusions Uses reasonable judgment Discriminates rationally Synthesizes data Views information critically	Argues succinctly Discusses issues thoroughly Shows intellectual honesty Justifies decisions Assimilates information
3 - Competent	Asks insightful questions Detects bias. Categorizes content. Identifies inconsistencies Recognizes context	Formulates conclusions Recognizes arguments Notices differences Evaluates data Seeks out information	Argues clearly Identifies issues Attributes sources naturally Suggests solutions Incorporates information
2 - Developing	Identifies some questions Notes some bias Recognizes basic content States some inconsistencies Selects sources adequately	Identifies some conclusions Sees some arguments Identifies some differences Paraphrases data Assumes information valid	Misconstructs arguments Generalizes issues Cites sources Presents few options Overlooks some information
1 - Beginning	Fails to question data Ignores bias Misses major content areas Detects no inconsistencies Chooses biased sources	Fails to draw conclusions Sees no arguments Overlooks differences Repeats data Omits research	Omits arguments Misrepresents issues Excludes data Draws faulty conclusions Shows intellectual dishonesty

图 5-7 《整体批判性思维评分量表》内容架构

4	Consistently does all or almost all of the following: Accurately interprets evidence, statements, graphics, questions, etc. Identifies the salient arguments (reasons and claims) pro and con. Thoughtfully analyzes and evaluates major alternative points of view. Draws warranted, judicious, non-fallacious conclusions. Justifies key results and procedures, explains assumptions and reasons. Fair-mindedly follows where evidence and reasons lead.
3	Does most or many of the following: Accurately interprets evidence, statements, graphics, questions, etc. Identifies relevant arguments (reasons and claims) pro and con. Offers analyses and evaluations of obvious alternative points of view. Draws warranted, non-fallacious conclusions. Justifies some results or procedures, explains reasons. Fair-mindedly follows where evidence and reasons lead.
2	Does most or many of the following: Misinterprets evidence, statements, graphics, questions, etc. Fails to identify strong, relevant counter-arguments. Ignores or superficially evaluates obvious alternative points of view. Draws unwarranted or fallacious conclusions. Justifies few results or procedures, seldom explains reasons. Regardless of the evidence or reasons, maintains or defends views based on self-interest or preconceptions.

1	Consistently does all or almost all of the following:
	Offers biased interpretations of evidence, statements, graphics, questions,
	    information, or the points of view of others.
	Fails to identify or hastily dismisses strong, relevant counter-arguments.
	Ignores or superficially evaluates obvious alternative points of view.
	Argues using fallacious or irrelevant reasons, and unwarranted claims.
	Does not justify results or procedures, nor explain reasons.
	Regardless of the evidence or reasons, maintains or defends views based on
	    self-interest or preconceptions.
	Exhibits close-mindedness or hostility to reason.

图 5-8 《整体批判性思维评分量表》描述语节选

5.4.2.3　ETS 开发的《HEIghten 批判性思维测试》

　　《HEIghten 批判性思维测试》是目前国际上常见的批判性思维能力测试之一，广泛应用于公司、学校等招聘中的批判性思维能力测试，该测试的内容架构和描述语节选见图 5-9 和图 5-10。EST 是全球最权威的测试机构，作为一个非营利的教育评估和研究机构，其利用 70 年的专业知识和能力测试的丰富经验，为教师和学生开发出多种能力测试工具。在语言能力测试方面，《HEIghten 批判性思维测试》主要评估使用者两个方面的能力：分析能力和综合能力。对于分析能力，该测试主要评估：（1）分析论证结构，主要包括识别结论及其支持论证、特定论证要素的功能及共情策略等。（2）评估论证结构，包括识别推理中隐含的假设或缺陷。（3）评估论据及其使用，如寻找其他相关信息确认论证的科学性；评估论据与结论的相关性；通过加强或削弱论点或结论来评估证据的说服力。对于综合能力，该测试主要评估：（1）选择有效的信息或陈述作为某一论点的论据，以证明论点的有效性和全面性；（2）了解结论和观点的启示意义。《HEIghten 批判性

Analytic Skills:

- evaluating evidence and its use, including evaluating the evidence itself and evaluating it in light of its larger context, its relevance to the argument, appropriateness of sources, possibilities of bias and the degree of support the evidence lends to the claims made in the argument

- analyzing and evaluating arguments, including understanding or assessing the structure of the argument independent of the evidence offered, such as identifying stated and unstated premises, conclusions and intermediate steps

- understanding the language of argumentation and recognizing linguistic cues

- distinguishing between valid and invalid arguments, including recognizing structural flaws that may be present in an invalid argument (e.g., "holes" in reasoning)

Synthetic Skills:

- understanding implications and consequences, including identifying unstated conclusions or implications and consequences that go beyond the original argument

- developing arguments that are valid (i.e., exhibiting good reasoning) and sound (i.e., built on strong evidence)

图 5-9　《HEIghten 批判性思维测试》的内容架构

- *Evaluate evidence and its use:* Students are able to evaluate evidence apart from the position advanced by an argument. For example, they are able to:
  - Evaluate evidence in a larger context, which may include general knowledge, additional background information provided, or additional evidence included within an argument.
  - Identify inconsistencies of conclusions drawn or posited with evidence presented, or inconsistencies within the evidence presented.
  - Identify additional information that might be needed to evaluate the argument.
  - Evaluate sources, considering such factors as relevant expertise of sources and access to information.
  - Recognize potential biases in persons or other sources providing or organizing data, including potential motivations a source may have for providing truthful or misleading information.
  - Evaluate the extent to which the evidence provided in an argument is relevant to its conclusion.
  - Evaluate how strongly the evidence provided in argument supports the conclusion offered or implied, including identifying circumstances that, if true, would strengthen or weaken the argument being evaluated.

- *Analyze and evaluate arguments*: Students are able to analyze and evaluate the structure of an argument. For example, they are able to:
  - Analyze argument structure by identifying stated and unstated premises, conclusions, and intermediate steps.
  - Identify a particular statement's role in an argument.
  - Identify appeals to emotion.
  - Evaluate argument structure, distinguishing valid from invalid arguments, including recognizing structural flaws that may be present in an invalid argument and identifying unstated assumptions.

图 5-10 《HEIghten 批判性思维测试》描述语节选

思维测试》为分析能力和综合能力的测试提供了一个科学的工具，也是笔者设计的《商务外语批判性思维能力量表》的重要参考量表。

5.4.2.4 《加利福尼亚批判性思维倾向量表》

《加利福尼亚批判性思维倾向量表》是目前国际上评估批判性思维倾向的主要工具，可测试使用者在解决问题和决策时使用批判性思维的倾向。该量表通过"意愿"和"能力"两个尺度测试使用者的批判性思维"意愿"，等级越高，表明学习者越渴望在决策和解决问题中运用批判性思维技能。该量表是为成年人设计的，目前在包括美国在内的全球 40 多个国家被广泛使用。由于批判性思维倾向是本批判性思维能力理论框架的重要组成部分，所以《加利福尼亚批判性思维倾向量表》对《商务外语批判性思维能力量表》的设计具有一定的参考意义。该量表的内容架构和描述语节选见图 5-11 和图 5-12。

Scale Name	Scale Description
Learning Orientation	A disposition toward increasing one's knowledge and skill base. Valuing the learning process as a means to accomplish mastery over a task. Interested in challenging activities. Uses information seeking as a personal strategy in problem solving.
Creative Problem Solving	A disposition toward approaching problem solving with innovative or original ideas and solutions. Feeling imaginative, ingenious, original, and able to solve difficult problems. Desire to engage in activities such as puzzles, games of strategy, and understanding the underlying function of objects.
Mental Focus	A disposition toward being diligent, systematic, task oriented, organized, and clearheaded. Feeling at ease with engaging in problem solving. Feeling systematic and confident in ability to complete tasks in timely way. Feeling focused and clearheaded.
Cognitive Integrity	A disposition toward interacting with differing viewpoints for the sake of learning the truth or reaching the best decision. The expression of strong intellectual curiosity. Valuing the fair-minded consideration of alternative perspectives.

图 5-11　《加利福尼亚批判性思维倾向量表》的内容架构

I love learning new things.
I always look forward to learning challenging things.
Being eager to learn about different things is one of my strong points.
No matter what the topic, I am eager to know more about it.
Learning new things all my life would be fun.
I want to learn everything I can because it might come in handy someday.
Complicated problems are fun to try to figure out.
If given a choice, I would pick a challenging activity over an easy one.
I really enjoy trying to figure out how things work.
Easy problems are less fun than challenging problems.
I hate dealing with anything that is complicated.
I am good at making plans for how to solve difficult problems.
I am one of the smartest kids in my class.
I have trouble concentrating in school.
My trouble is I stop paying attention too soon.
It's easy for me to stay focused when working on a problem.
It is difficult for me to finish my school assignments.
I keep my schoolwork organized.
It is easy for me to organize my thoughts.
When I need to solve a problem, I have difficulty knowing where to begin.
It is just not that important to keep trying to solve difficult problems.
I only look for facts that support my beliefs, not for facts that disagree.
Thinking about other points of view is a waste of time.
I know what I think, so why should I pretend to consider choices.
Thinking about what others believe means you cannot think for yourself.

图 5-12　《加利福尼亚批判性思维倾向量表》描述语节选

5.4.3 《商务外语批判性思维能力量表》的研制

5.4.3.1 《商务外语批判性思维能力量表》

在 Valenzuela、Halpern、Facione 等学者对批判性思维能力认知技能的研究和 Facione、Ennis 等学者对批判性思维能力认知倾向研究以及 Wigfield 对批判性思维能力认知动机研究的基础上，笔者建立了商务外语批判性思维能力模型和指标体系。通过对国际通用的批判性思维能力量表描述语的搜集、筛选、修订和增加，笔者设计了《商务外语批判性思维能力量表》（表 5-3 是其描述语节选）。

表 5-3 《商务外语批判性思维能力量表》描述语节选

Level	Item	Descriptors
1	1	CAN stay strictly within the guidelines of the assignment.
1	2	CAN use a single approach used to solve the problem.
1	3	CAN take information from source(s) without interpretation /evaluation.
1	4	CAN take information from source(s) without coherent analysis or synthesis.
1	5	CAN take viewpoints of experts without questioning.
1	6	CAN show an emerging awareness of present assumptions.
1	7	CAN begin to identify some contexts when presenting a position.
1	8	CAN state simplistic and obvious position, perspective or hypothesis.
1	9	CAN make oversimplified conclusions.
1	10	CAN explain information presented in mathematical forms, but draw incorrect conclusions about what the information means.

5.4.3.2 对《商务外语批判性思维能力量表》的分析

该量表的框架主要分为三部分：认知技能、认知倾向和认知动机。批判性思维能力共分为四个等级，共计 194 条描述语。

第一，认知技能是《商务外语批判性思维能力量表》的重要组成部分，主要包括阐释、分析、评估、推理、解释和自我调节等技巧。对于较低等级的学习者，他们只能勉强使用这些认知技能，如第 1 级第 5 条 "CAN take viewpoints of experts without questioning"，第 2 级第 62 条 "CAN draw conclusions only to the extent that those conclusions are supported by the facts and sound reasoning"；而较高等级的学习者能根据批判性思维任务，熟练地综合应用多种批判性思维认知技能，如第 3 级第 102 条 "CAN accurately and logically evaluate the traditions and practices that others often accept unquestioningly" 和第 4 级第 148 条 "CAN take information from source(s) with enough interpretation/evaluation to develop a coherent analysis or synthesis"。掌握批判性思维技能需要一个过程，通过在实践中不断应用这些认知技能，学习者可以逐步提高批判性思维能力。

第二，对于认知倾向，《商务外语批判性思维能力量表》主要评估学习者的学习倾向、问题解决创新能力、心理焦点、认知完整性、认知成熟度和追求真理。学习者应该善于学习，不能将学习局限在课堂中，要善于联系实际，寻找验证和丰富所学知识的机会，如第 3 级第 14 条 "CAN identify connections between life experiences and knowledge and ideas perceived as similar and related to one's own interests"。学习者需要具备创新意识，不能因循守旧，要创造性地解决问题，如第 3 级第 124 条 "CAN consider new directions or approaches without going beyond the guidelines of the assignment"。进行批判性思维时，学习者要学会心理聚焦，围绕一个问题进行发散性思维，最终把所有信息和论据都能归结在一个结论中，如第 4 级第 151 条 "CAN present in-depth information from relevant sources representing various points of view/approaches for one problem"。认知完整性和认知成熟度是评判批判性思维能力的两个重要指标，要求学习者对某一问题要全面收集信息，了解各种相关观点，从而得出全面、成熟、符合逻辑的结论，如第 4 级第 173 条 "CAN identify and provide a well-developed explanation of contextual issues with a clear sense of scope accurately" 和第 4 级第 175 条 "CAN identify conclusions, implications, and consequences with a well-developed explanation accurately"。追求真理是批判性思维倾向的本质，也是进行批判性思维的目的，学习者应该客观地看待各种观点，对某些观点不能有偏好或偏见，如第 4 级第 193 条 "CAN use good reasoning as the fundamental criterion by which to judge whether to accept or reject any beliefs or explanations"。

学习者对批判性思维的预期和价值是批判性思维认知动机的两大评估指标。要具备批判性思维自觉性，学习者应该对批判性思维任务赋予较高的预期和较大的价值。《商务外语批判性思维能力量表》中有多条有关认知动机的描述语，如第 1 级第 34 条 "CAN recognize that thinking critically can help to become a good professional"、第 4 级第 177 条 "CAN analyze and evaluate major alternative points of view thoughtfully"、第 4 级第 191 条 "CAN relate the subjects he/she studies to his/her experience and significant problems in the world"。学习者需要将批判性思维融入生活、工作和学习中，这样才能具有更强的批判性思维动机，提高运用批判性思维的自觉性。

《商务外语批判性思维能力量表》的描述语格式统一，采用 "CAN do" 短句，通过评估使用者完成批判性思维任务的能力，可确定他们的批判性思维能力等级。所有的描述语都经过审慎的修改，简单易懂，为商务外语学习者提供了一个评估自己批判性思维能力的工具。

第**6**章

商务实践能力量表

随着全球化的发展，一些公司在全球开展业务活动，在世界各地生产和销售商品，跨国公司在世界各地迅速增长和扩张。全球化对商业的影响也在很大程度上改变着高等教育。随着全球经济的增长，企业对商务人才的需求越来越大。

在中国快速融入世界经济的大背景下，为满足我国参与国际经济贸易的需要，商务外语专业应运而生。该专业培养的是掌握必要的知识和技能的合格的国际经济活动参与者。商务外语是一门交叉学科，涉及贸易、管理、金融、营销、法律等学科（陈准民，王立非，2009）。它的主要教学目标是培养学习者的专业语言技能与丰富的商业知识和技能。商务外语在中国的兴起和迅速发展，有力地证明了经济发展与商务人才需求之间的相关性。

商务外语人才的高要求对人才的培养提出了挑战。商务外语专业需要培养能熟练进行商务活动的复合型人才。随着中国进一步改革开放和"一带一路"的发展，社会对实践能力强的商务外语人才的需求不断增加。英语教学的目标也由培养英语语言技能向培养英语实践能力转变，实践能力越来越成为商务外语专业学生的核心能力。

6.1 商务实践能力的国内外相关研究

对于商务外语学习者来说，语言能力和商务实践能力是两个最重要的能力

（雷春林，2006）。目前，国内很多高校对学生的培养目标和教学内容与企业对人才的知识、能力要求存在着不小的差距。多年来，在商务外语教学中，教师和学习者往往为语言能力的提高付出了很大的努力，而在一定程度上忽视了商务实践能力的培养。

如今，随着商务英语理论框架的建立和发展，越来越多的商务英语教师和相关管理人员已经认识到商务知识和技能对商务英语学习者的重要性（孙毅，2016）。商务外语人才需要掌握复合型知识和技能。学习者不仅要经过严格的语言和沟通技能的系统训练，而且要系统学习经济、商务、金融和商法等相关学科的课程，掌握其基本理论和知识框架。这些相关学科的课程是构成商务外语课程体系的重要模块，学生从中学到的不仅仅是相关学科的知识和技能，还有不同的思维模式、研究方法和处理问题的方式（王关富，2012）。

笔者梳理了有关研究商务外语实践能力的文献，发现关于商务外语实践能力量表和指标体系的研究不多，大部分研究是关于造成实践能力不足的原因或提升实践能力的途径。

6.1.1　国外商务实践能力的相关研究

国外高校系统培养大学生的实践能力始于 20 世纪 60 年代。20 世纪 80 年代，一些学者开始在企业层面对商务实践能力进行研究，并建立了特定领域的模型。经过几十年的发展，国外有关商务实践能力培养的模式已比较成熟，其有以下几个特点。

（1）在课程设置上，因材施教。注重课程的针对性，为不同阶段、不同水平的学生提供不同的课程；注重课程的开发与创新，学校出资支持以学生为主导的创新活动。此外，国外普遍重视实践课程在课程体系中的比重（如德国的"双轨制"培养方式），增加学时数，鼓励学生运用所学内容设计出体现创新意识的方案。

（2）在教学方式上，采用合同教学法、独立学习法、个性教学法、问题教学法等具有研究式、探索式、启发式、互动式的教学方法，培养学生的创新意识与实践能力。

（3）在实践活动中，鼓励学生参加各种社团活动和竞赛活动，弥补课堂教学的不足，锻炼学生才干，这是培养学生创新能力与实践能力的必要环节和重要组成部分。

（4）创业教育在一些经济发达国家，如美国、英国、法国、德国、日本、新加坡、韩国等都较早地受到重视并得到广泛、深入的开展，这些国家的创业教育已进入成熟阶段，对学生实践能力的提升有很大帮助。

（5）在人才培养上，重视学生研究能力的培养。开设专门的研究课程；组织学生参与科研；为学生开展创新研究提供示范和实践基地，走产学研一体化道路，通过导师制、科研训练计划和科技孵化，为学生的创新性实践活动提供试验田（商应美等，2011）。

6.1.2　国内商务实践能力的相关研究

总体来说，国内对商务外语商务实践能力的研究较为有限。目前，许多专家认为商务外语专业学生的实践能力普遍不强。李晶等经过调研发现，90% 以上的企业对商务外语专业学生的理论知识表示满意或基本满意，但对该专业学生的职业能力的满意度普遍较低（李晶，付爱玲，李淑芳，2018）。造成商务外语专业学生实践能力不足的主要原因有：理论与实践脱节、教学过程中的情景缺失、课程设置不合理、教师队伍的商务实践能力不足、教学评估与监督机制不完善等。

为此，一些学者从五个方面提出了培养学生实践能力的方法和途径。

（1）教学模式。2013 年，陈冬纯提出"商务"依托式大学英语语言实践能力培养模式，使用情景教学法将语言学习与专业学习相结合，使学生通过反复多样的模拟交际活动将英语技能提升为英语实践能力。这种教学模式在一定程度上弥补了传统英语教学中语境缺失的问题，但对教师也具有一定的挑战性，教师不但要有扎实的英语教学能力，还要熟知专业原理。

（2）阶梯式递进的课程设置。根据语言与相关专业的学习规律，商务外语专业学生学习的课程应包括五类：语言类、专业类、办公技能类、公共类、专业素养拓展类。这五类课程既独立又相互联系，是商务外语专业学生不可或缺的课程（吴寒，何宇，项伟锋，2006）。

（3）教师队伍。充分利用社会力量，建设"双师型"教师队伍。如聘请企业专业人员做学生的校外导师，邀请社会专业人士做讲座分享经验，实施"青年教师和骨干教师培养计划"，聘请外校优秀教师，实现校际师资共享等（郭汝惠，2013）。

（4）充分利用现代信息技术。门博良引进西方的多模态课堂教学方式，即利用现代教学工具，调动学生的多种感官以帮助其提高商务实践能力。这种教学模式能够丰富课堂教学信息的来源以及输入方式，保证教学知识与时俱进。该模式在高校教学中已大范围使用，但实际效果并不明显，目前仅限于 PPT 教学，且各项功能没有得到充分利用（门博良，2016）。

（5）技能竞赛。"外研社杯"全国商务外语实践大赛、"亿学杯"全国商务英语实践技能大赛、全国高校商务英语知识竞赛、"语通杯"全国大学生职场与商务英语沟通技能大赛等能够激发学生的竞争意识，提升学习兴趣，有助于形成良好的学习氛围，从而提高学生的实践能力。

6.1.3　商务实践能力的概念界定

在《普通高等学校本科专业类教学质量国家标准（外国语言文学类）》中，商务实践能力是学习者必备的五大能力之一。商业实践能力指在复杂而相互关联的国际商业环境中完成商业任务的能力。在这里，能力不是指某个特定的任务，而是在复杂和不断变化的环境中完成不同任务的技能的总称（Brown，1994）。

为了对商务实践能力进行全面评估，笔者想在收集一系列商务实践能力量表基础上设计一个较为全面的商务能力量表。此量表将为商务英语学习者提供必要的能力评估工具，包括他们在工作中需要的核心技能。

6.2　商务实践能力的理论框架

要建立能力量表，就必须先建立一个可靠的理论框架。1956 年，Benjamin Bloom 和其他教育工作者共同开发的教育目标分类法已经成为衡量教育目标的重要框架。在 Benjamin Bloom 的教育目标分类法中，学习被划分为三个领域（如图 6-1）：认知领域、情感领域和动作技能领域。随后，Bloom 的教育目标分类法被众多课程规划人员、教师使用，成为制订教学计划和评估教育目标的标准。这三个领域完美地涵盖了业务能力领域：认知领域是基于知识的领域，情感领域是基于态度的领域，动作技能领域是基于技能的领域。三个领域的目标设计能为商务外语学习者提供科学的指导，因此，笔者将基于这三个领域对商务实践能力进行解析，并构建量表。

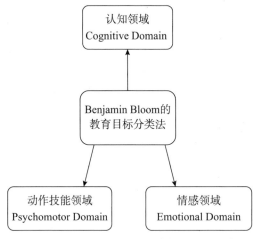

图 6–1　Benjamin Bloom 的教育目标分类法

6.2.1　Benjamin Bloom 的认知领域理论

认知领域是基于知识的领域，包括 6 个组成部分（见图 6–2）：知识、领会、应用、分析、综合和评价。（1）知识是对已学习的资料的掌握，主要指已知知识；（2）领会是指把握知识材料的意义；（3）应用是指人们在新的场景下使用所学知识的能力；（4）分析是指分解信息以了解其组织结构的能力；（5）综合则是将各个组织结构整合，获得综合信息的能力；（6）评价是根据明确的内部和／或外部标准判断某一特定目的的信息价值的能力。在认知领域中，不仅要评估学习者对商业知识的掌握，还要评估他们如何解读并使用商业知识。

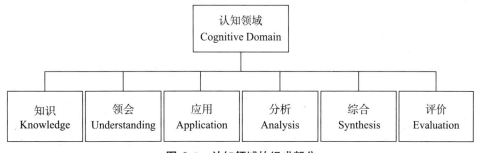

图 6–2　认知领域的组成部分

6.2.2 Benjamin Bloom 的情感领域理论

本杰明·布鲁姆（Benjamin Bloom）的情感领域理论主要关注学习者的情感、态度、价值观和兴趣等方面的变化。情感领域的目标分为五个层次，从低到高依次是：

1. 接受/注意（Receiving or Attention）：学习者对学习内容产生最基本的觉知和关注。例如，愿意倾听或观察。

2. 反应（Responding）：学习者对学习内容产生积极的反应。例如，通过参与讨论或表达对某个主题的兴趣。

3. 价值化（Valuing）：学习者开始将特定的价值观念内化，并在自己的行为中体现出来。例如，认为诚实是一种重要的品质，并在行动中体现。

4. 组织价值观念系统（Organizing）：学习者将不同的价值观念组织成一个系统，并开始形成自己的价值体系。例如，将对家庭、友谊和职业的价值观念整合成一个协调的系统。

5. 价值体系个性化（Characterization）：学习者的价值观念已经高度内化，并成为其个性的一部分。例如，学习者的行为和决策始终体现出对自由和公正的承诺。

这些层次反映了学习者在情感领域从简单的接受到高度内化和个性化的价值观念的逐步发展。情感领域的目标旨在帮助学习者在情感、态度和价值观方面得到全面的发展，从而更好地适应社会和生活。情感领域是基于态度的领域，包括学习者对商务活动的态度和价值观。对于商务外语学习者来说，笔者认为情感领域的能力可以细化为服务意识、创业精神、全球意识、职业道德（见图 6-3）。

图 6-3 情感领域的组成部分

服务意识指满足客户需求的欲望。不管从事何种职业、身处什么岗位或地位，都要为客户竭诚服务，积极快速地响应客户不断变化的需求，提供高标准的服务。

创业精神是一个发现和捕捉机会并由此创造出新颖的服务或实现其潜在价值的过程。创业精神是对创业活动自觉的反映，即对创业者行为起到促进和动力作用的个人心理倾向，它是一种创造能力，是创造新事物的能力。当今的中国乃至全世界，创业越来越成为经济发展的强劲推动力。培养大学生创新创业的意识、素质、精神和能力，有利于其未来发展。

全球意识包括了解全球问题对个人、商业组织甚至国家的影响的能力，如理解爱国主义和国际主义与解决全球问题的相互关系，理解维护和平对于各国人民具有的共同意义；理解生态问题、保护世界文化以及加强国际多边合作等对于人类持续发展的深远意义。全球意识也包括全球心态。每一个人都是世界的公民，应该将自己、祖国与世界联系起来。全球心态要求人们从宏观的角度思考问题，避免种族中心主义，平等对待所有文化，理解、尊重其他国家的不同文化。公民教育的重要使命是为人们参与公共生活做准备，使之成为积极的、有见识的公民。在今天这样一个全球化、信息化的时代，培养公民的全球意识尤为重要。

职业道德主要包括对自身商业活动的理解和对商业活动中的思维模式的理解两个方面。在竞争激烈的商业世界中，参与者需要遵循法律和道德原则，承担相应的社会责任。 职业道德教育要培养人们良好的职业态度、职业观念，提高职业道德认知能力和职业道德评价能力，具有良好的敬业精神、合作精神和创新精神等从业品质。职业道德教育不是简单的知识传递，而是价值观、能力和品质的培养。学习者要多参加各种实践活动，在实践中形成一整套独特的职业道德价值观体系。

6.2.3　丹尼尔·科伊尔的动作技能领域理论

动作技能领域也被称为基于技能的领域。技能可分为硬技能和软技能（见图6-4）。硬技能是指专业人员使用的固定技能或操作方式，是一种惯性的技能；软技能是指人际交往的技能，有相当大的灵活性。在企业招聘中，面试者已从过去主要强调应聘者的专业知识，即"硬技能"，转向强调应聘者的综合素质，重视"软技能"和"硬技能"。培养学生的职业软技能与硬技能同等重要。硬技能与软技能好比是马车的两个轮子，并驾齐驱才能行千里。下图是丹尼尔·科伊尔在《像高手一样行动》一书中对动作技能领域的分类。

图 6-4　动作技能领域的组成部分

（1）硬技能

硬技能是指完成某种任务或活动的技术和能力（**Parsons**，**2008**），是从事某一岗位所必须具备的知识和技能。现在，科技对商务英语学习者的商业技能产生了深远影响（**Mitchell**，**2010**），在进行商务活动前，他们必须发展出更多样化的硬技能。硬技能来自一个人的专业知识和实践。商务外语硬技能的教学是商务外语专业课程的重要组成部分，经过学习和训练，学习者可以掌握更多的硬技能。硬技能的学习对商务外语学习者来说可能是一个挑战，然而，掌握硬技能也是商务外语学习者的竞争优势。只有具备硬技能，学习者才能更专业地进行商务活动。

（2）软技能

软技能，又被称为非技术技能，是相对于硬技能而言的。**Kantrowitz** 把软技能定义为：非技术技能，个人内在和人际的、促进技术技能和知识应用的工作技能。软技能就是指一个人"激发自己潜能并通过赢得他人认可和合作放大自己的资源，以获得超越自身独立能力的更大成功的技能"的总和。

随着社会的发展，软技能已和专业技能同样重要，甚至更为重要。**Stanford** 国际咨询研究所和卡内基基金会所做的一项研究表明：长期工作的成功，**75%** 依赖于人际间的技能或软技能，只有 **25%** 依赖于技术技能。因此，现代教育如果只是一味传授专业知识和专业技能，忽略学生职业软技能的培养，很难满足企业的用人需要。

软技能的提高，意味着学习者综合素质的提高。一方面，这增强了学习者的职业适应能力，拓宽了就业的选择面，也提升了学生的心理素质；另一方面，这对于促进学生的自我发展、自我实现以及提升人生满意度影响深远。软技能的构成是多维度、复杂的，目前还没有统一的构成模式，许多研究者基于不同的研究目的，对软技能的内容进行了分析、研究。笔者结合商务外语的教学目标和教学大纲，总结商务外语学习者应该具备的软技能，作为商务外语学习者商务实践能力的重要评价指标。

6.3　商务实践能力模型的构建

基于 Bloom 的教育目标分类法框架，笔者构建了针对商务外语学习者的商务实践能力模型（见图 6-5）。

6.3.1　商务实践能力的认知领域

在商务外语商务实践能力的认知领域层面，主要包括知识、领会、分析、综合、应用和评价（见图 6-6），它要求学习者不仅要学习商务课程，积累商务知识，还要在商务实践中通过应用商务知识，不断提升商务能力。

《普通高等学校本科专业类教学质量国家标准（外国语言文学类）》规定，商务知识包括企业经营管理知识、经济学知识、跨国公司管理知识、国际商法知识、国际贸易知识五个方面的相关知识。在经济全球化的今天，国际金融知识也是必不可少的一项。因此，笔者认为商务知识包括六大类（见图 6-7）：（1）企业经营管理知识。商务外语学习者应该知道如何写工作计划、工作安排和工作报告，熟悉公司的运作流程。（2）经济学知识。商务外语学习者要从事各种经济活动，因此必须了解一些重要的经济学理论，如成本理论、消费者行为理论、市场理论和生产理论。（3）对于商务外语学习者来说，跨国公司管理知识也至关重要。跨国公司与本土公司的经营方式不同，面临的挑战也更多。在多元文化环境

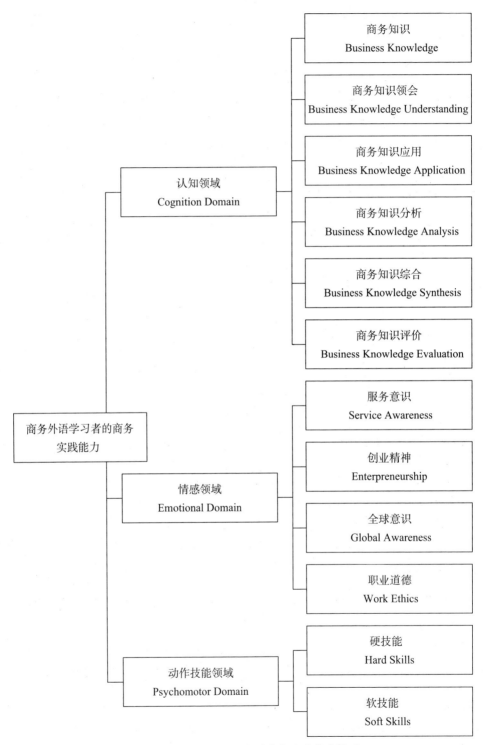

图6-5　商务外语学习者的商务实践能力模型

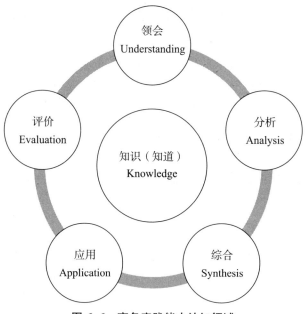

图 6-6　商务实践能力认知领域

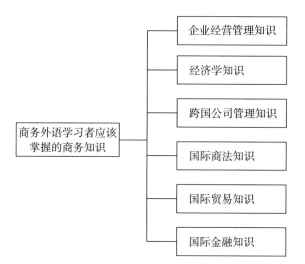

图 6-7　商务外语学习者应该掌握的商务知识

中工作，了解跨国公司的管理，有助于商务外语学习者适应环境，为企业的发展作出更大的贡献。（4）了解国际商法知识是商务外语学习者提升商务实践能力的一个重要途径，商务外语学习者需要了解民法和普通法的形式、结构和特点，掌握合同法、国际贸易公约、商业组织法、国际仲裁法等重要的国际商法知识。（5）商务外语学习者需要掌握的核心知识是国际贸易知识，如国际贸易的基本理论知识。国际贸易相当复杂，参与者需要遵守许多规则，只有掌握国际贸易知识，才能在商务活动中体现出自己的专业性。（6）国际金融知识对于学习者来说也很重要，特别是国际货币体系知识、汇率知识和金融市场知识对学习者的日常工作至关重要，商务外语学习者应该掌握一定的国际金融知识。

6.3.2　商务实践能力的情感领域

商务实践能力的情感领域主要包括四个方面：服务意识、创业精神、全球意识和职业道德。这四个方面都是针对学习者的思想意识提出的具体能力要求。

服务意识对商务外语学习者非常重要。国际贸易本质上是一种服务，作为国际经济贸易活动的参与者，商务外语学习者应该具备一定的服务意识。在商务活动中，学习者要尽量多地为客户考虑，为客户提供更好的服务。服务意识是衡量学习者商务实践能力的关键指标之一。

创业精神也是商务外语学习者需要具备的精神。国际贸易活动属于富有挑战性的工作，因此，优秀的商务外语学习者应该在实践过程中提升创新意识，培养创业精神。商务外语学习者在复杂和充满挑战的日常工作中会遇到很多问题，必须以创新的方式思考并灵活解决这些问题。他们需要通过收集数据、确定关键事实，从不同角度比较各种选择，作出果断和创新的判断。想在商战中抓住机会，商务外语学习者要有积极的态度并富有创业精神。

商务外语学习者必须具有全球意识，全球意识属于跨文化交际能力，它不仅是一种认知能力，还是一种生存能力和竞争力。

对于商务外语学习者而言，职业道德主要包括对自身商业活动的理解和在商务活动中要有正确的思维模式两个方面。在竞争激烈的商业世界中，商务外语学习者不仅要诚实守信，展示较高的道德水准，更要遵循法律和道德原则，承担社会责任。在商务思维模式中，契约精神应该是商务外语学习者高度敬业精神的核心表现之一。总之，在商务活动中，学习者要恪守商业道德，为客户保守商业秘密。

以上四个主要指标对于商务外语学习者至关重要，它们也是商务实践能力指标体系的重要组成部分。

6.3.3　商务实践能力的动作技能领域

动作技能领域的商务实践能力，又称为基于技能的商务实践能力，可分为硬技能和软技能。

（1）硬技能

笔者认为硬技能主要包括项目管理能力、营销和业务沟通能力、财务管理能力、国际业务战略能力、供应链基础管理能力和电子商务能力等（见图6-8）。

1）项目管理能力包括了解项目管理准则、项目的设计、执行和改进以及项目管理标准、法律法规。商务外语学习者应该了解通用的项目管理准则，策略性地利用、获得相应的资源以完成项目。通过比较项目设计，确定最佳的项目实施方案并对其不断进行优化，以得到更好的项目成果。商务外语学习者必须了解相关的标准和法律法规，保证项目执行过程中合法合规。

2）商务外语学习者应具有一定的营销和沟通能力。要顺利开展营销活动，商务外语学习者应该了解营销在市场中的作用，制定合适的营销方案，并应用恰当的营销策略执行营销方案。随着多媒体的发展，商务外语学习者还要具备网络营销能力，利用网络等平台提高品牌影响力。要提升业务沟通能力，商务外语学习者要了解商务沟通的重要性和功能，根据不同的沟通对象选择相应的沟通策略，以实现沟通目的。

3）商务外语学习者需要具备一定的财务管理能力。首先，学习者需要了解财务管理准则，具备一定的财务分析能力，能合理评估并避免财务风险，制订相关的财务计划。

4）商务外语学习者应具有国际业务战略能力，了解国际贸易，了解客户和市场，并战略性地制订运营计划。

5）供应链基础管理能力是商务外语学习者必须具备的一项重要能力。学习者应该了解供应链管理准则，合理管控供应链上下游，评估供应链网络，以便及时、有效地为客户提供更优质的服务。

6）电子商务能力主要包括电子商务分析能力、电子商务开发技能、电子商务营销技能。电子商务分析能力包括两个方面：数据分析能力和运用专业知识的能力。要分析商业数据，商务外语学习者必须具备一定的数学知识和统计能力，

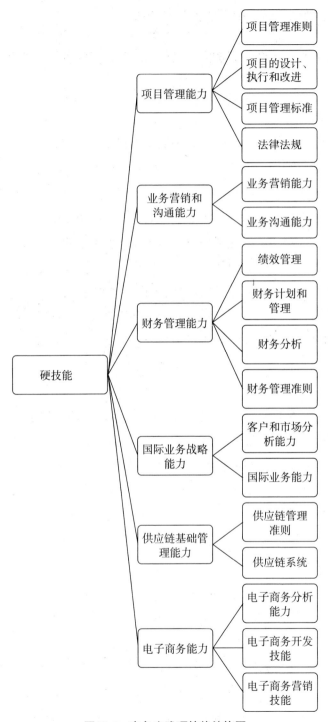

图6-8　商务实践硬技能结构图

整合数据来作出有效的业务决策。除此之外，运用专业知识的能力对于商务外语学习者来说也是至关重要的。众所周知，商务外语的实践性很强。商务专业知识不应仅仅储存在学习者的头脑中，还应该应用于实践中。学习者应通过各种途径培养自己运用专业知识的能力。例如，运用经济学原理，分析网络环境下经济发展中存在的问题。

互联网是影响全球经济的重要因素之一。有了互联网，各国开展商务活动越来越方便，它还为企业提供越来越多的平台从事国际商务。在当今数字化世界中，商务外语学习者应该掌握电子商务开发技能以及营销技能，熟悉电子商务的主要理论和知识，了解有关数据库的知识，具有一定的电子商务和应用程序开发能力。电子商务开发能力和营销能力是新时代对商务外语学习者提出的新要求。随着电商的不断发展，商务外语学习者要进一步强化电子商务开发能力和营销能力。

学习这些硬技能对商务外语学习者来说可能是一个挑战，然而，掌握了这些技能有助于提升商务外语学习者的竞争优势。只有具备这些技能，学习者才能更专业地从事国际商务工作。

（2）软技能

软技能主要包括人际交往能力、个人特质（含商业敏感度、沟通谈判能力、个人品质）、变化管理能力、战略思维能力、人力资源管理能力等。

人际交往能力是商务外语学习者应具备的重要软技能。有的学者认为人际技能是工作中最重要的技能（Smith，2007），对个人职业发展至关重要（Evenson，1999）。学习者需要掌握人际交往技巧，促进积极有效的客户沟通和团队沟通，与内外部利益相关者建立有效的联系（Klaus，2010）。

除了人际交往能力，个人特质也是软技能中不可或缺的。商业敏感度，涉及战略性地管理人力、财力和信息资源的能力。沟通谈判能力也是影响个人特质的重要因素之一。商务外语学习者经常需要与争议者进行讨论并寻求共识。谈判最好是实现双赢，也就是各方都能满足自己的需要和利益。个人品质是个人特质的重要内容，包括领导力和工作投入度、忠诚度等。

变化管理能力、战略思维能力和人力资源管理能力等也是重要的软技能，对商务外语学习者的职业发展具有重要作用。变化管理能力指学习者如何在变化的环境下，调整管理策略的能力；战略思维能力指学习者从公司、品牌、产品等角度进行长期规划的能力；人力资源管理能力指学习者利用各种人力资源实现效益最大化、效率最高化的能力。以上能力都是衡量商务外语学习者实践能力的重要指标，都会体现在笔者设计的《商务实践能力量表》中。

6.4 《商务实践能力量表》的设计

商务实践能力量表与语言应用能力量表是商务外语学习者能力评价体系中最基础的量表。为了更好地设计商务实践能力描述语，笔者参照一些世界范围内通用的商务实践能力量表，并仔细选择和修改描述语，以便更好地对学习者的商务实践能力进行评估。

6.4.1 商务实践能力指标体系

基于上文的商务实践能力模型，笔者构建了系统的商务实践能力指标体系。商务实践能力指标体系主要分为三个领域：认知领域、情感领域和动作技能领域，每个领域的商务实践能力又可细分为多个子能力，这些子能力就是衡量商务外语学习者商务实践能力的重要指标（见图6-9）。

在商务认知领域中，本量表主要评估的指标是学习者对经济学、企业经营管理、跨国公司管理、国际商法、国际金融、国际贸易等商务知识的理解、分析、应用、综合和评价。该量表不仅评估商务外语学习者商务知识的储备，更评估学习者在真实的商务交际场景中对商务知识的应用能力。在情感领域中，本量表主要评估服务意识、创业精神、全球意识和职业道德四项能力，这四项能力对商务外语学习者非常重要，只有具备这四项能力，学习者才能更好地应对充满各种挑战和机会的商务环境。在动作技能领域中，本量表评估商务外语学习者应该掌握的多项技能，这是商务实践能力量表的重点。商务实践技能分为硬技能和软技能。硬技能包括项目管理能力、业务营销和沟通能力、财务管理能力、国际业务战略能力、供应链基础管理能力和电子商务能力六大能力；软技能分为人际交往能力、个人特质、变化管理能力、战略思维能力和人力资源管理能力五大能力。笔者构建的

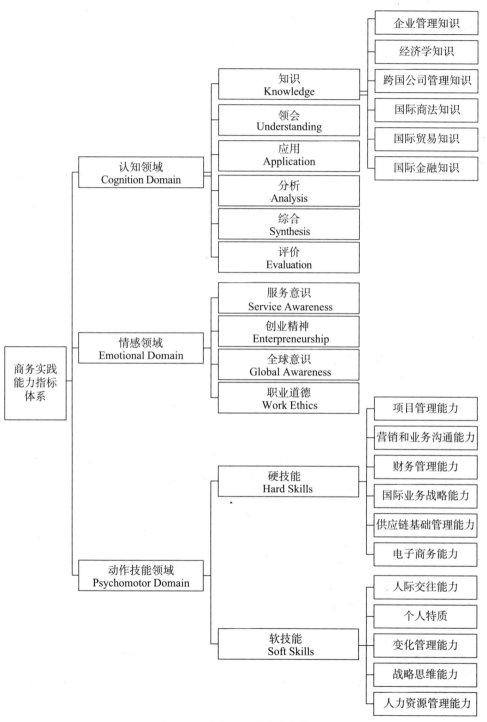

图 6-9　商务实践能力指标体系

商务外语商务实践能力指标体系，可以为商务外语学习者提供一个科学、便利的商务实践能力的自我评估工具。

6.4.2　商务实践能力描述语来源

为了提高《商务实践能力量表》的科学性，笔者进行了大量的资料收集工作，对相关商务实践能力量表仔细地进行梳理，主要收集了《特许全球管理会计师能力框架》《商务（通用）管理能力量表》《领导能力等级量表》《工作角色和熟练水平能力量表》四个具有国际权威性的商务实践能力量表作为《商务实践能力量表》描述语的来源（见表 6–1）。

上文中的四个能力量表都是近 10 年内出版的，保证了笔者设计的《商务实践能力量表》的时效性；同时，笔者参考的国际商务能力相关量表来源多样，有著名测试机构设计的商务能力评估量表，有协会制定的商务能力量表，有大学开发的用于评估学生商务能力的量表，甚至还有国家权威机构出版的商务能力标准。参考量表来源的多样性在一定程度上保证了笔者设计的《商务实践能力量表》应用的广泛性。

表 6–1　《商务实践能力量表》的描述语来源

类型	名称	开发者	年份	国别
协会量表	《特许全球管理会计师能力框架》(The Chartered Global Management Accountant Competency Framework)	美国注册会计师协会 (American Institute of Centified Public Accountants, AICPA) 和英国皇家特许管理会计师公会 (The Charted Institute of Management Accountant, CIMA)	2014	美国、英国
学校能力量表	《商务（通用）管理能力量表》[Business (General) Management Chart of Competency]	亚太国际学院 Asia Pacific International College	2011	澳大利亚

（续表）

类型	名称	开发者	年份	国别
国家能力量表	《领导能力等级量表》(*Proficiency Levels for Leadership Competencies*)	美国人事管理局 U.S. Office of Personnel Management	未知	美国
测试机构能力量表	《工作角色和熟练水平能力量表》(*Competence by Job Role and Proficiency Level*)	Workitect	2012	美国

6.4.2.1　《商务（通用）管理能力量表》

《商务（通用）管理能力量表》是 2011 年由亚太国际学院开发的能力量表，对商务能力的评估具有较大影响。《商务（通用）管理能力量表》将商务能力分为社会文化和个人能力、运营管理、营销和业务能力、金融管理、人力资源管理、国际贸易竞争战略和组织设计、领导力及变化管理、组织行为和内部沟通、创业创新和技术管理、供应链管理基础、高级供应链管理、战略信息系统、企业系统和业务流程整合、公司资产可持续化管理、复杂资产管理、环境可持续发展管理、排放计划管理、商业法和尽职调查、商业资产、公司管理 20 项能力，这 20 项能力又细分为 139 项子能力，系统定义了商务能力（见图 6–10）。基于商务实践能力的理论框架，笔者选取与商务知识、商务认知和商务技能相关的描述语见图 6–11，作为《商务实践能力量表》的语料参考。

6.4.2.2　《领导能力等级量表》

《领导能力等级量表》是由美国人事管理局开发的关于领导能力的量表。美国人事管理局是美国联邦政府的主要人力资源管理机构和人事政策制定机构，其出版的能力量表是联邦机构人才评估的重要工具，具有权威性。不论管理一支队伍，还是开展一个项目，领导能力都是学习者不可缺少的一项重要的商务实践能力。《领导能力等级量表》主要评估使用者六个方面的能力：领导变革、带领团队、成就导向性，商业敏感性、战略联合和基础能力（见图 6–12）。量表把每项能力

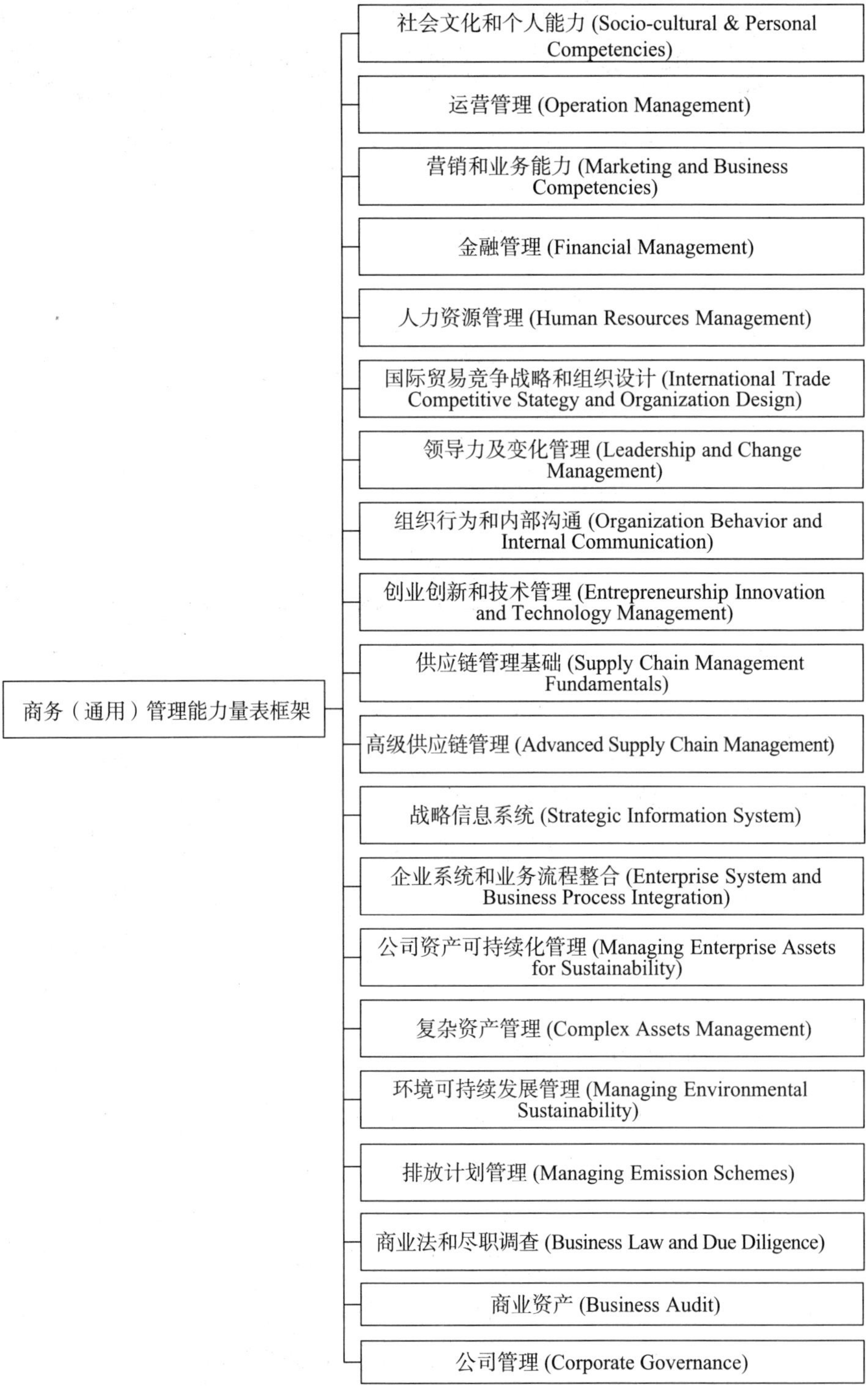

社会文化和个人能力 (Socio-cultural & Personal Competencies)

运营管理 (Operation Management)

营销和业务能力 (Marketing and Business Competencies)

金融管理 (Financial Management)

人力资源管理 (Human Resources Management)

国际贸易竞争战略和组织设计 (International Trade Competitive Stategy and Organization Design)

领导力及变化管理 (Leadership and Change Management)

组织行为和内部沟通 (Organization Behavior and Internal Communication)

创业创新和技术管理 (Entrepreneurship Innovation and Technology Management)

供应链管理基础 (Supply Chain Management Fundamentals)

高级供应链管理 (Advanced Supply Chain Management)

战略信息系统 (Strategic Information System)

企业系统和业务流程整合 (Enterprise System and Business Process Integration)

公司资产可持续化管理 (Managing Enterprise Assets for Sustainability)

复杂资产管理 (Complex Assets Management)

环境可持续发展管理 (Managing Environmental Sustainability)

排放计划管理 (Managing Emission Schemes)

商业法和尽职调查 (Business Law and Due Diligence)

商业资产 (Business Audit)

公司管理 (Corporate Governance)

商务（通用）管理能力量表框架

图 6–10　商务（通用）管理能力量表框架

Segmenting market and formulating marketing strategies, plans and activities

Applying techniques to deliver results at various stages of marketing

Development and improvement of network and e-marketing campaigns

Understanding the role and function of business communications

Understanding the relationships between marketing and business communications on the one hand, and organisational performance on the other

Determining the communication, information and documentation requirements of an organisation

Designing formal processes and supporting ICT infrastructure for effective business communications across the whole enterprise

图 6-11　《商务（通用）管理能力量表》描述语节选

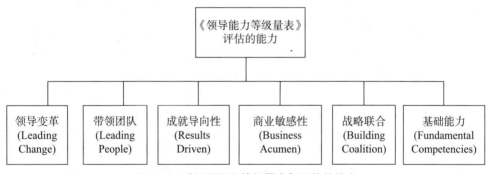

图 6-12　《领导能力等级量表》评估的能力

分为五个等级，对每项能力进行了清晰的定义并给出每个等级的描述语。如对客户服务能力的评估（见表 6-2），量表将其定义为"猜测和满足内部和外部客户的需求，交付高质量的产品和服务并持续改进"，该项能力被分为五个等级，并给出每个等级能力的定义和能力等级的描述。通过对能力等级清晰的表述，该量表易于使用，为科学评估使用者与领导力相关的能力提供了一个科学的工具。基于该量表的科学性、权威性和实用性，结合商务实践能力的理论框架，笔者主要挑选与领导变革、带领团队、商业敏感性和基础能力四大能力相关的描述语作为《商务实践能力量表》的描述语。

表 6-2 《领导能力等级量表》描述语节选

Proficiency Levels for Leadership Competencies

Customer Service—Anticipates and meets the needs of both internal and external customers. Delivers high-quality products and services; is committed to continuous improvement.

Proficiency Level	Proficiency Level Definition	Proficiency Level Descriptors
Level 5-Expert	• Applies the competency in exceptionally difficult situations • Serves as a key resource and advises others	• Develops innovative customer service initiative which significantly improves quality and enhances customer satisfaction • Implements organization—wide customer service initiative to raise employee skill levels and improve customer service
Level 4-Advanced	• Applies the competeney in considerably difficult situations • Generally requires little or no guidance	• Anticipates growing customer needs and expectations to continuously improve product development and service delivery • Creates work group consisting of stakeholders and neutral parties to develop solutions to customer service barriers
Level 3-Intermediate	• Applies the competency in difficult situations • Requires occasional guidance	• Designs and implements guidelines to improve products and services • Develops customer satisfaction surveys, analyzes results, and makes necessary improvements • Addresses customer service deficiencies by involving employees to identify solutions
Level 2-Basic	• Applies the competency in somewhat difficult situations • Requires frequent guidance	• Develops guides and user manuals for customers • Ensures products and services comply with customer requirements • Streamlines procedures based on customer feedback
Level 1-Awareness	• Applies the competency in the simplest situations • Requires close and extensive guidance	• Addresses customer questions in a timely manner • Updates agency website to reflect changes to services

6.4.2.3 《工作角色和熟练水平能力量表》

《工作角色和熟练水平能力量表》是国际著名人力资源与人才管理咨询和培训公司 Workitect 开发的一套在工作场所的能力评估工具。Workitect 成立于 1992 年，在帮助公司评估、选择、发展优秀员工，提供创新和有效的解决方案方面具有丰富的经验。《工作角色和熟练水平能力量表》是建立在坚实的研究基础上的，它能为人才评估和选择、绩效评估、职业道路规划、人才培训等提供重要工具。该量表主要评估人际交往相关能力、商务相关能力和自我管理能力，其内容架构图和表述节选见图 6–13 和表 6–3。由于该表的能力框架与商务实践能力理论框架在很大程度上吻合，因此笔者将其作为《商务实践能力量表》描述语的主要来源。

COMPETENCIES DEALING WITH PEOPLE

- *Leading Others Cluster*
  - Establishing Focus --- 2
  - Providing Motivational Support ---------------------------------- 3
  - Fostering Teamwork --- 6
  - Empowering Others --- 8
  - Managing Change -- 9
  - Developing Others --- 12
  - Managing Performance -- 14
  - Fostering Diversity -- 17
- *Communicating and Influencing Cluster*
  - Attention to Communication --------------------------------------- 19
  - Oral Communication -- 21
  - Written Communication -- 23
  - Persuasive Communication --- 26
  - Interpersonal Effectiveness -- 28
  - Influencing Others --- 31
  - Building Collaborative Relationships --------------------------- 34

COMPETENCIES DEALING WITH BUSINESS

- *Preventing and Solving Problems Cluster*
  - Diagnostic Information Gathering --------------------------------- 37
  - Analytical Thinking --- 40
  - Forward Thinking -- 42
  - Conceptual Thinking -- 44
  - Strategic Thinking --- 46
  - Technical Expertise --- 49
- *Achieving Results Cluster*
  - Initiative -- 51
  - Entrepreneurial Orientation -- 52
  - Fostering Innovation -- 54
  - Customer Orientation --- 56
  - Results Orientation -- 59
  - Thoroughness --- 61
  - Decisiveness --- 64
  - Business Acumen --- 65
  - Global Perspective --- 68

SELF MANAGEMENT COMPETENCIES

- Self Confidence -- 71
- Adaptability -- 73
- Personal Credibility --- 76
- Flexibility --- 78
- Personal Accountability -- 79

图 6–13 《工作角色和熟练水平能力量表》内容架构图

表 6-3 《工作角色和熟练水平能力量表》描述语节选

4- Empowering Others— Conveying confidence in employees' ability to be successful, especially at challenging new tasks; delegating significant responsibility and authority; allowing employees freedom to decide how they will accomplish their goals and resolve issues.

	Basic	Proficient	Advanced
Supervisor/ Manager	• Allows people some freedom and autonomy to make their own decisions in their own sphere of work • Allows others to make minor decisions, but wants to be involved in the major decisions • Allows individuals and groups to draft their own goals • Has faith in the ability of others to be successful • Is involved with groups to resolve problems; tends to prescribe solutions	• Gives people latitude to make decisions in their own sphere of work • Is able to let others make decisions and take charge • Encourages indviduals and groups to set their own goals, consistent with business goals • Expresses confidence in the ability of others to be successful • Encourages groups to resolve problems on their own; avoids prescribing a solution	• Coaches people to make decisions and gives them latitude to do so in their own sphere of work • Coaches others to take charge of all aspects of their work and make decisions, even in challenging new tasks • Empowers and enables individuals and groups to set their own goals, consistent with business goals • Conveys a sense of confidence and certainty in the ability of others to be successful • Coaches and encourages groups to resolve problems on their own; avoids prescribing a solution
Director/ Executive	• Gives people latitude to make decisions in their own sphere of work • Is able to let others make decisions and take charge	• Coaches people to make decisions and gives them latitude to do so in their own sphere of work	• Instills a culture in the organization to coach people to make decisions and give them latitude to do so in their own sphere of work

（续表）

	Basic	Proficient	Advanced
Director/ Executive	• Encourages individuals and groups to set their own goals, consistent with business goals • Expresses confidence in the ability of others to be successful • Encourages groups to resolve problems on their own; avoids prescribing a solution	• Coaches others to take charge of all aspects of their work and make decisions, even in challenging new tasks • Empowers and enables individuals and groups to set their own goals, consistent with business goals • Conveys a sense of confidence and certainty in the ability of others to be successful • Coaches and encourages groups to resolve problems on their own; avoids prescribing a solution	• Instills a culture in the organization to coach others to take charge of all aspects of their work and make decisions, even in challenging new tasks • Demonstrates a passion for empowering and enabling individuals and groups to set their own goals, consistent with business strategies and goals • Encourages and enables other leaders to convery a sense of confidence and certainty in the ability of others to be successful • Helps other leaders to coach and encourage groups to resolve problems on their own; avoids prescribing a solution

6.4.2.4　《特许全球管理会计师能力框架》

《特许全球管理会计师能力框架》是国际公认的管理会计师资格认证的重要框架（见图 6–14）。该框架主要评估四项技能：（1）专业技能，即各项专业的会计知识和能力；（2）商务技能，即商务环境中理解和应用商务知识的技术技能；（3）人际技能，即通过有效沟通影响组织和业务利益相关者的决策、行动和行为的技能；（4）领导能力，即领导各级别的工作伙伴实现共同的业务目标的能力。笔者把《特许全球管理会计师能力框架》中与商务技能、人际技能和领导能力相关的描述语有选择地融入《商务实践能力量表》的设计中（见图6–15）。

CGMA COMPETENCY FRAMEWORK，2023

TECHNICAL SKILLS	BUSINESS SKILLS	PEOPLE SKILLS	LEADERSHIP SKILLS	DIGITAL SKILLS
• Financial accounting and reporting • Cost accounting and management • Business planning • Management reporting and analysis • Corporate finance and treasurymanagement • Risk management and internal control • Accounting information systems • Tax strategy, planning and compliance	• Strategy • Business models • Market and regulatory environment • Process management • Business relations • Business ecosystems management • Project management • Macroeconomic analysis	• Influence • Negotiation and decision-making • Communication • Collaboration and partnering	• Team building • Coaching and mentoring • Driving performance • Motivating and inspiring • Change management	• Information and digital literacy • Digital content creation • Problem-solving • Data strategy and planning • Data analytics • Data visualisation

1   2   3   4   5

ETHICS, INTEGRITY AND PROFESSIONALISM

图 6–14 《特许全球管理会计师能力架构》（2014）

Strategy

This is the process of articulating the organisation's general sense of identity and direction, outlining why the organisation exists, for whom and what the stakeholders require.

Foundational	Intermediate	Advanced	Expert
• Aware of the organisation's business plan, immediate environment and the possible impact of events and activities on the organisation; understand current role in relation to executing the business plan • Observe and notice events that are out of the ordinary, make connections, draw conclusions and feed ideas and observations to senior finance colleagues • Understand the strategic direction of the organisation and highlight areas of potential value or risk	• Analyse the organisation's wider environment and draw conclusions about the impact of events and activities; guide the team to create solutions that deliver value in line with the business and finance plans • Link ideas or events, use insights to shape the views of managers and feed insights and observations to senior finance colleagues to influence business decisions • Understand the steps to achieve long-term business strategy, identify immediate threats or opportunities to the business and resolve or escalate them accordingly	• Evaluate the organisation's wider environment and offer insights based on an understanding of the business to influence change at tactical, team and individual levels and make informed business decisions and strategy • Explain the strategic direction of the organisation to others; develop a prioritised finance plan that both delivers the needs of the business and is consistent with the overall finance functional strategy and business plan • Ensure the team is focused on identified priorities; develop and implement solutions at an operational level to address actions emanating from insights, either to mitigate critical risk or capitalise on opportunity	• Offer unique insights based on a deep understanding of political, social, business, market and finance trends; use insights to lead and influence change at strategic, tactical, team and individual levels across the organisation • Develop finance strategy that is aligned with the organisation's long-term plan that anticipates and supports business need, ensures appropriate resources are allocated to deliver effectively including goals to expand capacity, improve productivity and surpass industry benchmarks • Identify and focus on future critical areas for the organisation and devise strategy to maximise opportunity and minimise risk

图 6–15 《特许全球管理会计师能力框架》描述语节选——"战略"部分

除以上国际量表外，笔者还收集了部分国内商务英语实践技能大赛的评价指标。这些评价指标也可为《商务实践能力量表》的设计和开发提供参考。例如，"亿学杯"全国商务英语实践技能大赛的评判指标（见表6-4）在某种程度上体现出对商务实践能力的要求。

表 6-4　"亿学杯"全国商务英语实践技能大赛的评判指标

职业功能	工作内容	技能要求	相关知识
国际商务综合基础知识	熟悉国际商务理论知识	能够了解并熟悉实际国际商务活动中所需要掌握的基础知识和理论	商务英语视听说 商务英语写作 商务谈判 商务礼仪 商务沟通 商务翻译 跨文化交际 跨境电子商务 国际市场营销 外贸函电 国际单证 国际物流 国际风险与保险 国际结算 商业伦理
	通晓国际商务专业词汇	能够知晓并写出国际商务活动中常用的中英文专业词汇	
国际商务综合技能	国际商务综合理解与沟通	1. 能够理解国际商务中各种场景的人物关系、沟通对话及场景要点，场景涵盖的主题包括求职面试、简历制作、职场新人、职场礼仪、客户接待、国际差旅、工厂参观、酒店入住、客户投诉、商务谈判、客户拜访、机场登机等 2. 能够通过观看音视频，知晓国际商务中的各种场景隐藏的业务知识、细节与国别文化差异，并进行相关英语语言的听、写、译	1. 英语听力、写作和翻译的基本语言能力 2. 国际商务综合基础知识 3. 跨文化商务沟通
国际商务综合技能	数据分析	1. 能够理解国际商务中各类图表数据的汇总规范、主要内容及其应用，图表数据涵盖的内容包括销售报告、参展数据、谈判数据、绩效评估表、提成核算表等 2. 能够通过对案例与数据的理解，对图表数据进行分析，总结其中的业务知识、细节、问题及相应的应对思路等	1. 数据分析与应用方法 2. 国际营销概论系统知识 3. 英语阅读与分析能力

（续表）

职业功能	工作内容	技能要求	相关知识
函电写作与沟通	函电阅读理解	能够阅读并知晓国际贸易及其他业务中的各种函电及其写作思路与策略，辨别并分析函电中隐藏的业务知识与细节	1. 商务知识 2. 函电写作要点 3. 英语阅读与分析
函电写作与沟通	函电写作	能够完成国际贸易及其他业务中不同环节的函电写作	1. 商务知识 2. 函电写作策略与方法 3. 英语写作与表达能力
单证操作	单证阅读理解	能够了解并知晓国际贸易业务中不同单据的缮制规范要点以及应用场景	1. 单证的类型及应用场景 2. 单证的缮制规范
单证操作	单证实操	能够根据提供的案例完成国际贸易业务中出口公司、货代、海关等组织机构常用的各种单据的缮制、审核、审改	1. 缮制单据 2. 审核单据
跨境电商	跨境电商运营推广	1. 能够运用阿里国际站、一达通平台完成不同行业产品 B2B 批发业务的实操，包括 RFQ 报价、租船订舱、出口报关等 2. 能够编写不同产品的详细描述、运用 Pinterest 进行特定营销、处理客户纠纷等 B2C 业务的相关实操 3. 能够通过 Amazon、Ebay、速卖通等平台完成不同行业产品的上架实操	1. 跨境电商实务 2. 电子商务产品运营与推广 3. 客户管理 4. 跨境电商平台实操系统知识 5. 跨境电商店铺运营与管理
商务案例的调研与分析	案例分析	1. 能够根据演讲主题进行正确的分析 2. 能够通过案例分析得出演讲要点	案例分析方法
商务案例的调研与分析	熟悉商业主题	1. 能够根据主题理解相关商务内容 2. 能够掌握相关的商务知识	1. 国际市场营销 2. 品牌管理 3. 新媒体运营 4. 企业社会责任 5. 客户关系与管理 6. 展会招展与参展 7. 供应链管理 8. 企业战略 9. 跨境电商战略 10. 商务沟通技巧 11. 跨文化交际
商务案例的调研与分析	信息调研分析	1. 能够针对演讲要点进行有效的信息调研 2. 能够对信息进行有效的分析 3. 能够从信息分析中得出有效的结论	1. 数据调研方法 2. 数据分析总结方法

（续表）

职业功能	工作内容	技能要求	相关知识
商务演讲稿件的制作	演讲稿的撰写	1. 能够针对听众明确演讲基调 2. 能够撰写结构完整的演讲框架 3. 能够在演讲稿中清楚地提出问题、分析问题、解决问题 4. 能够有效运用调研结论支撑演讲	1. 分析听众的方法 2. 不同报告的演讲结构 3. 演讲稿写作的策略与技巧 4. 英语写作 5. 应用信息的方法 6. 图表制作的方法
	演示 PPT 的制作	1. 能够制作清晰明了切题的演示 PPT 2. 能够有效借用视觉辅助材料	1. 商务 PPT 制作方法 2. 多媒体制作运用方法
	演讲语言的打磨	1. 能够撰写正确无误的英文 2. 能够生动运用英语进行演讲	1. 英语语言能力 2. 演讲的策略与技巧
发表商务演讲	发表演讲	1. 能够流利地发表演讲内容 2. 能够进行有效的团队合作 3. 能够有效地掌控演讲的进程	1. 英语口语演讲能力 2. 团队合作能力 3. 现场掌控能力
	个人形象和身体语言	1. 能够展现得体的商务形象 2. 能够展现自信、自然的身体语言 3. 能够有效控制自己的声音	1. 商务形象礼仪 2. 演讲中身体语言的使用策略与技巧 3. 演讲中声音的掌控策略与技巧
	提问及对答	1. 能够清楚理解提问人的意思 2. 能够及时给出有效的回复	1. 听力理解能力 2. 应对不同问题的处理策略与技巧 3. 反应能力 4. 团队合作能力

6.4.3 《商务实践能力量表》的研制

6.4.3.1 《商务实践能力量表》

　　笔者在 Benjamin Bloom 等的教育目标分类理论基础上，结合商务外语学习者的特点和现实社会需求，构建了商务实践能力模型和评价指标体系；以具有国际影响力的 4 个相关能力评价量表为基础，对其中的描述语进行分级、分类、筛选、修订，最终构建了《商务实践能力量表》（表 6-5 是该量表描述语的节选）。

表 6-5 《商务实践能力量表》节选

Fundamental	1	demonstrates the general awareness and knowledge of the professional accounting standards.
	2	understands and describes the main elements of financial statements and reports.
	3	understands and applies basic concepts of cost accounting to support entities' operational and financial requirements.
	4	can demonstrate basic understanding of techniques used to analyse and manage costs.
	5	can demonstrate understanding of basic principles and application of business tax.
Intermediate	61	understands and discusses routine tax matters such as income tax, indirect tax, corporate tax within clear guidelines.
	62	analyses the organisational wider environment and draw conclusions about the impact of events and activities.
	63	identifies immediate threats or opportunities to the business and resolve or escalate them accordingly.
	64	uses sound knowledge of the organisation's customers and competitors to analyse and challenge business cases.
	65	understands the elements that make up each process and the performance measures that can be applied to each.
Advanced	125	takes the lead in developing and implementing complex project plans that have implications across business units or the organisation.
	126	identifies new and innovative ways to achieve required outputs of projects.
	127	provides recommendations to macroeconomic analysis.
	128	evaluates and properly interprets the influence of the external environment on the organisation.
	129	identifies key environmental drivers and understands their impact upon business strategies and decisions.
	130	uses a combination of logic, personal passion, conviction and interpersonal skills to influence others.

（续表）

	292	understands the nature and limits of related organisations and government agencies, and uses that knowledge to influence and lead.
	293	takes ownership of compliance, ethical and other issues in order to protect the organisation's reputation and respect its obligations.
Expert	294	uses a variety of means to communicate the organisation's needs and strategic directions.
	295	develops a strategic direction for one's unit that connects the role of the team to the success of the organisation.
	296	ensures the initiatives and priorities in one's area are integrated with one another and aligned with the strategic priorities of the broader organisation.

6.4.3.2　对《商务实践能力量表》的分析

基于前文的理论框架和收集的描述语，笔者为商务外语学习者建构了一个科学、实用的《商务实践能力量表》。本量表将商务实践能力的各项子能力分为认知领域、情感领域和动作技能领域，可多角度、大范围综合评估商务外语学习者的商务实践能力。本量表将商务实践能力分为基础、中等、良好和优秀四个等级，共 305 条描述语。

在认知领域中，本量表主要测试学习者的商务基础知识，包括对商务知识的理解、应用、分析、综合和评价。根据《高等学校商务英语专业本科教学质量国家标准》，本量表评估的商务知识主要包括经济学知识、企业管理知识、跨国公司管理知识、国际商法知识和国际金融知识等。如量表第 2 条描述语 "understands and describes the main elements of financial statements and reports" 主要评估学习者对金融知识的理解和应用。为了解公司和市场形势，商务外语学习者应该具有分析各种报表的能力，基础和中等等级的商务外语学习者应该了解各种报表的基本构成，根据报表数据得出基本结论；良好和优秀等级的商务外语学习者应该能够综合分析多个报表，得出较复杂全面的结论，并根据结论预测发展趋势以用于市场分析和风险规避。

本量表不仅评估商务外语学习者商务知识的储备，还评估学习者在商务场景中对商务知识的应用，如描述语第 10 条 "can understand the strategic direction of the organisation and highlight areas of potential value or risk"，这条描述语不仅评估商务外语学习者对企业管理知识的掌握，还评估学习者根据企业管理知识采取正确的措施促进企业发展的能力。因此，学习者需要理解、应用、分析、综合和评价企业管理知识，从而达到相应的能力等级。

本量表还评估学习者情感领域的相关能力，主要包括服务意识、创业精神、全球意识和职业道德。服务意识不仅是针对外部客户，还要对内部客户和合作伙伴具有服务意识，如量表第 78 条 "proposes innovative business deals to potential customers, suppliers, and business partners" 和第 79 条 "talks to customers (internal or external) to find out their needs and meet their needs" 评估学习者的服务意识。学习者要善于发现商机，具备创新能力和批判性思维。全球意识对于商务外语学习者而言是一项重要能力，具有全球意识，学习者才能更好地融入国际商贸大环境。因此，本量表也测评商务外语学习者的全球意识，如第 93 条 "identifies the broader impact of problems in one's own work area and acts to minimize or address these" 和第 127 条 "provides recommendations to macroeconomic analysis" 分别评估学习者在商务行为对国际环境的影响和国际环境对商务行为的影响两方面的全球意识。职业道德是商务外语学习者的道德指标，合格的商务经济贸易活动的参与者应该遵守职业道德，合理合法合规地做好本职工作。本量表在职业道德方面也给出了一定的规范，如第 106 条 "admits to mistakes and takes responsibility" 和第 280 条 "promotes group morale and productivity by being clear about output expectations"。

本量表还评估学习者动作技能领域相关的子能力，包括软技能和硬技能，几乎涵盖了商务活动的核心技能。如第 67 条 "develops simple project plans including business case, contingencies, critical paths and applies project management tools and techniques" 评估学习者制定商务管理计划的能力。营销和业务管理能力对于商务外语学习者很重要，也是本量表评估的重要指标之一，第 77 条 "keeps abreast of business, industry and market information that may reveal business opportunities"、第 111 条 "knows marketing process, from assessing market needs to marketing products and services" 和第 118 条 "uses understanding of the organisation's commercial business and markets to tailor offerings to current and future needs"等评估学习者的营销和业务管理能力。财务管理能力、国际业务战略能力和供应链基础管理能力对商务外语学习者提出了更高要求，也是他们必不可少的能力。因此，本量表还测评学习者这三方面的能力。电子商务能力是新时代对商务外语学习者提出的能力要求，随着网络和信息化的发展，电子营销和电子商务对企业越来越重要。因此，笔者将电子商务能力作为重要的硬技能对商务外语学习者进行评估。如第 287 条"accurately hears and understands the unspoken thoughts or feelings of others and acts purposefully"评估学习者倾听他人想法的能力；第 55 条"motivates others to contribute through one's own enthusiasm"评估学习者在团队中发挥积极作用的个人特质；第 275 条"assesses group performance against goals and identifies areas for improvement"评估学习者根据团队目前表现制定相应的改进措施的变化管理能力；第 265 条"manages operations with a continual focus on the impact of decisions and actions on client"评估使用者在战略决策中始终关注客户关心的问题的战略思维；第 264 条"understands when and how to use personal power and relational power and relational power underpinned by integrity to influence outcomes"评估使用者利用个人能力和对他人的影响获取好的结果的人力资源管理能力。《商务实践能力量表》可根据学习者应对商务实践任务的能力，科学地衡量其商务实践能力。

结　语

　　商务外语人才能力标准的设计和研究是一个相当复杂和具有挑战性的课题，此课题对商务外语学科发展和人才培养具有重要意义。在收集、筛选、比对、修订资料的基础上，笔者进行了商务外语人才能力标准的前期研究工作，设计了商务外语人才能力标准指标体系，即《商务外语语言应用能力量表》（250 条描述语）、《商务外语跨文化交际能力量表》（235 条描述语）、《商务外语自主学习能力量表》（149 条描述语）、《商务外语批判性思维能力量表》（194 条描述语）和《商务实践能力量表》（305 条描述语）五个量表，共计 1 133 条描述语。期望此标准可以为商务外语人才培养的方案设计、学科建设、课程体系、教材体系、评估工具、评估体系等提供一定的参考。

　　首先，为了设计上述五个量表，笔者综述国内外研究，在充分分析和比对《普通高等学校本科专业类教学质量国家标准（外国语言文学类）》和《普通高等学校本科外国语言文学类专业教学指南》的基础上，针对商务外语学习者的特点，对五大能力进行清晰的界定，为商务外语人才能力标准的后续研究奠定了基础。

　　其次，笔者分别针对五个能力量表的理论框架进行分析和建构研究，构建了每一项能力的实践操作模型。五项能力可被视为一系列子能力的集合，因此，对这五项能力的评估不是片面的、武断的，而是较为科学和全面的。在每项能力的实践操作模型的基础上，笔者又对该能力的二级指标进行细分，建立了三级和四级指标，进而形成了对每项能力的系统的、清晰的评价指标体系，以期可以更加系统、全面、综合地评估这五项能力。

　　再次，笔者结合国际上较新的、成熟的、通用的相关量表，对五项能力的描述语进行了仔细的设计、筛选、修订、修改、增删等，最终研制出了商务外语人才的《商务外语语言应用能力量表》《商务外语跨文化交际能力量表》《商务外语自主学习能力量表》《商务外语批判性思维能力量表》《商务实践能力量表》五个量表，为语言政策的制定者、教材的设计者、一线教师的课堂教学和学生的自主学习提供了可靠的参考工具。此外，这些量表也为评价商务外语学习者的能力提供了工具，为我国商务外语测评体系的完善奠定了一定的基础，丰富了商务外语的研究。

由于时间、精力、人手、资源等条件限制，笔者设计的量表还有一些不足，仍需不断完善。例如，描述语还不够精准，量表尚未经过实际测试，信度和效度还有待验证。

笔者尽可能挑选来自不同领域的具有代表性的量表，这些量表的开发者具有权威性和多样性，其信度和效度已经被验证过。这在一定程度上弥补了作者设计的量表的缺陷。同时，笔者主要关注量表开发的前四个阶段：概念界定、操作模型建构、指标体系设计、描述语的收集。而能力量表设计的后两个阶段：量表有效性和可靠性验证，及能力量表体系的进一步的修改暂时没有涉及。

在未来的研究中，笔者将对商务外语五个能力量表的可靠性和有效性进行验证，继续改进这些量表，不断优化文本设计，验证量表的可信度、效度和稳定性。笔者认为每个能力量表都必须是动态发展的，随着时间的推移需不断更新修改，以满足新的学习需求。因此，笔者设计的量表不是最终产品，今后仍会不断对其进行完善与改进。同时，也希望更多的学者加入到这些量表的完善工作中。

商务外语人才能力标准的构建为完善商务外语能力评估体系奠定了基础，期待笔者设计的五个能力量表能对国家有关部门、教研院、课堂教学、教材开发等研究工作有一定的作用，也期待该成果能够在商务外语学习者的能力测试和培训中发挥一定的作用，为商务外语学习者进行能力自评、商务外语教学者进行教学设计和评估学生能力提供一定的参考。在能力测评的实践中，笔者会收集各方意见，不断优化量表，以保证其科学性。

参考文献

［1］毕继万.第二语言教学的主要任务是培养学生的跨文化交际能力［J］.中国外语，2005，（01）：66–70.

［2］蔡基刚.专门用途英语的信仰与理念的再认识：改革开放40周年我国高校外语教育的回顾与反思.外语研究，2018，（2）.

［3］陈波.批判性思维与创新型人才的培养.中国大学教学，2017（3）.

［4］陈波.中国逻辑学70年：历程与反思.社会科学文摘，2019（12）.

［5］陈建平，聂利亚.从目前的研究看商务英语学科体系的构建.外语教学，2009（5）.

［6］陈准民，王立非.解读《高等学校商务英语专业本科教学要求》（试行）.中国外语，2009（4）.

［7］陈准民，王立非.解读《高等学校商务英语专业本科教学要求》（试行）［J］.中国外语，2009，6（04）：4–11+21.

［8］崔诣晨，刘青玉，李凡妹.批判性思维的意蕴及其培养：基于激进建构主义的视角.当代教育论坛，2018（5）.

［9］杜瑞清.关于跨文化交际与素质培养的几点思考［J］.西安外国语学院学报，1998，（02）：19–20+33.

［10］对外经济贸易大学商务英语理论研究小组.论商务英语的学科定位、研究对象和发展方向.中国外语，2006（5）.

［11］方明.商务英语写作能力量表研究与构建.中国商界（下半月），2010（1）.

［12］方绪军，杨惠中，朱正才.语言能力"能做"描述的原理与方案：以CEFR为例".世界汉语教学，2011（2）.

［13］郭汝惠.基于实践能力培养的电子商务专业教学改革［J］.北京广播电视大学学报，2013，（01）：37–41.

［14］韩宝成.由国外语言能力量表看统一的学生英语能力标准的制定.第一届两岸外语大学院校学术研讨会论文集，2005.

［15］黄源深.思辨缺席［J］.外语与外语教学，1998（7）：2–2+18.

［16］雷春林.论基于商务内容的语言教学——兼论商务英语学科定位［J］.国际商务研究，2006，（01）：17–22.

［17］冷静，郭日发.在线协作平台中批判性思维话语分析研究.电化教育研究，2018（2）.

［18］李晶，付爱玲，李淑芳.构建以职业能力培养为核心的商务英语专业实践教学体系［J］.职业教育研究，2018，（06）：60–64.

［19］林大津，谢朝群.论言语交际的得体原则：争议与意义［J］.外语教学与研究，2005，（06）：21–26+82.

［20］刘法公.中国从无到有的商务英语学科.外语界，2009（6）.

［21］刘贵芹.推动高等教育内涵式发展提高本科人才培养质量［J］.重庆高教研究，2013，1（01）：1–4.DOI：10.15998/j.cnki.issn1673–8012.2013.01.001.

［22］吕世生.商务英语学科定位的学理依据.外语界，2013（4）.

［23］罗清旭，杨鑫辉.《加利福尼亚批判性思维倾向问卷》中文版的初步修订.心理发展与教育，2001（3）.

［24］门博良.多模态理论在商务英语专业课堂教学中的应用［J］.宿州教育学院学报，2016，19（06）：118–119.DOI：10.13985/j.cnki.34–1227/c.2016.06.056.

［25］彭美慈，汪国成，等.批判性思维能力测量表的信效度测试研究.中华护理杂志，2004（9）.

［26］商应美，仇云龙，牛鸿生，等.高校英语专业"全方位进阶型"学科竞赛体系构建的实践探索——基于广义的知识观［J］.现代教育科学，2011，（03）：131–133.DOI：10.13980/j.cnki.xdjykx.gjyj.2011.03.006.

［27］孙毅.《高等学校商务英语专业本科教学质量国家标准》的地方性解读：国标与校标的对照.外语界，2016（2）.

［28］王浈、张国建.国家语言能力视角下商务英语能力标准研究.北京：对外经济贸易大学出版社，2020.

［29］王浈，杨妍.商务英语口语能力量表研究.海外英语，2016（7）.

[30] 王淙, 张国建, 马青. 商务英语翻译能力量表研究. 电子测试, 2015 (24).

[31] 王关富. 商务英语学科的"交叉性"研究. 当代外语研究, 2012 (4).

[32] 王关富, 刘丽. 关于商务英语学科核心竞争力的理论探讨. 中国外语, 2012 (5).

[33] 王建娜. 商务英语阅读能力量表研究. 当代教育理论与实践, 2016 (7).

[34] 王建卿, 文秋芳. 国外思维能力量具评介及启示: 我国外语类大学生思维能力现状研究报告. 江苏技术师范学院学报, 2011 (7).

[35] 王立非, 江进林. 全国商务英语考试的设计与信效度研究. 外语与外语教学, 2011 (6).

[36] 王立非, 叶兴国, 严明, 等. 商务英语专业本科教学质量国家标准要点解读. 外语教学与研究, 2015 (2).

[37] 王丽, 范劲松. 国外商务英语能力等级量表研究述评. 解放军外国语学院学报, 2017 (5).

[38] 王瑞霞, 郭爱萍. 国内近三十年批判性思维研究: 现状、思考、展望. 太原师范学院学报(社科版), 2011 (5).

[39] 王淑花. 中国学生英语理解能力量表的构建及验证研究. 北京: 知识产权出版社, 2012.

[40] 文秋芳. 论外语专业研究生高层次思维能力的培养. 学位与研究生教育, 2008 (10).

[41] 文秋芳, 刘艳萍, 王海妹, 等. 我国外语类大学生思辨能力量具的修订与信效度检验研究. 外语界, 2010 (4).

[42] 文秋芳, 王海妹, 王建卿, 等. 我国英语专业与其他文科类大学生思辨能力的对比研究. 外语教学与研究, 2010 (5).

[43] 文秋芳, 王建卿, 赵彩然, 等. 构建我国外语类大学生思辨能力量具的理论框架. 外语界, 2009 (1).

[44] 文秋芳, 王建卿, 赵彩然, 等. 对我国大学生思辨倾向量具信度的研究. 外语电化教学, 2011 (6).

[45] 文秋芳, 张伶俐, 张旻. 外语专业学生的思辨能力逊色于其他专业的学生吗?. 现代外语, 2014 (6).

［46］文秋芳，周燕．评述外语专业学生思维能力的发展［J］．外语学刊，2006（5）：76–80.

［47］吴寒，何宇，项伟锋．高职商务英语人才培养模式——以就业为导向、以职业能力为本位的探索与实践［J］．广东轻工职业技术学院学报，2006，（03）：47–50.

［48］徐强，苏晓军．夸张和低调的语用对比分析［J］．山东外语教学，2000，（01）：41–45.DOI：10.16482/j.sdwy37–1026.2000.01.012.

［49］薛荣．当代语言测试：理论发展与未来趋势［J］．外语与外语教学，2008（10）：44–47.

［50］严明.大学英语自主学习能力培养实证研究.外语电化教学，2010（2）.

［51］严明.跨文化商务交际能力体系的构建.黑龙江社会科学，2009（6）.

［52］严明.基于体裁的商务英语话语能力研究:构念界定与测试开发.上海外国语大学，2012.

［53］杨惠中.关于我国外语能力测评体系建设的几点思考.中国考试，2015（1）.

［54］杨惠中，桂诗春.制定亚洲统一的英语语言能力等级量表.中国外语，2007（2）.

［55］杨盈，庄恩平．构建外语教学跨文化交际能力框架［J］．外语界，2007，（04）：13–21+43.

［56］叶兴国．我国商务英语专业教育的起源、现状和发展趋势．当代外语研究，2014（5）.

［57］张蔚磊.加拿大第二语言测评二十年实践经验及其对我国的启示.比较教育学报，2022（4）.

［58］张蔚磊.外语教育政策研究：理论基础与参考框架.西安外国语大学学报，2022（3）.

［59］张蔚磊．英语专业课程思政元素融入的路径、评价与成效：以"英语教学研究"课程为例.北京第二外国语学院学报，2022（4）.

［60］张蔚磊."流"理论及其在计算机辅助外语教学中的应用.山东外语教学，2010（1）.

［61］张蔚磊.NCSSFL-ACTFL 全球外语能力"Can-do"绩效指标体系研究及其对我国"学习者自我评价量表"的启示.外语教学理论与实践，2022（4）.

［62］张蔚磊. 从宏观生态哲学视角来解读我国大学外语政策的发展. 江苏外语教学研究, 2011（1）.

［63］张蔚磊. 大学外语教师绩效评估指标体系研究. 中国外语, 2012（4）.

［64］张蔚磊. 大学外语教师评价与质量提升研究. 中国外语, 2014（6）.

［65］张蔚磊. 大学英语教改转型期的政策研究：以《上海市大学英语教学参考框架》为例. 外语教学理论与实践, 2018（4）.

［66］张蔚磊. 大学英语教师评估现状研究. 上海对外经贸大学学报, 2014（5）.

［67］张蔚磊. 大学英语教学大纲对比分析——生态化视角. 现代教育科学, 2011（5）.

［68］张蔚磊. 发达国家外语能力标准比较研究与我国外语能力标准构建. 外语界, 2016（6）.

［69］张蔚磊. 非英语国家外语教育政策与规划的焦点问题探究. 外国中小学教育, 2018（11）.

［70］张蔚磊. 国外语言政策与规划理论研究述评. 外国语（上海外国语大学学报）, 2017（5）.

［71］张蔚磊. 计算机语言学习游戏研究初探. 外语电化教学, 2011（5）.

［72］张蔚磊. 论计算机教育游戏与外语学习. 广东外语外贸大学学报, 2011（5）.

［73］张蔚磊. 美国21世纪初外语教育政策述评. 外语界, 2014（2）.

［74］张蔚磊. 美国ACTFL外语能力指导方针研究及启示. 外国语文研究（辑刊）, 2021（1）.

［75］张蔚磊. 美国语言政策研究:《语言学习的世界标准》的内涵与启示. 浙江外国语学院学报, 2019（2）.

［76］张蔚磊. 数据包络分析方法在平衡大学外语教师教学与科研工作中的实证研究. 复旦外国语言文学论丛, 2014（1）.

［77］张蔚磊. 外语能力标准的国别研究:加拿大与英国. 上海：上海交通大学出版社, 2022.

［78］张蔚磊. 外语能力标准的国别研究:美国与澳大利亚. 上海：上海交通大学出版社, 2022.

［79］张蔚磊. 外语学习的理想状态:"流"体验. 当代外语研究, 2011（1）.

［80］张蔚磊.微观语言规划理论在我国外语课程政策实施中的探究.解放军外国语学院学报,2016（6）.

［81］张蔚磊.我国高校教师绩效评价的现状评析.现代教育科学,2012（7）.

［82］张蔚磊.我国商务英语的研究热点及发展趋势:基于10年来CNKI论文的知识图谱分析.上海交通大学学报（哲学社会科学版）,2021（3）.

［83］张蔚磊.我国外语教育政策的实然现状与应然选择.外语教学,2015（1）.

［84］张蔚磊.新文科背景下的商务外语人才培养策略分析.外国语文,2021（2）.

［85］张蔚磊.中国外语教育的创新、融合与发展:第七届全国外国语学院院长论坛述评.中国外语,2011（4）.

［86］张蔚磊,雷春林.我国英语能力标准的研究热点及趋势:基于近10年来CNKI论文的知识图谱计量分析.外语教学,2020（6）.

［87］张蔚磊,李馨,赵云建.高等教育数字化学习的未来:访哈佛大学教育技术学专家克里斯·德迪教授.中国电化教育,2014（12）.

［88］张蔚磊,宋秋逸,魏冬亮.《世界各种语言教学实用指南》与我国各学段英语教学实用指南开发.当代外语研究,2019（6）.

［89］张蔚磊,王光林.经济全球化背景下的商务英语人才培养战略.中国ESP研究,2016（2）.

［90］张蔚磊,王辉.微观语言规划理论及其对我国外语教育规划的启示.外语研究,2022（1）.

［91］赵婷婷,杨翀,刘欧,等.大学生学习成果评价的新途径:EPP（中国）批判性思维能力试测报告.教育研究,2015（9）.

［92］赵雯,金檀,王勃然.大学英语语言能力标准的研制——理论、实践及启示［J］.现代外语,2015,38（01）:102–111+147.

［93］郑敏.自主性学习的缘起和发展［J］.西安外国语学院学报,2000,（03）:100–105.

［94］中华人民共和国教育部.中国英语能力等级量表.北京:教育部,2018.

［95］朱正才.关于我国英语能力等级量表描述语库建设的若干问题.中国考试,2015（4）.

［96］朱智贤,林崇德.思维发展心理学.北京:北京师范大学出版社,2002.

[97] Alderson, J. "Brand and scores," In Alderson J. and North B. (eds.). *Language Testing in the 1990s.* London：Modern English Publication and the British Council, 1991.

[98] Allen, J. P. B. and H. G. Widdowson, *English in Focus: English in Social Studies.* London：Oxford University Press, 1978.

[99] Alsaker F D. School Achievement, Perceived Academic Competence and Global Self-esteem 1[J]. *School Psychology International*, 1989, 10(2): 147–158.

[100] Ang, S., L. Van Dyne, C. Koh, K. Y. Ng, K. J. Templer, C. Tay, and N. A. Chandrasekar, "Cultural Intelligence: Its Measurement and Effects on Cultural Judgment and Decision-Making, Cultural Adaptation and Task Performance," *Management and Organization Review*, 2007(3), pp. 335–371.

[101] Arasaratnam, L. A, "The Development of a New Instrument of Intercultural Communication Competence." *Journal of Intercultural Communication*, 2009(2), pp.1–11.

[102] Bachman, L. F., *Fundamental Considerations in Language Testing.* Oxford：Oxford University Press, 1990.

[103] Beechler, S. and M. Javidan, "Leading with a Global Mindset," *Advances in International Management*, 2007(19), pp. 131–169.

[104] Bennett, M. J., "Towards Ethnorelativism：A Developmental Model of Intercultural Sensitivity," In R. M. Paige (Ed.), *Education for the Intercultural Experience.* Yarmouth, ME：Intercultural Press, 1993.

[105] Bennett, M. J, "A Developmental Approach to Training for Intercultural Sensitivity'. *International Journal of Intercultural Relations*, 1986(2), pp. 179–196.

[106] Benson B A, Valenti-Hein D. Cognitive and social learning treatments [A]. In Dosen, A. and Day, K. (eds.), *Treating mental illness and behavior disorders in children and adults with mental retardation*, 2001: 101–118.

［107］Benson H H. *Socratic wisdom: the model of knowledge in Plato's early dialogues* [M]. Oxford: Oxford University Press, 2000.

［108］Benson P. *Teaching and Researching: Autonomy in Language Learning* [M]. London: Routledge, 2011.

［109］Berry J W, Kim U, Power S, et al. Acculturation attitudes in plural societies[J]. *Applied Psychology*, 1989, 38(2): 185–206.

［110］Black, J. S., W. H. Mobley and E.W. Weldon, "The Mindset of Global Leaders: Inquisitiveness and Duality." *Advances in Global Leadership*, 2005(4), pp.181–200.

［111］Boeckx C, Hornstein N, Nunes J. Control as Movement[M]. Cambridge: Cambridge University Press, 2010.

［112］Boekaerts M. *Context sensitivity: Activated motivational beliefs, current concerns and emotional arousal*[A]. In S. Volet & S. Järvelä (Eds.), *Motivation in learning contexts: Theoretical advances and methodological implications* (pp. 17–32). Oxford: Pergamon Press. 2001.

［113］Bok, D., *Our Underachieving Colleges: A Candid Look at How Much Students Learn and Why They Should Be Learning More.* Princeton: Princeton University Press, 2006.

［114］Bradford G, Gary M, Wallach G. *The Politics of Culture: Policy Perspectives for Individuals, Institutions, and Communities*[M]. New York: The New Press, 2000.

［115］Brenneman M W, Klafehn J, Burrus J, et al. Assessing cross-cultural competence: a working framework and prototype measures for use in military contexts [J]. *Critical Issues in Cross Cultural Management*, 2016: 103–131.

［116］Brown R B. Refrain the competency debate: Management knowledge and meta-competence in graduate education [J]. *Management Learning*, 1994, 25(2): 289–299.

[117] Brown, J.D. and T. Hudson, *Criterion-referenced Language Testing.* Cambridge: Cambridge University Press, 2002.

[118] Bryony, H. and U. Fredriksson, *Learning to Learn: What Is It and Can It Be Measured?* Publication Office of the European Union, 2008.

[119] Burkert A, Schwienhorst K. Focus on the student teacher: The European portfolio for student teachers of languages (EPOSTL) as a tool to develop teacher autonomy[J]. *International Journal of Innovation in Language Learning and Teaching*, 2008, 2(3): 238–252.

[120] Byram, M. *Teaching and Assessing Intercultural Communicative Competence.* Clevedon, UK: Multilingual Matters, 1997.

[121] Calculator, S. N., "Augmentative and Alternative Communication (AAC) and Inclusive Education for Students with the Most Severe Disability," *International Journal of Inclusive Education*, 2009(1), pp. 93–113.

[122] Campbell, R. and R. Wales, "The Study of Language Acquisition," In J. Lyons (ed.), *New Horizons in Linguistics*, Harmondsworth: Penguin Books, 1970.

[123] Canale, M. and M. Swain, "Theoretical Bases of Communicative Approaches to Second Language Teaching and Testing". *Applied Linguistics,* 1980(1), pp. 1–47.

[124] Canale, M., "From Communicative Competence to Communicative Language Pedagogy" In J.C. Richards and R.W. Schmidt (eds). *Language and Communication,* London: Longman Group Ltd., 1983.

[125] Candy P C. *Self-Direction for Lifelong Learning. A Comprehensive Guide to Theory and Practice* [M]. San Francisco, CA : Jossey-Bass, 1991.

[126] Carol, A. G., S. W. Blohm and T. Urdan, "Assessing Secondary Students' Disposition toward Critical Thinking: Development of the California Measure of Mental Motivation," *Educational and Psychological Measurement*, 2004(2), pp. 347–364.

［127］Chen, G.M. and W. J. Starosta, "Intercultural communication competence: A synthesis," *Communication Yearbook*, 1996(1), pp. 353–383.

［128］Chomsky, N. *Reflections on Language*. New York：Pantheon, 1975.

［129］Cole, J.R., E.G. Barber and S.R. Graubard. *The Research University in a Time of Discontent*. Baltimore: Johns Hopkins University Press, 1994.

［130］Collier, M. J., "Cultural and Intercultural Communication Competence: Current Approaches and Directions for Future Research," *International Journal of Intercultural Relations*, 1989(3), pp. 287–302.

［131］Deardoff, D.K., "The Identification and Assessment of Intercultural Competence as a Student Outcome of Internationalization," *Journal of Studies in International Education*, 2006(3), pp. 241–266.

［132］Deardorff, D. K, "Internationalization: In Search of Intercultural Competence," *International Educator*, 2004(3), pp. 13–15.

［133］Deci E L, Connell J P, Ryan R M. A motivational analysis of self-determination and self-regulation in the classroom[J]. *Research on motivation in education*, 1985, 2: 13–52.

［134］Delahaye B L, Smith H E. The validity of the learning preference assessment [J]. *Adult Education Quarterly*, 1995, 45(3): 159–173.

［135］Dickinson, L., *Self-instruction in Language Learning*. Cambridge：Cambridge University Press, 1987.

［136］Dunnette, M. D., "Aptitudes, Abilities and Skills," In M.D. Dunnette and L.M. Hough (eds.), *Handbook of Industrial and Organizational Psychology*, Chicago: Consulting Psychologist Press, 1976.

［137］Durlak J A, Weissberg R P, Dymnicki A B, et al. The impact of enhancing students' social and emotional learning: A meta-analysis of school-based universal interventions[J]. *Child Development*, 2011, 82(1): 405–432.

［138］Durr R E. An examination of readiness for self-directed learning and selected personnel variables at a large Midwestern electronics development and manufacturing corporation [D]. Doctoral dissertation. Florida Atlantic University, 1992.

［139］ Dweck C S. *Self-theories: their Role in Motivation*[J]. Personality, and Development, 2000.

［140］ Dweck C. *Self-theories: Impact on motivation, personality and development*[M]. London: Psychology Press, 1999.

［141］ Earley, P. C., and R. S. Peterson, "The Elusive Cultural Chameleon: Cultural Intelligence as a New Approach to Intercultural Training for the Global Manager," *Academy of Management Learning & Education*, 2004, (1), 100–115.

［142］ Eccles J S, Wigfield A. Motivational beliefs, values, and goals[J]. *Annual Review of Psychology*, 2002, 53(1): 109–132.

［143］ Egel İ P. The impact of the European language portfolio on the learner autonomy of Turkish primary school students[D]. Anadolu University (Turkiye), 2003.

［144］ Elias M J, Arnold H. *The educator's guide to emotional intelligence and academic achievement: Social-emotional learning in the classroom* [M]. Thousand Oaks, CA : Corwin Press, 2006.

［145］ Elliott D J. Puerto Rico: A Site of Critical Performative Pedagogy[J]. *Action, Criticism & Theory for Music Education*, 2007, 6(1).

［146］ Ellis, M. and C. Johnson, *Teaching Business English*. Oxford：Oxford University Press, 1994.

［147］ Ennis R H. Critical thinking dispositions: Their nature and assessability [J]. *Informal Logic*, 1996, 18(2).

［148］ Ennis R H. The extent to which critical thinking is subject-specific: Further clarification [J]. *Educational Researcher*, 1990, 19(4): 13–16.

［149］ Evenson R. Soft skills, hard sell[J]. *Techniques*, 1999, 74(3): 29–30.

［150］ Facione P A, Facione N C, Giancarlo C A. Professional judgment and the disposition toward critical thinking [J]. Retrieved Nov, 1997, 21: 2020.

［151］ Facione P A, Facione N C, Giancarlo C A. *Test manual: The California critical thinking dispositions inventory*[M]. San Jose, CA: California Academic Press 1992.

［152］Facione P A. The disposition toward critical thinking: Its character, measurement, and relationship to critical thinking skill [J]. *Informal Logic,* 2000, 20(1).

［153］Facione P. Critical thinking: A statement of expert consensus for purposes of educational assessment and instruction [J]. *The Delphi Report*, 1990.

［154］Facione, P. A, C. A. Giancarlo, N. C. Facione, "The Disposition toward Critical Thinking," *The Journal of General Education*, 1995(1), pp. 1–25.

［155］Fantini A E. Assessing intercultural competence: Issues and tools[A]// *The SAGE handbook of intercultural competence*. SAGE Publications, Inc, 2009: 456–476.

［156］Fantini, A. E., "Introduction—Language, Culture, and World View: Exploring the Nexus," *International Journal of Intercultural Relations*, 1995(2), pp. 143–153.

［157］Fantini, A. E., F. Arias-Galicia and D. Guay, "Globalization and 21st Century Competencies: Challenges for North American Higher Education," Boulder, Colorado: Western Interstate Commission for Higher Education, 2001.

［158］Fennes H, Hapgood K. *Intercultural Learning in the Classroom: Crossing Borders* [M]. London : Cassell, 1997.

［159］Fischer, G. and S. Masanori, "Supporting Self-directed Learners and Learning Communities with Sociotechnical Environments. *Research and Practice in Technology Enhanced Learning*, 2006(1), pp. 31–64.

［160］Friedman D S. Campus design as critical practice [J]. *Places Journal*, 2005, 17(1).

［161］Gallois C, Callan V J. Communication accommodation and the prototypical speaker: Predicting evaluations of status and solidarity[J]. *Language & Communication*, 1988.

［162］Gallois C, Franklyn-Stokes A, Giles H, et al. Communication accommodation in intercultural encounters [J]. *Theories in Intercultural Communication*, 1988, 158: 185.

［163］Galloway V B. *A design for the improvement of the teaching of culture in foreign language classrooms*[J]. ACTFL Project Proposal, 1985.

［164］Giancarlo C A, Facione P A. A look across four years at the disposition toward critical thinking among undergraduate students [J]. *The Journal of General Education*, 2001: 29–55.

［165］Giancarlo C A, Facione P A. A look across four years at the disposition toward critical thinking among undergraduate students [J]. *The Journal of General Education*, 2001: 29–55.

［166］Grant H, Dweck C S. *Cross-cultural response to failure: Considering outcome attributions with different goals*[J]. Student motivation: The culture and context of learning, 2001: 203–219.

［167］Griffith, D. A., and M. G. Harvey, "An Intercultural Communication Model for Use in Global Interorganizational Network," *Journal of International Marketing*, 2001(3), pp. 87–103.

［168］Gross J J. The emerging field of emotion regulation: An integrative review [J]. *Review of General Psychology*, 1998, 2(3): 271–299.

［169］Gudykunst W B, Matsumoto Y, Ting-Toomey S, et al. *Measuring self construals across cultures: A derived etic analysis*[C]//International Communication Association Convention in Sydney, Australia. 1994.

［170］Guerrero-Nieto C H. National standards for the teaching of English in Colombia: A critical discourse analysis[M]. The University of Arizona, 2009.

［171］Gundling E. *Working GlobeSmart: 12 people skills for doing business across borders*[M]. Nicholas Brealey, 2003.

［172］Hacker, D. J, Dunlosky, J, & Graesser, A. C. *Metacognition in educational theory and practice*[M]. London: Routledge, 1998.

［173］ Halliday M A K. *Cohesion in English*[M]. London: Routledge, 1976.

［174］ Halliday M A K. *Language as social semiotic: The social interpretation of language and meaning*[J]. London: Edward Arnold, 1978.

［175］ Halpern D F. Teaching critical thinking for transfer across domains: Disposition, skills, structure training, and metacognitive monitoring [J]. *American Psychologist*, 1998, 53(4): 449.

［176］ Halpern D F. Teaching critical thinking for transfer across domains: Disposition, skills, structure training, and metacognitive monitoring [J]. *American Psychologist*, 1998, 53(4): 449.

［177］ Hammer M R, Wiseman R L, Rasmussen J L, et al. A test of anxiety/uncertainty management theory: The intercultural adaptation context[J]. *Communication quarterly*, 1998, 46(3): 309–326.

［178］ Hardré P L, Huang S H, Chen C H, et al. High school teachers' motivational perceptions and strategies in an East Asian nation[J]. *Asia-Pacific Journal of Teacher Education*, 2006, 34(2): 199–221.

［179］ Howard-Hamilton M F, Richardson B J, Shuford B. Promoting multicultural education: A holistic approach[J]. *College Student Affairs Journal*, 1998, 18(1): 5.

［180］ Hunter, B., G. P. White and G. C. Godbey, "What Does It Mean to Be Globally Competent?," *Journal of Studies in International Education*, 2006(3), 267–285.

［181］ Hutchinson, T. and A. Waters. *English for Specific Purpose*：*A Learning-Centred Approach*, Cambridge：Cambridge University Press, 1987.

［182］ Hymes, D., "On Communicative Competence," In J.B. Pride and J. Holmes (Eds.) *Sociolinguistics. Selected Readings.* Harmondsworth：Penguin, 1972.

［183］ Imahori T T, Lanigan M L. Relational model of intercultural communication competence[J]. *International Journal of Intercultural Relations*, 1989, 13(3): 269–286.

［184］ Jay M. For theory[J]. *Theory and Society*, 1996: 167–183.

［185］ Jones E A, Ratcliff G. Critical Thinking Skills for College Students [J]. 1993.

［186］ Katzell R A, Thompson D E. Work motivation: Theory and practice[J]. *American Psychologist*, 1990, 45(2): 144.

［187］ Kim Y Y, Gudykunst W B. *Theories in Intercultural Communication* [M]. Newbury Park, CA : Sage Publications, Inc. , 1988.

［188］ Kim Y Y. Synchrony and intercultural communication[C]//*Global Interdependence: Simulation and Gaming Perspectives Proceedings of the 22nd International Conference of the International Simulation and Gaming Association* (ISAGA) Kyoto, Japan: 15–19 July 1991. Springer Japan, 1992: 99–105.

［189］ Kim, Y. Y., *Becoming Intercultural: An Integrative Theory of Communication and Cross-cultural Adaptation*. Thousand Oaks, CA: SAGE Publications, Inc, 2000.

［190］ King, P.M. and M. B. Baxter Magolda, "A Developmental Model of Intercultural Maturity," *Journal of College Student Development*, 2005(6), pp. 571–592.

［191］ Kitchener K S. 10 Wisdom and Reflective Judgment: knowing in the face of uncertainty[J]. *Wisdom: Its Nature, Origins, and Development*, 1990: 212.

［192］ Klaus J N. High School Career Education: Student's Perceptions of The Life Planning Course [J]. *Journal High School University*, 2010, 2(1).

［193］ Kuada J, Sorensen O J. *Internationalization of companies from developing countries*[M]. New York: Haworth Press Inc., 2004.

［194］ Kuada, J., *Intercultural Competence: Development of Danish Managers*, International Business Economics Working Paper Series, 2001.

［195］ Kupka B, Kennan W R. Toward a theory based approach for intercultural communication training[J]. *Intercultural Communication Studies*, 2003, 12(2): 93–110.

［196］ Kupka B. *Creation of an instrument to assess intercultural communication competence for strategic international human resource management*[D]. University of Otago, 2008.

［197］ Kurfiss J G. Critical Thinking: Theory, Research, Practice, and Possibilities. ASHE-ERIC Higher Education Report No. 2, 1988 [R]. ASHE-ERIC Higher Education Reports, The George Washington University, 1988.

［198］ Lambert R D. Problems and processes in US foreign language planning[J]. *The Annals of the American Academy of Political and Social Science*, 1994, 532(1): 47–58.

［199］ Levy, O., S. Beechler, S. Taylor and N.A. Boyacigiller, "What We Talk about When We Talk about 'global mindset': Managerial Cognition in Multinational Corporations," *Journal of International Business Studies*, 2007(2), pp. 231–258.

［200］ Lewln K. A dynamic theory of personality[J]. New York: McGraw-hill Book Company, 1935.

［201］ Litman J. Curiosity and the pleasures of learning: Wanting and liking new information[J]. *Cognition and Emotion*, 2005, 19(6): 793–814.

［202］ Little, D. Learner autonomy: A theoretical construct and its practical application [J]. *Die Neuere Sprache*, 1994, 93(5).430–442.

［203］ Loewenstein G. The psychology of curiosity: A review and reinterpretation[J]. *Psychological Bulletin*, 1994, 116(1): 75.

［204］ Long H B. *Self-Directed Learning: Emerging Theory & Practice* [M]. Oklahoma Research Center for Continuing Professional and Higher Education, 1989.

［205］ Louis, R.S., "Helping Students Become Autonomous Learners: Can Technology Help?," *Teaching English with Technology*, 2006(3), pp. 47–59.

［206］ Lund S K, Light J. *Long-term outcomes for individuals who use augmentative and alternative communication: Part III–contributing factors* [J]. *Augmentative and Alternative Communication*, 2007, 23(4): 323–335.

[207] Lustig M W, Koester J. Cultural identity, cultural biases, and intercultural contact[J]. *Chap*, 2003, 6: 136–171.

[208] Lustig M W, Koester J. Cultural identity, cultural biases, and intercultural contact[J]. *Chap*, 2003, 6: 136–171.

[209] Lustig M W, Koester J. *Intercultural Competence: Intercultural Communication across Cultures*[M]. New York: Pearson, 1996.

[210] Mitchell G W, Skinner L B, White B J. Essential soft skills for success in the twenty-first century workforce as perceived by business educators[J]. *Delta Pi Epsilon Journal*, 2010, 52(1).

[211] Morrow K, Johnson K. Meeting some social language needs of overseas students[J]. *Canadian Modern Language Review*, 1977, 33(5): 694–707.

[212] Munby J. *Communicative syllabus design: A sociolinguistic model for designing the content of purpose-specific language programmes*[M]. Cambridge: Cambridge University Press, 1981.

[213] Navas, M., M. C. García, J. Sánchez, A. J. Rojas, P. Pumares and J. S. Fernández, "Relative Acculturation Extended Model (RAEM): New Contributions with Regard to the Study of Acculturation," *International Journal of Intercultural Relations*, 2005(1), pp. 21–37.

[214] Norris C. Truth and the Ethics of Criticism[M]. Manchester University Press, 1994.

[215] Norris S P, Ennis R H. *Evaluating Critical Thinking. The Practitioners' Guide to Teaching Thinking Series*[M]. Pacific Grove, CA : Critical Thinking Press and Software, 1989.

[216] North, B., *The Development of a Common Framework Scale of Language Proficiency*. New York: Peter Lang Inc., 2000.

[217] Nunan D, Lai J, Keobke K. Towards autonomous language learning: Strategies, reflection and navigation[J]. *Learner autonomy in language learning: Defining the field and effecting change*, 1999, 8: 69–78.

[218] Nunan D. *Autonomy and Independence in Language Learning* [M]. London: Routledge , 1997.

[219] Olebe M, Koester J. Exploring the cross-cultural equivalence of the behavioral assessment scale for intercultural communication[J]. *International Journal of Intercultural Relations*, 1989, 13(3): 333–347.

[220] Oller J W. *Language tests at school: A pragmatic approach* [M]. London: Longman, 1979.

[221] Orr J B, Klein M F. Instruction in critical thinking as a form of character education[J]. *Journal of Curriculum & Supervision*, 1991, 6(2).

[222] Paige R M. On the nature of intercultural experiences and intercultural education[J]. *Education for the Intercultural Experience*, 1993, 2: 1–19.

[223] Palmer J, Carliner G, Romer T. Leniency, learning, and evaluations[J]. *Journal of Educational Psychology*, 1978, 70(5): 855.

[224] Parsons S, Bynner J. Insights into basic skills from a UK longitudinal study[A]//*Tracking adult literacy and numeracy skills*. London: Routledge, 2008: 47–78.

[225] Paul R, Elder L. Critical thinking: Thinking to some purpose [J]. *Journal of Developmental Education*, 2001, 25(1).

[226] Paul R. The state of critical thinking today [J]. *New directions for community colleges*, 2005, (130): 27–38.

[227] Paul, R. W., "Critical Thinking：How to Prepare Students for a Rapidly Changing World," Santa Rosa，CA：Foundation for Critical Thinking, 1995.

[228] Rathje, S., "Intercultural Competence: The Status and Future of a Controversial Concept," *Language and Intercultural Communication*, 2007(4), pp. 254–266.

[229] Reinders, H., "Towards a Classroom Pedagogy for Learner Autonomy：A Framework of Independent Language Learning Skills," *Australian Journal of Teacher Education*, 2010(5), pp. 40–55.

〔230〕 Rivers W M. *Speaking in many tongues: Essays in foreign-language teaching*[J]. Rowley, Mass.: Newbury House, 1972.

〔231〕 Robles, M. M., "Executive Perceptions of the Top 10 Soft Skills Needed in Today's Workplace," *Business Communication Quarterly*, 2012(4), pp. 453–465.

〔232〕 Salomon W. The Critical I[J]. *Philosophy and Literature*, 1994, 18(1): 138–139.

〔233〕 Schulz R A. Discrete-point versus simulated communication testing in foreign languages[J]. *The Modern Language Journal*, 1977, 61(3): 94–101.

〔234〕 Sears A, Parsons J. Towards critical thinking as an ethic [J]. *Theory & Research in Social Education*, 1991, 19(1): 45–68.

〔235〕 Smith P H. The Hard Road Back to Soft Power [J]. *Georgetown Journal of International Affairs*, 2007: 115–123.

〔236〕 Spitzberg B H. Issues in the development of a theory of interpersonal competence in the intercultural context[J]. *International Journal of Intercultural Relations*, 1989, 13(3): 241–268.

〔237〕 Spitzberg Jr I J. *Movers and Doers: International Exchange, the International Knowledge System, and Public Policy*[M]. Washington, DC: Education Resources Information Center, 1984.

〔238〕 Stern H H. *Fundamental concepts of language teaching: Historical and interdisciplinary perspectives on applied linguistic research* [M]. Oxford: Oxford university press, 1983.

〔239〕 Sternberg R J. Teaching critical thinking, Part 1: Are we making critical mistakes?[J]. *The Phi Delta Kappan*, 1985, 67(3): 194–198.

〔240〕 Tassinari, M. G., "Evaluating Learner Autonomy: A Dynamic Model with Descriptors," *Studies in Self-Access Learning Journalism*, 2012(1), pp. 24–40.

〔241〕 Terrell, S. R. and Rosenbusch, K., "How Global Leaders Develop", *Journal of Management Development*, 2013(10), 1056–1079.

［242］Ting-Toomey S, Kurogi A. Facework competence in intercultural conflict: An updated face-negotiation theory[J]. *International journal of intercultural relations*, 1998, 22(2): 187–225.

［243］Ting-Toomey S. *Communicating across Cultures*[J]. New York: The Guilford Press , 1999.

［244］Tishman S. Thinking dispositions and intellectual character[C]// American Educational Research Association Meetings, New Orleans, LA. 1994.

［245］Tratnik, A, "Key Issues in Testing English for Specific Purposes," *Scripta Manent*, 2008(1), 3–13.

［246］Trim J L M. *Some Possible Lines of Development of an Overall Structure for a European Unit/Credit Scheme for Foreign Language Learning by Adults*[J]. 1978.

［247］Tucker G R, Scott M S. Error analysis and English—language strategies of Arab students 1[J]. *Language Learning*, 1974, 24(1): 69–97.

［248］Valenzuela, J., A. M. Nieto and C. Saiz, "Critical Thinking Motivational Scale: A Contribution to the Study of Relationship Between Critical Thinking and Motivation," *Electronic Journal of Research in Education Psychology*, 2011(2), pp. 823–848.

［249］Walberg S M. Motivational Effects on Test Scores of Elementary Students[J]. *The Journal of Educational Research*, 2011: 133–136.

［250］Widdowson H G. *Stylistics and the Teaching of Literature* [M]. London: Routledge, 1975.

［251］Widdowson H G. *Teaching language as communication* [M]. Oxford: Oxford University Press, 1978.

［252］Widdowson, H. G, "Knowledge of Language and Ability for Use," *Applied Linguistics*, 1989(2), 128–137.

［253］Wigfield A, Eccles J S. Children's competence beliefs, achievement values, and general self-esteem: Change across elementary and middle school[J]. *The Journal of Early Adolescence*, 1994, 14(2): 107–138.

［254］Wigfield A, Eccles J S. Expectancy–value theory of achievement motivation [J]. *Contemporary Educational Psychology*, 2000, 25(1): 68–81.

［255］Wigfield A. Expectancy-value theory of achievement motivation: A developmental perspective[J]. *Educational Psychology Review*, 1994, 6: 49–78.

［256］Wigfield, A. and J. S. Eccles, "The Development of Achievement Task Value：A Theoretical Analysis," *Developmental Review*, 1992(3), pp. 265–310.

［257］Wiley K. Effects of a self-directed learning project and preference for structure on self-directed learning readiness[J]. *Nursing Research*, 1983, 32(3): 181–185.

［258］Wilkins, D. A., *Teaching Language as Communication*. London: Oxford University Press, 1978.

［259］Zins, J. E. *Building academic success on social and emotional learning: What does the research say?*[M]. New York: Teachers College Press, 2004.

附 录

附录1:《商务外语语言应用能力量表》
(Business Foreign Language Application Competence Scale)〔250 条描述语〕

Levels	Items	Descriptors
A1	1	CAN understand short reports or product descriptions on familiar matters, if these are expressed in simple language and the contents are predictable.
A1	2	CAN write a simple routine request to a colleague.
A1	3	CAN understand a simple travel itinerary, including places, dates, and times.
A1	4	CAN understand a simple time-sheet.
A1	5	CAN understand a colleague's introduction when repeated.
A1	6	CAN follow a simple imperative instruction.
A1	7	CAN recognise a request for the time.
A1	8	CAN recognise a very simple question that has been learned as a fixed expression, such as, "What is your name?"
A1	9	CAN use appropriate leave-taking expressions.
A1	10	CAN provide personal information, such as name and address, and spell some of the words orally.
A1	11	CAN follow a short simple instruction.
A1	12	CAN identify price, tax and total on a receipt for supplies.
A1	13	CAN choose words from a list to match illustrations of common familiar objects.
A1	14	CAN copy information from an invoice to complete a cheque.
A1	15	CAN address an envelope for mailing by following a model.
A1	16	CAN understand a short goodwill expression from a co-worker.
A1	17	CAN read a simple two-step instruction for a work task.
A1	18	CAN locate a specific short piece of information on a simple invoice.
A1	19	CAN read a simple customer comment and identify whether it is positive or negative.

（续表）

Levels	Items	Descriptors
A1	20	CAN fill out a simple form with date, first and last name, address, postal code, phone number, date of birth, age.
A2	21	CAN state simple requirements within own job area.
A2	22	CAN understand most short reports or manuals of a predictable nature within his/her own area of expertise, provided that enough time is given.
A2	23	CAN write a short, comprehensible note of request to a colleague or a known contact in another company.
A2	24	CAN understand a simple work schedule.
A2	25	CAN understand short, simple emails on work-related topics.
A2	26	CAN understand simple meeting titles in a work-related calendar.
A2	27	CAN understand short, simple user tips in a software interface.
A2	28	CAN understand simple requests or instructions to carry out concrete work-related tasks.
A2	29	CAN understand the main information in a simple work-related phone message.
A2	30	CAN conduct very simple business transactions using basic language.
A2	31	CAN ask what an employee likes or dislikes about their job.
A2	32	CAN answer simple work-related questions on the phone using fixed expressions.
A2	33	CAN leave simple, clear and appropriately expressed work-related phone messages.
A2	34	CAN place a simple written order for goods or services.
A2	35	CAN post short, simple work-related messages on professional social networks.
A2	36	CAN write simple lists as part of a work-related task.
A2	37	CAN write a simple email accepting a work-related invitation.
A2	38	CAN write a simple email issuing a work-related invitation.
A2	39	CAN complete a simple job application form requiring basic professional information.
A2	40	CAN write a short, clear subject line for a business email/letter.
A2	41	CAN get the gist of a new supervisor's formal introduction.
A2	42	CAN understand a manager giving permission to leave work early.
A2	43	CAN identify basic courtesy formulas, communication problems in a short exchange between two speakers
A2	44	CAN understand a short description of work tasks when accompanied by a simple list of the same tasks.

（续表）

Levels	Items	Descriptors
A2	45	CAN get the gist of a short, simple announcement about a company event.
A2	46	CAN participate in a very short informal conversation with a supportive colleague.
A2	47	CAN ask a colleague for help performing a basic task.
A2	48	CAN write a few sentences about the daily work routine.
A2	49	CAN complete a checklist to indicate that a routine cleaning inspection has been conducted.
A2	50	CAN read a brief email from a co-worker to identify the location of a meeting.
A2	51	CAN understand a co-worker's account of plans for the weekend.
A2	52	CAN give a brief description of the daily workplace routine.
B1	53	CAN offer advice to clients within own job area on simple matters.
B1	54	CAN understand the general meaning of non-routine letters and theoretical articles within own work area.
B1	55	CAN make reasonably accurate notes at a meeting or seminar where the subject matter is familiar and predictable.
B1	56	CAN extract key details from conversations between colleagues about familiar topics.
B1	57	CAN understand what people like or dislike about their workplace in some detail.
B1	58	CAN understand the main points of feedback about what he/she is doing well and what he/she needs to improve on.
B1	59	CAN identify the main action points in a work-related meeting conducted in clear, standard speech.
B1	60	CAN understand conversations about rules or regulations related to the workplace.
B1	61	CAN understand the main points of a work-related recorded presentation.
B1	62	CAN recognise appropriate pauses during discussions in meetings in order to politely take his/her turn.
B1	63	CAN extract the key details from discussions in meetings conducted in clear, standard speech.
B1	64	CAN respond to simple work-related messages from colleagues on professional social networks.
B1	65	CAN write a short online profile.
B1	66	CAN write work-related correspondence on familiar topics using a limited range of grammar and expressions.
B1	67	CAN reply to a work-related email confirming arrangements.
B1	68	CAN write the agenda for a meeting on a work-related topic in a simple way.

（续表）

Levels	Items	Descriptors
B1	69	CAN write a simple email, giving details of work-related events or plans.
B1	70	CAN write a simple email of introduction in a professional context.
B1	71	CAN write descriptions of familiar job roles and responsibilities.
B1	72	CAN prepare a simple questionnaire in order to gather data.
B1	73	CAN write simple questions to get written feedback from employees or customers.
B1	74	CAN write a simple email requesting work-related information, emphasizing the most important points.
B1	75	CAN write a short, simple comparison of products and services from different companies.
B1	76	CAN write answers to open-ended questions in a survey about familiar products or services.
B1	77	CAN write a short, simple marketing document, describing products or services.
B1	78	CAN listen to questions from a customer about a product in order to provide information.
B1	79	CAN listen to an announcement with instructions for evacuating a building.
B1	80	CAN respond to a routine request from a customer on the phone.
B1	81	CAN ask a supplier for the cost of a product.
B1	82	CAN greet a customer and ask whether assistance is required.
B1	83	CAN lead a completed form to locate client contact details and preferences.
B1	84	CAN read a brief description of an item in an online catalogue.
B1	85	CAN write a list of tasks for a co-worker to carry out on the next shift.
B1	86	CAN write a brief email to request supplies.
B1	87	CAN enter amount of purchase into a payment terminal.
B1	88	CAN fill out a requisition form to identify items required and reasons for a purchase.
B1	89	CAN complete an inventory form by recording quantities of goods in stock.
B1	90	CAN listen to questions from a customer about a product in order to provide information.
B1	91	CAN inform the manager of a problem and suggest how it CAN be resolved.
B1	92	CAN exchange information with a supervisor to clarify information and coordinate work.
B1	93	CAN lead a brief weekly staff meeting to provide information about goals and priorities.

（续表）

Levels	Items	Descriptors
B1	94	CAN write a project quote describing work to be carried out over several stages, along with materials and labor requirements.
B1	95	CAN write an email to customers to inform them of an upcoming promotion.
B2	96	CAN put his/her point across persuasively when talking about a familiar product.
B2	97	CAN take dictation provided that is delivered clearly, at a reasonable pace and one is given the opportunity to check the vocabulary.
B2	98	CAN express his/her own opinion, and present arguments to a limited extent.
B2	99	CAN follow a presentation/demonstration concerning a physical object, e.g. a product.
B2	100	CAN understand most of what takes place.
B2	101	CAN ask for factual information and understand the answer.
B2	102	CAN write a summary to describe a product and its intended uses for a retailer website.
B2	103	CAN write a report to propose changes to operating procedures.
B2	104	CAN take or leave routine messages, ask for clarification or elaboration where these are not expressed clearly, with only occasional misunderstanding of facts.
B2	105	Can record relatively precise summaries in a symposium or conference when the content is common and foreseeable.
B2	106	CAN write a simple report of a factual nature and begin to evaluate, advise the report.
B2	107	CAN write and check a continuous set of instructions, for example, a section of an operating manual with limited length.
B2	108	CAN understand the general meaning of a report even if the topic is not entirely predictable.
B2	109	CAN understand most factual product literature within own work area.
B2	110	CAN understand in detail the agenda for a work-related meeting.
B2	111	CAN infer the meaning of words from context in work-related documents or publications on unfamiliar topics.
B2	112	CAN distinguish between facts and opinions in extended, unstructured meeting notes.
B2	113	CAN understand a complex form for company-offered services
B2	114	CAN identify relevant articles and reports on a range of professional topics.

Levels	Items	Descriptors
B2	115	CAN understand a list of linguistically complex written questions to ask during a job interview.
B2	116	CAN understand specialized vocabulary used in presentations or discussions within his/her field.
B2	117	CAN distinguish between ambiguity and certainty in speech.
B2	118	CAN recognise indirect disagreement expressed through modifiers used during a negotiation.
B2	119	CAN understand a course of action suggested during a negotiation.
B2	120	CAN understand the details of a complex telephone order for goods or services.
B2	121	CAN politely express dissatisfaction for products and services offered by a company or institution.
B2	122	CAN express specific concerns about a work-related issue.
B2	123	CAN discuss a plan of action for dealing with a work-related task.
B2	124	CAN express understanding about someone's reaction to change.
B2	125	CAN clearly describe his/her professional background.
B2	126	CAN express general concern about a work-related issue (e.g. project completion, deadlines).
B2	127	CAN make a factual comparison of products and services from different companies.
B2	128	CAN answer complaints from dissatisfied employees and customers politely.
B2	129	CAN clearly and concisely describe a product or a service within his/her field.
B2	130	CAN confirm decisions at the end of a meeting or teleconference.
B2	131	CAN deal with dissatisfied clients or customers politely.
B2	132	CAN describe in detail why he/she agrees or disagrees with a suggested work-related change.
B2	133	CAN summarize the action items at the end of a meeting.
B2	134	CAN give feedback to an employee about what he/she is doing well and what he/she needs to improve on.
B2	135	CAN discuss specific comments made on a performance evaluation form.
B2	136	CAN describe changes in a company or department that will affect an employee's job or responsibilities.
B2	137	CAN ask for detailed feedback about specific points of a business idea or proposal.
B2	138	CAN explain the main points of a negotiating position with some precision.
B2	139	CAN express concern about a business situation, giving specific reasons and details (e.g. project completion, deadlines).

Levels	Items	Descriptors
B2	140	CAN emphasise key information in a negotiation.
B2	141	CAN give a detailed update on a work-related project.
B2	142	CAN describe the results and consequences of a specific action taken by an employee.
B2	143	CAN justify points made during a presentation by referring to information in graphs and charts.
B2	144	CAN lead a discussion so that the group is able to make a decision.
B2	145	CAN redirect a discussion that has become wordy or off-topic.
B2	146	CAN politely respond to interruptions during a discussion and return to the main topic.
B2	147	CAN adjust the precision of questions in order to obtain more detailed information.
B2	148	CAN participate in on-going dialogue during a negotiation.
B2	149	CAN encourage employees using motivational language.
B2	150	CAN describe a business proposal in detail.
B2	151	CAN summarize relevant data or research in support of an argument in a debate or discussion.
B2	152	CAN bring a work-related discussion back to the main points when the participants have gone off topic.
B2	153	CAN give a presentation or lecture in his/her field of specialisation.
B2	154	CAN use persuasive language to convince others to agree with his/her recommended course of action during a discussion.
B2	155	CAN repair communication breakdowns caused by cultural misunderstandings during phone calls.
B2	156	CAN listen to a brief presentation about new equipment during a staff meeting.
B2	157	CAN listen to a customer describe his/her needs in order to make suggestions about services that CAN be offered.
B2	158	CAN listen to a customer's opinions and suggestions about a new menu item.
B2	159	CAN listen to a voicemail message from a dissatisfied client to understand concerns and identify a way to address him/her.
B2	160	CAN coordinate tasks and discuss delays with a co-worker.
B2	161	CAN interpret a line graph to learn about sales trends.
B2	162	CAN read a detailed incident report to infer probable causes.
B2	163	CAN read a procedure to learn how to handle a customer request.

Levels	Items	Descriptors
B2	164	CAN exchange information with a supervisor to clarify information and coordinate work.
B2	165	CAN write a letter of apology to a customer to explain how a problem occurred and relate actions taken to avoid a recurrence.
B2	166	CAN prepare minutes of a meeting.
C1	167	CAN give detailed information and state detailed requirements within familiar area of work.
C1	168	CAN argue his/her case effectively, justifying, if necessary, a need for service and specifying needs precisely.
C1	169	CAN engage in an extended conversation with a visitor on matters within his/her authority/competence.
C1	170	CAN give detailed information and deal with most routine problems that are likely to arise.
C1	171	CAN make notes on unfamiliar matters.
C1	172	CAN understand correspondence expressed in non-standard language.
C1	173	CAN understand at least the general meaning of more complex articles without serious misunderstanding.
C1	174	CAN understand instructions giving detailed warnings, advice, conditions etc.
C1	175	CAN distinguish between facts and opinions in linguistically complex written proposals.
C1	176	CAN understand complex technical work-related documents in detail.
C1	177	CAN understand complex arguments in technical journals.
C1	178	CAN present detailed, evidence-based arguments during work-related meetings.
C1	179	CAN summarize complex diagrams and visual information during a formal presentation when requested by a member of the audience.
C1	180	CAN make a linguistically complex business presentation with the help of notes.
C1	181	CAN give a progress report including key milestones and highlighting risks.
C1	182	CAN answer questions in a job interview in detail, interacting authoritatively, developing points fluently, and managing interjections.
C1	183	CAN adjust tone or language to build rapport in situations where there may be an unequal power dynamic.
C1	184	CAN carry out complex business transactions with vendors and suppliers.

Levels	Items	Descriptors
C1	185	CAN summarize the position at the end of a negotiation in detail, outlining his/her own and other people's positions.
C1	186	CAN explain the main points of a negotiating position with precision.
C1	187	CAN effectively discuss the meaning and implications of research data.
C1	188	CAN conduct a job interview, interacting authoritatively, developing points fluently, and managing interjections.
C1	189	CAN participate in extended, detailed professional discussions and meetings with confidence.
C1	190	CAN make proposals to resolve conflicts in complex negotiations.
C1	191	CAN propose a range of different options in a complex negotiation.
C1	192	CAN adapt the language and organisation of a project communication to the needs of different audiences.
C1	193	CAN write a report describing business plans and strategies in detail.
C1	194	CAN correct structural errors in someone else's written report.
C1	195	CAN write an executive summary of plans or strategies for a business presentation.
C1	196	CAN take full notes on points made during meetings on a wide range of work-related topics.
C1	197	CAN write a review of a product or service using complex language.
C1	198	CAN recommend changes to the style or structure in a collaboratively written report.
C1	199	CAN employ high-level vocabulary and structures to enhance impact in written correspondence.
C1	200	CAN listen to a panel discussion to gain insight into ways of modifying the work environment to meet the needs of individuals with disabilities.
C1	201	CAN listen to an audio recording from a web-based meeting to prepare meeting minutes.
C1	202	CAN listen to detailed descriptions of equipment failures extending over a period of time, as part of a problem-solving process with supervisory staff and equipment manufacturers.
C1	203	CAN listen to instructions and requests for information from police, fire department and medical staff during a workplace incident.
C1	204	CAN listen to extended discussions between co-workers and business partners during a strategic planning session.
C1	205	CAN give detailed feedback to an employee during a performance review.

（续表）

Levels	Items	Descriptors
C1	206	CAN discuss a patient's treatment options with colleagues during a weekly team meeting.
C1	207	CAN negotiate a contract with a supplier in order to receive favorable terms and conditions.
C1	208	CAN propose a solution to a client who is upset about an error made to an account.
C1	209	CAN make a presentation to managers and co-workers to share the results of a survey and provide evidence to support a set of recommendations.
C1	210	CAN advise clients on collective bargaining matters in order to influence decisions.
C1	211	CAN read a magazine or newsletter article to stay current on industry trends.
C1	212	CAN prepare an annual report to summarize a company's activities throughout the preceding year.
C1	213	CAN write an article for a company newsletter to present an analysis of industry trends.
C1	214	CAN write a detailed report that describes test objectives and procedures, discusses results, and offers conclusions and recommendations for technical experts.
C1	215	CAN write a marketing plan detailing strategies and opportunities.
C1	216	CAN complete an extensive development and build permit application form by combining information from several sources.
C1	217	CAN complete a detailed planning document about a student to indicate learning objectives, strengths, needs, accommodations and recommendations.
C1	218	CAN interpret information contained in complex tables and graphs to make predictions.
C1	219	CAN read a legal contract to understand the terms and conditions and to identify any risks.
C1	220	CAN read a project proposal to understand scope, timelines, finances, objectives and anticipated challenges, and to evaluate suitability.
C1	221	CAN write a business plan to detail strategic direction and steps to implementation.
C1	222	CAN write an evaluation report to present an analysis of a program's strengths and challenges, and to offer recommendations.

（续表）

Levels	Items	Descriptors
C1	223	CAN ask questions outside own immediate area of work (e.g. asking for external legal or financial advice).
C1	224	CAN advise on/handle complex, delicate or contentious issues (e.g. legal or financial situations).
C2	225	CAN argue effectively for or against a case, and has sufficient language to be able to talk about/discuss most aspects of his/her work.
C2	226	CAN both follow and give a presentation, demonstration or explanation of, for example, a product or system, dealing with information of a complex nature.
C2	227	CAN use the telephone confidently, even if the line is bad or the caller has a non-standard accent.
C2	228	CAN handle a wide range of routine and non-routine situations in which professional services are requested from colleagues or external contacts.
C2	229	CAN make full and accurate notes on all routine meetings.
C2	230	CAN participate a meeting or seminar and make full and accurate notes.
C2	231	CAN make notes that are useful to both himself/herself and to colleagues, even where the subject matter is complex and/or unfamiliar.
C2	232	CAN write any type of letter necessary in the course of his/her work.
C2	233	CAN write quite lengthy reports with only the occasional, minor error, and without taking much longer than a native speaker.
C2	234	CAN write a set of instructions with clarity and precision, addressing the reader effectively.
C2	235	CAN understand correspondence, including letters etc. of a specialist for example those dealing with legal points, contracts and similar specialist letters.
C2	236	CAN understand the reports that he/she is likely to come across, including the finer points, implications, etc. of a complex report.
C2	237	CAN understand most articles likely to be encountered during the course of his/her work, including complex ideas expressed in complex language.
C2	238	CAN understand complex arguments in technical or academic journals.
C2	239	CAN answer questions from a panel of interviewers, matching the linguistic complexity style of responses to those of each interviewer.
C2	240	CAN listen to project results and recommendations regarding proposed market positioning, growth, promotional and operational strategies in order to decide on future direction of a company.

（续表）

Levels	Items	Descriptors
C2	241	CAN listen to focus group participants' responses to understand and analyse views on a complex social issue and identify ways to probe for additional insights.
C2	242	CAN listen to a variety of professionals giving assessments of a proposed large-scale equipment purchase, including a cost-benefit analysis and projected impacts on the workforce in order to decide whether to proceed.
C2	243	CAN make an extended, formal presentation to a board of directors to propose a major change in an organisation's direction.
C2	244	CAN build a case using evidence from financial and human resources, specifying the advantages of the proposed change and the risks associated with the status quo.
C2	245	CAN mediate a dispute between management and a bargaining unit.
C2	246	CAN facilitate discussions between land developers, funding partners and government representatives for jointly-funded projects.
C2	247	CAN use complex tables, schedules, graphs, scale drawings, assembly drawings and schematics to evaluate and improve an electrical system.
C2	248	CAN examine survey plans and existing surveys, drawings, aerial photographs, topographical maps, land titles and other historical information to establish boundaries.
C2	249	CAN assess the quality and accuracy of scientific articles to determine if they should be published in an academic journal.
C2	250	CAN write a business plan to detail strategic direction and steps to implementation.

附录2:《商务外语跨文化交际能力量表》
(Business Foreign Language Intercultural Communication Competence Scale) （235 条描述语）

Level	Items	Descriptors
Benchmark 1	1	shows minimal awareness of own cultural rules and biases.
Benchmark 1	2	demonstrates partial understanding of the complexity of elements important to members of another culture in relation to its history, values, politics, communication styles, economy, or beliefs and practices.

（续表）

Level	Items	Descriptors
Benchmark 1	3	views the experience of others but does so through own cultural worldview.
Benchmark 1	4	has a minimal level of understanding of cultural differences in verbal and nonverbal communication.
Benchmark 1	5	is unable to negotiate a shared understanding.
Benchmark 1	6	has difficulty suspending any judgment in his/her interactions with culturally different others, but is unaware of own judgment.
Benchmark 1	7	uncomfortable with identifying possible cultural differences with others.
Benchmark 1	8	states minimal interest in learning more about other cultures.
Benchmark 1	9	identifies some connections between an individual's decision-making and certain local and global issues.
Benchmark 1	10	identifies multiple perspectives while maintaining a value preference for own positioning (such as cultural, disciplinary, and ethical).
Benchmark 1	11	describes the experiences of others historically or in contemporary contexts primarily through one cultural perspective, demonstrating some openness to varied cultures and worldviews.
Benchmark 1	12	identifies basic ethical dimensions of some local or national decisions that have global impact.
Benchmark 1	13	identifies global challenges in basic ways, including a limited number of perspectives and solutions.
Benchmark 1	14	identifies the basic role of some global and local institutions, ideas, and processes in the human and the natural worlds.
Benchmark 1	15	is receptive to interacting with culturally different others.
Benchmark 1	16	has limited global experience: to some degree considers problems and opportunities from a global perspective.
Benchmark 1	17	understands global issues; lacks international experience.
Benchmark 1	18	tends to be more pessimistic toward others and their motivation or intent about situation or people.
Benchmark 1	19	prefers to maintain current habit, traditions and way of thinking.
Benchmark 1	20	dislikes or avoids ambiguity and uncertainty.

Level	Items	Descriptors
Benchmark 1	21	reacts negatively when it's unclear what is happening.
Benchmark 1	22	avoids foreign things, will be very insular when it comes to international event.
Benchmark 1	23	feels uncomfortable replacing old and familiar activities with new ones.
Benchmark 1	24	acts with annoyance when daily routines are disturbed or removed.
Benchmark 1	25	is not really proactive in interacting and developing friendship with people who are different from oneself.
Benchmark 1	26	is little awareness of how people are feeling or what they are thinking.
Benchmark 1	27	rarely attempts to consider the situations or challenges that others may face.
Benchmark 1	28	is unconcerned about knowing oneself or how one behavior affects others.
Benchmark 1	29	dislikes adjusting one's own social behavior even though situation may require such adjustment.
Benchmark 1	30	is unaware of the role that technology plays in enabling a global economy.
Benchmark 1	31	is quick to compromise own value in order to fit in or avoid a conflict.
Benchmark 1	32	knows at a very superficial level that technology links individuals from different nations.
Benchmark 1	33	does not understand that economies of nations impact one another.
Benchmark 1	34	is unaware of the impact of economic considerations on political decision-making.
Benchmark 1	35	is largely unaware of political events and international economic conditions.
Benchmark 1	36	has no knowledge of the impacts of decisions made by national/international organisations.
Benchmark 1	37	has little knowledge of national/international organisations or their functions.
Benchmark 1	38	is unaware of the ways in which culture impacts national/personal political decision-making.
Benchmark 1	39	is unaware that political ideologies and culture impact individuals' access to these resources.
Benchmark 1	40	is not aware that people in other nations directly influence his/her life socially, politically, and economically.

（续表）

Level	Items	Descriptors
Benchmark 1	41	asks simple or surface questions about other cultures.
Benchmark 1	42	finds it difficult to handle psychologically and emotionally challenging experiences; takes a long time to recover from such experiences.
Benchmark 1	43	reacts with stress or highlights anxiety and tension.
Benchmark 1	44	rarely uses stress reduction strategies or inadequately employs a narrow range of such techniques.
Benchmark 1	45	has difficulty suspending any judgment in his/her interactions with culturally different others.
Benchmark 1	46	has some understanding of the ways in which technology has been an essential part of the global economy.
Benchmark 1	47	has little knowledge of specific considerations and national/international policies.
Benchmark 2	48	is aware that national economies impact one another, but this knowledge is general and sparse.
Benchmark 2	49	seeks information from others who have different personalities, backgrounds and styles.
Benchmark 2	50	interacts with others who have a diversity of cultural and demographic backgrounds.
Benchmark 2	51	tries to make it easy for others to feel valuable regardless of diversity in personality, culture, or background.
Benchmark 2	52	attempts to include in conversations people with diverse cultural backgrounds.
Benchmark 2	53	listens actively, considers people's concerns and adjusts own behaviour in a helpful manner.
Benchmark 2	54	is culturally aware of business in local terms.
Benchmark 2	55	understands global and local impacts on day-to-day activities.
Benchmark 2	56	aligns global strategy with local considerations.
Benchmark 2	57	keep track of worldwide innovations.
Benchmark 2	58	can give example of cultural differences from personal experiences.
Benchmark 2	59	enjoys talking with people from different cultures.
Benchmark 2	60	has the ability to accurately understand the feeling of people from other cultures.
Benchmark 2	61	tries to understand people from another culture by imagining how something looks from their perspectives.
Benchmark 2	62	can change his/her behavior to suit different cultural situation and with culturally different people.

Level	Items	Descriptors
Benchmark 2	63	is aware of the culture knowledge he/she uses when interacting with someone from another culture.
Benchmark 2	64	thinks a lot about the influence that culture has on his/her behavior and that of others who are culturally different.
Benchmark 2	65	plans action when in different cultural situations and with culturally different people.
Benchmark 2	66	enjoys interacting with people from different cultures.
Benchmark 2	67	often gives positive responses to his/her culturally different counterpart during interacting.
Benchmark 2	68	likes to be with people from different cultures.
Benchmark 2	69	accepts the opinions of people from different cultures.
Benchmark 2	70	is pretty sure of himself/herself in interacting with people from different cultures.
Benchmark 2	71	is confident when interacting with people from different cultures.
Benchmark 2	72	is as sociable as he/she wants to be when interacting with people from different cultures.
Benchmark 2	73	feel useful when interacting with people from different cultures.
Benchmark 2	74	is sensitive to his/her culturally-distinct counterpart's subtle meanings during their interaction.
Benchmark 2	75	is very observant when interacting with people from different cultures.
Benchmark 2	76	tries to obtain as much information as he/she can when interacting with people from different cultures.
Benchmark 2	77	is aware how a specific context affects/alters his/her interaction with others.
Benchmark 2	78	expresses negative feelings constructively.
Benchmark 2	79	is attentive when doing projects, assignments or interacting with people from different countries and backgrounds.
Benchmark 2	80	tries to deal with the emotions and frustrations caused by his/her participation in the other culture.
Benchmark 2	81	tries to communicate and to behave in ways judged "appropriate."
Benchmark 2	82	is aware how he/she is viewed by members of the foreign cultures.
Benchmark 2	83	demonstrates flexibility when interacting with persons from the foreign cultures.
Benchmark 2	84	uses models appropriate to the culture and avoids offending his/her hosts with his/her behavior, dress, etc.

（续表）

Level	Items	Descriptors
Benchmark 2	85	can cite a basic definition of culture and identify its components.
Benchmark 2	86	knows the essential norms and taboos.
Benchmark 2	87	recognises signs of cultural stress and knows strategies for overcoming them.
Benchmark 2	88	identifies own cultural rules and biases (e.g. with a strong preference for those rules shares with own cultural group and seeks the same in others.)
Benchmark 2	89	identifies components of other cultural perspectives but responds in all situations with own worldview.
Benchmark 2	90	identifies some cultural differences in verbal and nonverbal communication.
Benchmark 2	91	is aware when misunderstandings occur.
Benchmark 2	92	expresses openness to most of people, and interacts with culturally different others.
Benchmark 2	93	explains and connects two or more cultures historically or in contemporary contexts with some acknowledgement of power structures, demonstrating respectful interaction with varied cultures and worldviews.
Benchmark 2	94	examines the historical and contemporary roles, interconnections, and differential effects of human organisations and actions on global systems within the human and the natural worlds.
Benchmark 2	95	maintains objectivity when one's own positions or opinions are challenged by peers or stakeholders.
Benchmark 2	96	remains objective when facing criticism.
Benchmark 2	97	communicates and cooperates with others who have a diversity of cultural and demographic backgrounds.
Benchmark 2	98	makes it easy for others to feel valuable regardless of diversity in personality, culture, or background.
Benchmark 2	99	makes conversations with people who come from diverse cultural backgrounds, and invites them to be part of informal work-related activities, such as attending company social events.
Benchmark 2	100	has global experience：considers problems and opportunities from a global perspective.
Benchmark 2	101	is culturally aware and demonstrates ability to conduct business in local terms.

Level	Items	Descriptors
Benchmark 2	102	understands and takes into account global and local impacts on day-to-day activities.
Benchmark 2	103	keeps abreast of global influences on the local business.
Benchmark 2	104	understands the reason behind, or motivation for someone's actions.
Benchmark 2	105	is proactive in preparing locally to support global activities.
Benchmark 2	106	is empathetic and sensitive to global issues, but may lack international experience.
Benchmark 2	107	is willing to withhold or suspend negative judgement about situation or people.
Benchmark 2	108	looks at a new and different situation as an opportunity for variety change and learning.
Benchmark 2	109	exhibits the capacity to be comfortable with ambiguity and uncertainty.
Benchmark 2	110	is willing to explore interests or hobbies and tries things that differ from one's norm routine.
Benchmark 2	111	is willing to take the initiative to meet and engage others in interaction, including strangers from other cultures.
Benchmark 2	112	is aware of one's own value, belief, capacities and limitations.
Benchmark 2	113	understands how one's value, belief, capacities and limitations affect others.
Benchmark 2	114	is able to read motions and understand the feelings and concerns of others.
Benchmark 2	115	is able to regulate and adopt one's behavior to fit in and builds positive relationship with others.
Benchmark 2	116	holds positive mental outlook toward people and situations generally when living or working in a foreign culture.
Benchmark 2	117	is able to maintain own values and beliefs while being able to accept those who are different.
Benchmark 2	118	has emotional strength and ability to cope well with setbacks, mistakes and frustration.
Benchmark 2	119	responds with calmness and serenity to the stress he/she faces.
Benchmark 2	120	believes in his/her own ability to succeed by hard work and effort.
Benchmark 2	121	uses a variety of effective strategies when interacting with culturally different people.
Benchmark 2	122	demonstrates the capacity to interact appropriately in a variety of situations within the foreign culture.

Level	Items	Descriptors
Benchmark 2	123	can explain at least one model for understanding learning processes, strategies and implications for learning about and adjusting to another culture.
Milestone 3	124	recognizes new perspectives about own cultural rules and biases.
Milestone 3	125	demonstrates adequate understanding of the complexity of elements important to members of another culture in relation to its history, values, politics, communication styles, economy, or beliefs and practices.
Milestone 3	126	recognises intellectual and emotional dimensions of more than one worldview and sometimes uses more than one worldview in interactions.
Milestone 3	127	recognizes and participates in cultural differences in verbal and nonverbal communication and begins to negotiate a shared understanding based on those differences.
Milestone 3	128	asks deeper questions about other cultures and seeks out answers to these questions.
Milestone 3	129	begins to initiate and develop interactions with culturally different others.
Milestone 3	130	can suspend judgment in valuing his/her interactions with culturally different others.
Milestone 3	131	can evaluate the global impact of one's own and others' specific local actions on the natural and human world.
Milestone 3	132	synthesises other perspectives (such as cultural, disciplinary, and ethical) when investigating subjects within natural and human systems.
Milestone 3	133	analyses substantial connections between the worldviews, power structures, and experiences of multiple cultures historically or in contemporary contexts, incorporating respectful interactions with other cultures.
Milestone 3	134	reacts purposefully to frustrations.
Milestone 3	135	proactively obtains and uses information from others who have different personalities, backgrounds, and styles; effectively includes them in decision-making and problem solving.
Milestone 3	136	communicates, cooperates, and works extremely well with others who have a diversity of cultural and demographic backgrounds.
Milestone 3	137	makes full interactions with people of different cultures and invites them to participate life-related activities, such as going to lunch.

（续表）

Level	Items	Descriptors
Milestone 3	138	is willing to invite people to be part of informal work-related activities.
Milestone 3	139	analyses the ethical, social, and environmental consequences of global systems and identifies a range of actions informed by his/her sense of personal and civic responsibility.
Milestone 3	140	analyzes major elements of global systems, including their historic and contemporary interconnections and the differential effects of human organizations and actions, and poses elementary solutions to complex problems in the human and the natural worlds.
Milestone 3	141	plans and evaluates more complex solutions to global challenges that are appropriate to his/her contexts using multiple disciplinary perspectives (such as cultural, historical, and scientific).
Milestone 3	142	identifies and responds to underlying attitudes or behaviour patterns, such as cultural norms and personality differences.
Milestone 3	143	phrases ideas in a way that avoids negative reactions (internally as well as externally).
Milestone 3	144	has extensive global experience: clearly considers problems and opportunities from a global perspective.
Milestone 3	145	is culturally knowledgeable and successfully conducts business in local terms.
Milestone 3	146	successfully prepares for global and local impacts on day-to-day activities.
Milestone 3	147	understands some of the effects technology has had in linking nations/individuals and enabling exchange of goods, services, and information.
Milestone 3	148	is aware that economic conditions of one nation can impact those of other nations.
Milestone 3	149	understands some specific ways in which culture impacts national/personal political decision-making.
Milestone 3	150	is aware how his/her values and ethics are expressed in specific contexts.
Milestone 3	151	recognizes his/her own role as an individual in a global society.
Milestone 3	152	is aware of his/her own values that affect his/her approaches to dilemmas and his/her resolution.
Milestone 3	153	is aware of differing cultural styles and language use and their effect on the workplace or institutional context.

Level	Items	Descriptors
Milestone 3	154	engages with others and tries to understand differences in his/her behavior, values, and attitude.
Milestone 3	155	interacts in a variety of ways, some quite different from those to which he/she is accustomed.
Milestone 3	156	utilizes several cultural frameworks to improve his/her professional interactions.
Milestone 3	157	engages the challenges of linguistic and cultural diversity as they occur in professional and community settings.
Milestone 3	158	communicates effectively with people from various cultures in a range of social domains, considering age, gender, social status, and other factors.
Milestone 3	159	utilizes relevant culture-specific information to improve his/her working style and professional interaction with workmates and customers.
Milestone 3	160	monitors his/her behavior and its impact on his/her learning, growth, and on others.
Milestone 3	161	successfully utilizes relevant frameworks to improve his/her managerial role in intercultural and multicultural settings.
Milestone 3	162	devises strategies to adapt his/her professional habits to the appropriate learning and styles of the workplace.
Milestone 3	163	is aware of his/her own level and stage of intercultural development (e.g., in terms of sensitivity, empathy, ethical issues, language proficiency, etc.)
Milestone 3	164	can cite various publications about understanding cultures, including those related to the domains of work, teaching, etc.
Milestone 3	165	can describe and explain the interactional behaviors common to persons from a specific other culture in social and professional domains.
Milestone 3	166	can compare and contrast his/her professional area of interest in his/her own culture and a specific other culture.
Milestone 3	167	can describe several models of cross-cultural entry and strategies for successful entry and adaptation.
Milestone 3	168	can discuss models for understanding learning styles and strategies, and describe prevailing styles in his/her own culture and another culture and their implications.

（续表）

Level	Items	Descriptors
Capstone 4	169	articulates insights into his/her own cultural rules and biases.
Capstone 4	170	Demonstrate an in-depth understanding of the intricacy of elements significant to people of another nation regarding their literature, philosophy, science, technology, law or social institutions and behaviors.
Capstone 4	171	interprets intercultural experience from the perspectives of own and more than one worldview.
Capstone 4	172	demonstrates ability to act in a supportive manner that recognizes the feelings of another cultural group.
Capstone 4	173	articulates a complex understanding of cultural differences in verbal and nonverbal communication.
Capstone 4	174	demonstrates understanding of the degree to which people use physical contact while communicating in different cultures or use direct/indirect and explicit/ implicit meanings.
Capstone 4	175	is able to skillfully negotiate a shared understanding based on those differences.
Capstone 4	176	asks complex questions about other cultures.
Capstone 4	177	seeks out and articulates answers to these questions that reflect multiple cultural perspectives.
Capstone 4	178	initiates and develops interactions with culturally different others.
Capstone 4	179	suspends judgment in valuing his/her interactions with culturally different others.
Capstone 4	180	effectively addresses significant issues in the natural worlds and human worlds based on articulating one's identity in a global context.
Capstone 4	181	evaluates and applies diverse perspectives to complex subjects within natural and human systems in the face of multiple and even conflicting positions.
Capstone 4	182	adapts and applies a deep understanding of multiple worldviews, experiences, and power structures while initiating meaningful interaction with members of other cultures to address significant global problems.
Capstone 4	183	takes informed and responsible action to address ethical, social, and environmental challenges in global systems and evaluates the local and broader consequences of individual and collective interventions.

（续表）

Level	Items	Descriptors
Capstone 4	184	uses deep knowledge of the historic and contemporary role and differential effects of human organizations and actions on global systems to develop and advocate for informed, appropriate action to solve complex problems in the human and the natural worlds.
Capstone 4	185	applies knowledge and skills to implement sophisticated, appropriate, and workable solutions to address complex global problems using interdisciplinary perspectives independently or with others.
Capstone 4	186	knows when to stand firm and when to accommodate.
Capstone 4	187	makes his/her case tactfully, especially when dealing with the highest level of government officials.
Capstone 4	188	accurately hears and understands the unspoken thoughts or feelings of others and acts purposefully.
Capstone 4	189	anticipates global influences on the local business.
Capstone 4	190	is extremely proactive in anticipating and preparing locally to support global activities.
Capstone 4	191	is empathetic and sensitive to global issues.
Capstone 4	192	waits to understand the situation or people before making a judgement, at the meantime, assume positive attribution.
Capstone 4	193	is open and curious about new things; energetically pursues an understanding of new idea, possibilities and experiences.
Capstone 4	194	tolerates ambiguity and uncertainty well and even welcome it in almost all situations.
Capstone 4	195	is intense interesting in travelling abroad and learning about foreign places; strive to stay the current on world and international events.
Capstone 4	196	is comfortable replacing familiar activities with different one in new situations.
Capstone 4	197	easily changes daily routines and adopts to new situations.
Capstone 4	198	is naturally interested in learning about and getting to know people who are different especially those from other cultures and ethic groups.
Capstone 4	199	is very proactive about developing and maintaining friendship with people who are different and engaging them in interesting conversation.
Capstone 4	200	is aware of and sensitive to the emotion and feeling of others.

Level	Items	Descriptors
Capstone 4	201	is highly attentive to how people feel and likely to respond with empathy.
Capstone 4	202	is aware of his/her own value, strengths, limitation and behavior along with their impacts on others.
Capstone 4	203	continually evaluates oneself and own impact.
Capstone 4	204	is versatile at adopting own behavior to fit in to various social situations and fosters positive social and interpersonal environment.
Capstone 4	205	maintains a naturally positive outlook toward people, events and outcomes.
Capstone 4	206	feels able to do anything; can stick it out.
Capstone 4	207	is aware of core personal values and never violate them, yet open and conformable around those who have different beliefs and values.
Capstone 4	208	responds with emotional resilience to potential challenging and frustrating situations; recovers quickly from difficult or challenging experiences.
Capstone 4	209	calmly responds to various stresses faced in life; keeps cool and rarely feels flustered.
Capstone 4	210	actively uses a variety of stress reduction strategies and techniques on a regular and daily basis.
Capstone 4	211	has an excellent understanding of the ways in which culture impacts decision-making of specific nations/groups (This understanding is fair and takes into account multiple cultural perspectives).
Capstone 4	212	has specific and well-developed knowledge of ways in which access to technology/information is impacted by culture and political ideology.
Capstone 4	213	is able to transfer this knowledge when learning about similar issues with which he/she is unfamiliar.
Capstone 4	214	seeks to understand the global impact of personal actions (e.g., consumerism based on company policies, consumption of energy, or recycling) , and acts accordingly.
Capstone 4	215	is aware of the levels and stages of intercultural development of those he/she works with (students, program participants, colleagues, etc.)
Capstone 4	216	is aware of factors which help and hinder his/her own intercultural development and ways to overcome them.

（续表）

Level	Items	Descriptors
Capstone 4	217	is aware how he/she perceives himself/herself as a communicator, facilitator, mediator in intercultural/multicultural situations.
Capstone 4	218	is aware how he/she is perceived by others as a communicator, facilitator, mediator in intercultural/multicultural situations.
Capstone 4	219	is aware of the multiple perspectives, complexities, and implications of choices in intercultural and multicultural contexts.
Capstone 4	220	exhibits appreciation for and interest in individuals and groups in particular cultural contexts.
Capstone 4	221	is flexible in communicating and interacting with those who are linguistically and culturally different (and with limited knowledge of his/her own language and culture).
Capstone 4	222	suspends judgment and appreciates the complexities and subtleties of intercultural and multicultural communication and interaction.
Capstone 4	223	extends a sense of empathy to those oppressed because of their sociocultural status.
Capstone 4	224	can explain a range of models for understanding cultures and the dominant and emerging theories which underpin these.
Capstone 4	225	utilizes language ability and cultural models to anticipate the behavior of persons from various cultures in most domains of social and professional interaction.
Capstone 4	226	helps resolve cross-cultural conflicts and misunderstandings.
Capstone 4	227	develops new concepts, models, and strategies for presentations at professional meetings and publications in appropriate journals.
Capstone 4	228	provides professional and educational services in the intercultural and multicultural fields.
Capstone 4	229	describes and explains in depth the behavior of persons from specific other cultures in important domains of social and professional interaction.
Capstone 4	230	discusses aspects of specific other cultures within the professional domain of intercultural training.
Capstone 4	231	explains and utilizes several models for mediating and resolving conflict among peoples of different cultures.
Capstone 4	232	participates in global initiatives.
Capstone 4	233	analyses ways that human actions influence the natural and human worlds.

（续表）

Level	Items	Descriptors
Capstone 4	234	identifies and explains multiple perspectives (such as cultural, disciplinary, and ethical) when exploring subjects within natural and human systems.
Capstone 4	235	explains the ethical, social, and environmental consequences of local and national decisions on global systems.

附录3:《商务外语自主学习能力量表》
(Business Foreign Language Learning Autonomy Competence Scale) （149 条描述语 ）

Level	Items	Descriptors
Benchmark 1	1	makes vague references to previous learning to new situation
Benchmark 1	2	accesses new information randomly
Benchmark 1	3	retrieves information that lacks relevance and quality.
Benchmark 1	4	reviews prior learning at a surface level
Benchmark 1	5	begins to look beyond classroom requirements
Benchmark 1	6	explores a topic at a surface level
Benchmark 1	7	provides little insight and/or information beyond the very basic facts
Benchmark 1	8	begins to look beyond classroom requirements
Benchmark 1	9	applies knowledge and skills to demonstrate comprehension and performance in novel situations
Benchmark 1	10	has difficulty defining the scope of the research question or thesis
Benchmark 1	11	has difficulty determining key concepts
Benchmark 1	12	presents examples, facts, or theories from one field of study or perspective
Benchmark 1	13	completes required work
Benchmark 1	14	is not very familiar about useful information resources or websites
Benchmark 1	15	cannot find target information effectively
Benchmark 1	16	has limited capacity in searching the information
Benchmark 1	17	uses no strategies in information search
Benchmark 1	18	describes own performances with general descriptors of success and failure

（续表）

Level	Items	Descriptors
Benchmark 1	19	can list a learning plan
Benchmark 1	20	begins to show interest in pursuing knowledge independently
Benchmark 1	21	amenable to fresh thoughts
Benchmark 1	22	has a need to learn
Benchmark 1	23	wants to learn new information
Benchmark 1	24	can set learning goal
Benchmark 1	25	tends to get upset when he/she has trouble learning something
Benchmark 1	26	struggles to learn something because he/she is not very bright
Benchmark 1	27	has difficulty in dealing with new learning tasks
Benchmark 1	28	gives up all too easily when the going gets tough
Benchmark 1	29	can find at least one person who is an important guide for him/her in learning
Benchmark 1	30	explores a topic at a surface level
Benchmark 1	31	searches new information from a few information sources
Benchmark 1	32	selectes sources using limited criteria
Benchmark 1	33	can only find limited sources
Benchmark 1	34	communicates information from fragmented sources
Benchmark 1	35	chooses a few information sources
Benchmark 1	36	is not very familiar about the criteria of effective resource
Benchmark 2	37	identifies connections between life experiences and those academic texts and ideas perceived as similar and related to own interests
Benchmark 2	38	presents examples, facts, or theories from one field of study or perspective
Benchmark 2	39	uses skills, abilities, theories, or methodologies gained in one situation in a new situation in a basic way
Benchmark 2	40	explores a topic with some evidence of depth
Benchmark 2	41	chooses a variety of information sources
Benchmark 2	42	communicates and organizes information from sources
Benchmark 2	43	can use two or more information strategies like citation, reference
Benchmark 2	44	can prioritize his/her work
Benchmark 2	45	is able to focus on a problem

Level	Items	Descriptors
Benchmark 2	46	tries to know himself/herself better
Benchmark 2	47	knows how to plan a time and place for learning
Benchmark 2	48	can make a research design
Benchmark 2	49	can set individual learning task by himself/herself
Benchmark 2	50	knows what the task needed to complete to achieve a learning goal
Benchmark 2	51	can carry out the systematically learning plan
Benchmark 2	52	can recognize what prevent him/her from completing a task
Benchmark 2	53	can evaluate personal competencies generally
Benchmark 2	54	can complete learning step by step
Benchmark 2	55	likes to question the things he/she is learning
Benchmark 2	56	likes to learn about things that really matter to him/her
Benchmark 2	57	likes learning new things that make sense
Benchmark 2	58	needs to know why
Benchmark 2	59	is open to new learning opportunities
Benchmark 2	60	is open to new ideas
Benchmark 2	61	enjoys a challenge
Benchmark 2	62	is willing to take risk
Benchmark 2	63	shows interest in pursuing knowledge independently
Benchmark 2	64	recognises opportunities for self-development
Benchmark 2	65	is aware of one's motivation for learning and reflects on it
Benchmark 2	66	treats the role of the teacher as a resource person
Benchmark 2	67	is willing to accept advice from others
Benchmark 2	68	can learn with and from others
Benchmark 2	69	goes on learning for a long time
Benchmark 2	70	prefers to solve problems on his/her own
Benchmark 2	71	prefers to plan his/her own learning
Benchmark 2	72	can set specific times for his/her study
Benchmark 2	73	seeks answers and asks questions of his/her data positively
Benchmark 2	74	fulfills the assignment(s) in an appropriate form
Benchmark 2	75	is willing to try new material and resources
Benchmark 2	76	explores a topic in depth
Benchmark 3	77	learns from his/her mistakes

（续表）

Level	Items	Descriptors
Benchmark 3	78	Applies advanced knowledge and complex skills to demonstrate thorough comprehension and performance in a challenging and unprecedented situations
Benchmark 3	79	can transfer the skills, abilities, theories, or methodologies gained in one situation to a new situation
Benchmark 3	80	can recognise one's strengths and weaknesses
Benchmark 3	81	illuminates concepts/ theories/ frameworks of fields of study by effectively selecting and developing examples of life experiences, drawn from a variety of contexts
Benchmark 3	82	connects examples, facts, or theories from more than one field of study or perspective independently
Benchmark 3	83	is confident in his/her ability to search out information
Benchmark 3	84	regards that getting to the bottom of things is more important than getting a good mark
Benchmark 3	85	is able to improve the way he/she does things
Benchmark 3	86	solves problems using a plan
Benchmark 3	87	likes to evaluate what he/she does
Benchmark 3	88	chooses a variety of information sources
Benchmark 3	89	extracts and structures Keep Points from various sources
Benchmark 3	90	Can proficiently use various advanced information strategies like precise citation, accurate reference, and skillful paraphrasing
Benchmark 3	91	can list a systematical and effective learning plan
Benchmark 3	92	chooses a variety of information sources appropriate to the scope and discipline of the research question
Benchmark 3	93	communicates, organises and synthesizes information from sources
Benchmark 3	94	evaluates changes in his/her own learning over time
Benchmark 3	95	can carry out the systematically learning plan
Benchmark 3	96	can reflect on materials and resources which he/she has used
Benchmark 3	97	prefers to set his/her own learning goals
Benchmark 3	98	has high beliefs in his/her abilities
Benchmark 3	99	is aware of his/her own limitations
Benchmark 3	100	needs to be in control of what he/she learns
Benchmark 3	101	thinks about how he/she tackles new things
Benchmark 3	102	finds new and better ways of doing things
Benchmark 3	103	takes ownership of new experiences and new situations
Benchmark 3	104	attends professional conferences to maintain technical knowledge

Level	Items	Descriptors
Benchmark 3	105	articulates one's strengths and challenges to increase effectiveness in different contexts
Benchmark 3	106	recognises areas needing improvement and take training to increase skills
Benchmark 3	107	can motivate oneself in a way that works
Benchmark 3	108	asks for help in his/her learning when necessary
Benchmark 3	109	can control his/her feeling when learning
Benchmark 3	110	can work with ambiguity and risk
Benchmark 3	111	can deal with frustration
Benchmark 3	112	can usually think of something to do to get round the problem when get stuck with a learning task
Benchmark 3	113	can decide when one needs to cooperate with others
Benchmark 3	114	makes connections between new things he/she is learning and things he/she already knew
Benchmark 3	115	sets strict time frames
Benchmark 3	116	evaluates new ideas critically
Benchmark 3	117	likes to gather the facts before making a decision
Benchmark 3	118	finds out information for himself/herself
Benchmark 3	119	chooses different methods and strategies
Benchmark 3	120	can complete individual learning task
Benchmark 3	121	solicits periodic feedback to continually improve quality of his/her own work
Benchmark 3	122	defines the scope of the research question or thesis completely
Benchmark 4	123	applies new knowledge and skills as the need arises
Benchmark 4	124	compares life experiences and academic knowledge to infer differences, as well as similarities
Benchmark 4	125	indicates broader perspectives about educational or life events
Benchmark 4	126	can structure his/her learning independently
Benchmark 4	127	is willing to change his/her ideas
Benchmark 4	128	uses the imagination productively
Benchmark 4	129	manages his/her time well
Benchmark 4	130	has good management skills
Benchmark 4	131	is systematic in his/her learning
Benchmark 4	132	alters his/her practices when necessary
Benchmark 4	133	sets his/her own criteria on which to evaluate his/her performance

Level	Items	Descriptors
Benchmark 4	134	manages learning processes, become aware of thoughts, feelings and actions as a learner
Benchmark 4	135	selects sources using multiple criteria
Benchmark 4	136	is familiar with a variety of learning methods and strategies
Benchmark 4	137	always tries out new learning in different ways
Benchmark 4	138	recognizes learning as one of life's pre-requisites and an essential tool in "moving with the times", recognizing opportunity and addressing life's challenges
Benchmark 4	139	is ready to persevere in the development of personal learning power even in an alien environment
Benchmark 4	140	flourishes educational interests and pursuits outside classroom requirements
Benchmark 4	141	is responsible for his/her own decisions/actions
Benchmark 4	142	can remotivate oneself when the initial motivation is wearing thin
Benchmark 4	143	changes the way he/she does things as a result of what he/she has learned
Benchmark 4	144	learns with and from others but also be able to manage without them
Benchmark 4	145	can continually improve as a learner
Benchmark 4	146	finds answers "outside the box" regularly
Benchmark 4	147	can set multiple learning task simultaneously
Benchmark 4	148	uses the intuition productively
Benchmark 4	149	gets the best ideas when thinking freely and independently

附录4：《商务外语批判性思维能力量表》
(Business Foreign Language Critical Thinking Competence Scale)（194条描述语）

Level	Item	Descriptors
1	1	CAN stay strictly within the guidelines of the assignment.
1	2	CAN use a single approach to solve the problem.
1	3	CAN take information from source (s) without interpretation /evaluation.
1	4	CAN take information from source (s) without coherent analysis or synthesis.

（续表）

Level	Item	Descriptors
1	5	CAN take viewpoints of experts without questioning.
1	6	CAN show an emerging awareness of present assumptions.
1	7	CAN begin to identify some contexts when presenting a position.
1	8	CAN state simplistic and obvious position, perspective or hypothesis.
1	9	CAN make oversimplified conclusions.
1	10	CAN explain information presented in mathematical forms, but draw incorrect conclusions about what the information means.
1	11	CAN explain the trend data shown in a graph, but will frequently misinterpret the nature of that trend.
1	12	CAN complete conversion of information but it may be inappropriate or inaccurate.
1	13	CAN use the quantitative analysis of data to make tentative, basic judgments.
1	14	CAN identify connections between life experiences and knowledge and ideas perceived as similar and related to own interests.
1	15	CAN transfer thinking skills gained in one situation into another situation in a basic way.
1	16	CAN demonstrate a limited ability in identifying a problem statement or related contextual factors.
1	17	CAN propose a vague and unclear solution/hypothesis which indirectly addresses the problem statement.
1	18	CAN review results superficially in terms of the problem defined with no consideration of need for further work.
1	19	CAN hastily identify strong, relevant arguments.
1	20	CAN evaluate obvious alternative points of view superficially.
1	21	CAN use fallacious or irrelevant reasons, and unwarranted claims in reasoning.
1	22	CAN maintain or defend views based on self-interest or preconceptions.
1	23	CAN identify a topic that is far too general and wide-ranging as to be manageable and doable.
1	24	CAN demonstrate a misunderstanding of the methodology or theoretical framework in inquiry design.
1	25	CAN state an ambiguous, illogical, or unsupportable conclusion from inquiry findings.
1	26	CAN identify one or more approaches for solving the problem that do not apply within a specific context.

（续表）

Level	Item	Descriptors
1	27	CAN understand everything related to thinking in a rigorous way.
1	28	CAN learn how to think in a rigorous way.
1	29	CAN learn how to reason correctly.
1	30	CAN recognize that it is important to learn how to reason correctly.
1	31	CAN recognize that it is important to good at reasoning.
1	32	CAN recognize that it is important to use his/her intellectual skills correctly.
1	33	CAN recognize that it is important to be good at solving problems.
1	34	CAN recognise that thinking critically can help to become a good professional.
1	35	CAN recognize that thinking critically will be useful in future development.
1	36	CAN recognize that thinking critically is useful in other subjects and courses.
1	37	CAN reason in a rigorous way.
1	38	CAN express in his/her own words clearly and precisely the most important information.
1	39	CAN distinguish the following related but different concepts: facts, information, experience, research, data, and evidence.
1	41	CAN explain in his/her own words the purpose of the subject or discipline being studied.
1	42	CAN explain in his/her own words the purpose of reasoning through a problem or issue.
1	43	CAN notice when straying from the purpose at hand, and redirect the thinking back toward the purpose.
1	44	CAN demonstrate the ability to adopt realistic ends when selecting a goal or purpose.
1	45	CAN choose reasonable secondary (instrumental) goals that make sense in working toward the accomplishment of a more ultimate goal.
1	46	CAN regularly adjust his/her thinking to fit his/her ultimate purposes.
1	47	CAN choose purposes and goals that are fair-minded, considering the relevant needs and rights of others
1	48	CAN consider and reject less acceptable approaches to solving problems.
1	49	CAN review prior learning at a surface level.

（续表）

Level	Item	Descriptors
2	50	CAN express in own words clearly and precisely the question at issue.
2	51	CAN re-express a question in a variety of ways with clarity and precision.
2	52	CAN divide complex questions into sub-questions accurately delineating the complexities in the issue.
2	53	CAN formulate fundamental and significant questions within any particular disciplines or subjects.
2	54	CAN accurately categorize the question, determining whether it is a question of fact or preference, or one that calls for reasoned judgment before reasoning through a question.
2	55	CAN distinguish conceptual questions from factual questions.
2	56	CAN distinguish significant questions from trivial ones, relevant from irrelevant ones.
2	57	CAN demonstrate sensitivity to the assumptions built into the questions.
2	58	CAN analyse and assess assumptions for justifiability.
2	59	CAN state his/her evidence for a view clearly and fairly.
2	60	CAN distinguish relevant from irrelevant information when reasoning through a problem.
2	61	CAN actively search for information against, not just for, his/her own position.
2	62	CAN draw conclusions only to the extent that those conclusions are supported by the facts and sound reasoning.
2	63	CAN demonstrate the ability to objectively analyze and assess information in coming to conclusions based on the information.
2	64	CAN demonstrate understanding of the difference between information and inferences drawn from that information.
2	65	CAN demonstrate understanding of the types of information used within particular subjects and disciplines, as well as understanding of how professionals within fields use information in reasoning through problems.
2	66	CAN state, elaborate and exemplify the meaning of an inference.
2	67	CAN distinguish between inferences and conclusions.
2	68	CAN distinguish between clear and unclear inferences.
2	69	CAN make only those inferences that follow logically from the evidence or reasons presented.

（续表）

Level	Item	Descriptors
2	70	CAN distinguish from deep and superficial inferences.
2	71	CAN make superficial inferences when reasoning through complex issues.
2	72	CAN make superficial assumptions and persuppositions when reasoning through complex issues.
2	73	CAN reason to logical conclusions after considering relevant and significant information.
2	74	CAN distinguish from consistent and inconsistent inferences.
2	75	CAN make inferences consistent with one other.
2	76	CAN distinguish from assumptions and inferences.
2	77	CAN uncover and accurately assess the assumptions underlying inferences.
2	78	CAN notice inferences or judgments made within particular disciplines.
2	79	CAN accurately identify his/her own assumptions, as well as those of others.
2	80	CAN make assumptions that are reasonable and justifiable, given the situation and evidence.
2	81	is aware of the natural tendency in humans to use stereotypes, prejudices, biases and distortions in their reasoning.
2	82	CAN regularly identify their own stereotypes, prejudices, biases and distortions.
2	83	CAN demonstrate skill in accurately identifying the stereotypes, prejudices, biases and distortions in the thinking of others.
2	84	CAN demonstrate understanding of the fact that assumptions function primarily at the unconscious or subconscious level of thought.
2	85	CAN demonstrate recognition that the mind naturally (egocentrically) seeks to hide unjustifiable assumptions in the mind in order to maintain its belief system or pursue selfish ends.
2	86	CAN seek out, in thinking, unjustifiable assumptions generated and maintained through native egocentric tendencies hidden at the unconscious level of thought.
2	87	CAN accurately identify assumptions within subjects, disciplines and texts.
2	88	CAN identify the assumptions embedded in the concepts he/she use and the theories he/she study.
2	89	CAN state, elaborate and exemplify what a concept is.
2	90	CAN demonstrate understanding of the following distinctions: theories, principles, definitions, laws, and axioms.

Level	Item	Descriptors
2	91	CAN identify the key concepts and ideas he/she and others use.
2	92	CAN accurately explain the implications of the key words and phrases he/she use.
2	93	CAN distinguish nonstandard uses of words from standard ones.
2	94	CAN think deeply about the concepts he/she use.
2	95	CAN analyze concepts and to draw distinctions between related but different concepts.
2	96	CAN demonstrate awareness of the mind's naturally to maintain a particular viewpoint or set of beliefs.
2	97	CAN show a propensity to identify when concepts are being misused.
2	98	CAN distinguish, clearly and precisely, the difference from (and overlap between) an implication and a consequence.
3	99	CAN demonstrate understanding of intellectual autonomy by stating, elaborating and exemplifying what it means in numerous ways.
3	100	CAN avoid passively or mindlessly accepting the beliefs of others.
3	101	CAN thoughtfully form principles of thought and action.
3	102	CAN accurately and logically evaluate the traditions and practices that others often accept unquestioningly.
3	103	CAN incorporate knowledge and insight into his/her thinking, independent of the social status of the source.
3	104	CAN respond positively to the reasonable suggestions of others.
3	105	CAN demonstrate understanding of the concept of egocentricity, with its many complexities.
3	106	CAN demonstrate understanding of the concept of rationality and can describe in detail how it differs from egocentricity.
3	107	CAN manifest the recognition that egocentric thinking needs to be "corrected" by more reasonable thinking.
3	108	CAN identify egocentric emotions that affect his/her thinking.
3	109	CAN accurately identify egocentric thought in others.
3	110	CAN give multiple examples from history of negative consequences that have resulted from sociocentric thought.
3	111	CAN accurately analyze any subjects he/she is studying.
3	112	CAN routinely raise important questions about what he/she is studying.
3	113	CAN demonstrate the distinction between rote memorization and genuine understanding.

（续表）

Level	Item	Descriptors
3	114	CAN regularly assess himself/herself as he/she is learning, to determine the extent of his/her understanding.
3	115	CAN use reading and writing as principal tools in learning.
3	116	CAN identify through questioning the basic structures in thinking.
3	117	CAN distinguish questions that admit of a definite answer from questions that call for reasoned judgment.
3	118	CAN question both dogmatic absolutism and subjective relativism.
3	119	CAN question concepts—his/her own use of concepts, as well as others' use of concepts.
3	120	CAN ask complex interdisciplinary questions.
3	121	CAN ask questions that help him/her make better decisions and solve problems.
3	122	CAN routinely ask questions that enable him/her to evaluate reasoning.
3	123	CAN adapt appropriate reasons to specifications.
3	124	CAN consider new directions or approaches without going beyond the guidelines of the assignment.
3	125	CAN create a novel or unique idea, question, format, or product.
3	126	CAN connect ideas or solutions in novel ways.
3	127	CAN identify several relevant contexts when presenting a position.
3	128	CAN be aware of others' assumptions.
3	129	CAN acknowledge different sides of an issue from one specific position.
3	130	CAN get a conclusion tied to known information.
3	131	CAN identify a manageable/doable topic that is too narrowly focused of the topic.
3	132	CAN present information from relevant sources representing limited points of view/approaches.
3	133	CAN develop some critical elements of the methodology or theoretical framework.
3	134	CAN organize evidence, but the organization is not effective enough.
3	135	CAN state a general conclusion according to inquiry findings.
3	136	CAN present relevant and supported implications for his/her findings.
3	137	CAN compare life experiences and academic knowledge to infer differences, as well as similarities.
3	138	CAN prompte, connect examples, facts, or theories from more than one field of studies or perspectives.

（续表）

Level	Item	Descriptors
3	139	CAN use skills, abilities, theories, or methodologies gained in one situation in a new situation to contribute to understanding of problems or issues.
3	140	CAN articulate personal strengths and challenges to increase effectiveness in different contexts.
3	141	CAN implement the solution in a manner that addresses the problem statement but ignores relevant contextual factors.
3	142	CAN describe assumptions explicitly.
3	143	CAN identify and provide an explanation of contextual issues accurately.
3	144	CAN identify meaning and/or bias of one reasoning and provide a brief explanation.
4	145	CAN develop a logical, consistent plan among alternatives to solve the problem.
4	146	CAN incorporate divergent, or contradictory perspectives or ideas in an exploratory way.
4	147	CAN synthesize ideas or solutions into a coherent whole.
4	148	CAN take information from source(s) with enough interpretation / evaluation to develop a coherent analysis or synthesis.
4	149	CAN identify own and others' assumptions in several relevant contexts when presenting a position.
4	150	CAN get a conclusion logically with a range of information.
4	151	CAN present in-depth information from relevant sources representing various points of views/approaches for one problem.
4	152	CAN develop the methodology or theoretical framework appropriately.
4	153	CAN organise evidence to reveal important patterns, differences, or similarities related to focus.
4	154	CAN state a sound conclusion focused solely on the inquiry findings.
4	155	CAN discuss relevant and supported limitations and implications.
4	156	CAN select and develop examples of life experiences drawn from a variety of contexts to illuminate concepts/ theories/ frameworks of fields of study effectively.
4	157	CAN connect examples, facts, or theories from more than one field of studies or perspectives independently.
4	158	CAN adapt and apply skills, abilities, theories, or methodologies gained in one situation to new situations to solve problems or explore issues.

Level	Item	Descriptors
4	159	CAN evaluate changes in own learning over time, recognising complex contextual factors.
4	160	CAN construct a detailed problem statement with evidence of most relevant contextual factors.
4	161	CAN identify multiple approaches for solving the problem within a specific context.
4	162	CAN propose one or more solutions/hypotheses for a problem.
4	163	CAN make solutions/hypotheses sensitive to contextual factors.
4	164	CAN evaluate solutions adequately and critically.
4	165	CAN implement the solution in a manner that addresses multiple contextual factors of the problem.
4	166	CAN examine results relative to the problem with some consideration of further work.
4	167	CAN provide accurate explanations of information.
4	168	CAN convert relevant information into an appropriate and desired form.
4	169	CAN use the quantitative analysis of data to draw reasonable and appropriately qualified conclusions.
4	170	CAN describe assumptions and provide compelling rationale for why assumptions are appropriate explicitly.
4	171	CAN identify the problem/question accurately and provide a well-developed summary.
4	172	CAN provide a well-developed examination of the evidence for its accuracy, relevance, and completeness.
4	173	CAN identify and provide a well-developed explanation of contextual issues with a clear sense of scope accurately.
4	174	CAN identify others' meaning and/or potential bias accurately.
4	175	CAN identify conclusions, implications, and consequences with a well-developed explanation accurately.
4	176	CAN provide an objective reflection of own assertions.
4	177	CAN analyze and evaluate major alternative points of view thoughtfully.
4	178	CAN draw warranted, judicious, non-fallacious conclusions.
4	179	CAN justify key results and procedures, explain assumptions and reasons.
4	180	CAN make inferential connections.
4	181	CAN follow the logic of an argument.

（续表）

Level	Item	Descriptors
4	182	CAN understand logical relationships between assertions/arguments and supporting information.
4	183	CAN identify implicit assumptions and evidence that support or undermine a claim.
4	184	CAN distinguish causation from correlation.
4	185	CAN identify needed evidence and implicit assumptions.
4	186	CAN identify possible alternative causes or explanations.
4	187	CAN recognise alternative explanations.
4	188	CAN explain in own words clearly and precisely the purpose of the subject or discipline being studied.
4	189	CAN communicate in a rational, rather than egocentric way.
4	190	CAN accurately identify core concepts within subjects and state the meaning of those concepts, as well as elaborate, exemplify, and interrelate them.
4	191	CAN relate the subjects he/she studies to his/her experience and significant problems in the world.
4	192	CAN demonstrate the ability to ask questions within academic discipline which enable him/her to understand the discipline and think within it.
4	193	CAN use good reasoning as the fundamental criterion by which to judge whether to accept or reject any beliefs or explanations.
4	194	CAN control irrational emotions when reasoning through problems and issues.

附录5:《商务实践能力量表》
(Business Practice Competence Scale)（305 条描述语）

Level	Items	Descriptors
Fundamental	1	demonstrates the general awareness and knowledge of the professional accounting standards.
Fundamental	2	understands and describes the main elements of financial statements and reports.
Fundamental	3	understands and applies basic concepts of cost accounting to support entities' operational and financial requirements.
Fundamental	4	can demonstrate basic understanding of techniques used to analyse and manage costs.

（续表）

Level	Items	Descriptors
Fundamental	5	can demonstrate understanding of basic principles and application of business tax.
Fundamental	6	can prepare basic tax returns in area of specialisation.
Fundamental	7	can apply basic tax accounting principles to appropriately record taxes.
Fundamental	8	can demonstrate basic understanding of taxation strategies.
Fundamental	9	can understand the organizational business plan, immediate environment and the possible impact of events and activities on the organization.
Fundamental	10	can understand the strategic direction of the organization and highlight areas of potential value or risk.
Fundamental	11	is aware of key business processes and key metrics associated with each business relevant to his/her area of work.
Fundamental	12	understands the interests and profiles of key stakeholders of the organization.
Fundamental	13	participates in the development of project plans (i.e. actions, resources required and timelines), and understands the development of project plans.
Fundamental	14	communicates project aims and plans.
Fundamental	15	supports negotiations by providing information and being part of the team.
Fundamental	16	makes decisions based on facts, common sense, previous experience.
Fundamental	17	establishes working level relationships with third-party counterparts to resolve routine issues.
Fundamental	18	listens actively to others and acknowledges hearing different perspectives.
Fundamental	19	provides fact-based information to others based on requests.
Fundamental	20	establishes relationships and credibility with business partners.
Fundamental	21	analyses needs of business partners.
Fundamental	22	proactively listens to, considers and embraces diverse ideas and styles
Fundamental	23	applies an understanding of available resources and uses them effectively
Fundamental	24	understands the fundamentals of the domestic economy.
Fundamental	25	possesses knowledge of basic macroeconomic measures and has a general understanding of the effects.

（续表）

Level	Items	Descriptors
Fundamental	26	takes time to understand customer needs and provides explanations.
Fundamental	27	understands how own job and actions affect customers.
Fundamental	28	demonstrates an awareness of the need to work as part of a team.
Fundamental	29	readily contributes to team initiatives and team meetings.
Fundamental	30	shares knowledge and information with colleagues when asked.
Fundamental	31	presents facts and figures when seeking agreement.
Fundamental	32	acknowledges the rights of others to express their views.
Fundamental	33	steps into work of colleagues when needed to do so.
Fundamental	34	has a basic understanding of what the business is trying to achieve.
Fundamental	35	uses computer databases and spreadsheets locating and retrieving data from storage systems.
Fundamental	36	uses technology appropriately, and is able to record information correctly, sort information, and provide totals.
Fundamental	37	uses MS Word and Excel to a basic level.
Fundamental	38	compiles or enters numerical data and accurately calculates totals.
Fundamental	39	understands the context of the figures.
Fundamental	40	understands, analyses and interprets basic financial information.
Fundamental	41	ensures inventory accounting is accurate and complete.
Fundamental	42	monitors income and expenditure for projects.
Fundamental	43	expresses disagreements, but often in a critical or disparaging way.
Fundamental	44	tends to give only positive feedback to other team members.
Fundamental	45	provides assistance, information, or other support to others when asked.
Fundamental	46	prepares a personal development plan with general goals.
Fundamental	47	seeks to develop skills needed for effectiveness in current job.
Fundamental	48	presents information or data that communicates to others.
Fundamental	49	uses graphics or slides that display information.
Fundamental	50	presents an argument in support of a position.
Fundamental	51	notices business opportunities.
Fundamental	52	becomes aware of business, industry and market information.
Fundamental	53	demonstrates some willingness to take certain risks to achieve business goals.
Fundamental	54	appreciates and supports the contributions of others.

（续表）

Level	Items	Descriptors
Fundamental	55	motivates others to contribute through own enthusiasm.
Fundamental	56	is aware of own personal strengths and development needs.
Fundamental	57	maintains composure in dealing with others.
Fundamental	58	responds to workmates in a timely and courteous manner.
Fundamental	59	is approachable and receptive to others.
Fundamental	60	responds promptly to the needs of the client even when under pressure.
Intermediate	61	understands and discusses routine tax matters such as income tax, indirect tax, corporate tax within clear guidelines.
Intermediate	62	analyses the organizational wider environment and draw conclusions about the impact of events and activities.
Intermediate	63	identifies immediate threats or opportunities to the business and resolves or escalates them accordingly.
Intermediate	64	uses sound knowledge of the organization's customers and competitors to analyse and challenge business cases.
Intermediate	65	understands the elements that make up each process and the performance measures that can be applied to each.
Intermediate	66	proactively identifies process improvement opportunities.
Intermediate	67	develops simple project plans including business case, contingencies, critical paths and applies project management tools and techniques.
Intermediate	68	understands stakeholder's positions and bargaining power and is able to negotiate and/or participate in negotiations with some support.
Intermediate	69	manages internal stakeholders prior to and during negotiations.
Intermediate	70	researches and uses data from a range of sources to make robust fact-based decisions.
Intermediate	71	understands the big picture by listening and leveraging non-verbal cues.
Intermediate	72	identifies the appropriate audience for sharing information and proactively shares appropriate fact-based information in a balanced and timely manner.
Intermediate	73	makes practical suggestions to improve customer service.
Intermediate	74	sees complaints as a high priority and is proactive and responsive to these.

（续表）

Level	Items	Descriptors
Intermediate	75	actively develops his/her own knowledge and skills by learning roles of other team members.
Intermediate	76	understands what other colleagues need to know and keeps them informed.
Intermediate	77	keeps abreast of business, industry and market information that may reveal business opportunities.
Intermediate	78	proposes innovative business deals to potential customers, suppliers, and business partners.
Intermediate	79	talks to customers (internal or external) to find out their needs and meet their needs.
Intermediate	80	deals with conflicting demands quickly and calmly.
Intermediate	81	plans carefully and sets goals for improving performance.
Intermediate	82	delivers high quality output.
Intermediate	83	understands and applies commercial principles to own area of business.
Intermediate	84	knows marketing process, from assessing market needs to marketing products and services.
Intermediate	85	understands legal and commercial frameworks required in a business team.
Intermediate	86	uses appropriate communication methods for effective interactions with a preference for personal interactions.
Intermediate	87	is persuasive and confident in communicating ideas.
Intermediate	88	negotiates win-win outcomes by exploring different positions and building consensus.
Intermediate	89	manages his/her emotions effectively within the workplace context.
Intermediate	90	produces clear client correspondence and reports selecting most appropriate style to achieve desired outcome.
Intermediate	91	portrays the organization and work area in a positive manner.
Intermediate	92	builds trust in relationships through maintaining confidentiality and keeping commitments.
Intermediate	93	identifies the broader impact of problems in one's own work area and acts to minimize or address these.
Intermediate	94	understands the contribution of operational actions to the strategic goals.
Intermediate	95	actively participates in team meetings through sharing ideas and contributing to discussions.

Level	Items	Descriptors
Intermediate	96	accomplishes shared goals through accepting joint responsibility.
Intermediate	97	exercises tact, tolerance and humour to promote team harmony.
Intermediate	98	analyzes business culture, structure, processes, data, management and performance criteria based on the scope of work.
Intermediate	99	understands the nature of the management consulting market, competitors and capabilities.
Intermediate	100	demonstrates understanding of, and where appropriate uses, systematic methods to promote consultancy services for external and internal clients.
Intermediate	101	understands and defines client requirements as evidenced by client agreement.
Intermediate	102	presents clear comprehensive written proposals.
Intermediate	103	demonstrates competent use of planning tools and techniques, and sets appropriate milestones for the size and scale of the assignment.
Intermediate	104	works effectively in a team with others and seeks support from others where appropriate.
Intermediate	105	uses a variety of data gathering, problem solving and analytical techniques that take into account client and own values and objectives.
Intermediate	106	admits to mistakes and takes responsibility.
Intermediate	107	manages own behavior to prevent or reduce feelings of stress.
Intermediate	108	quickly adjusts and constructively reacts to unforeseen circumstances and setbacks.
Intermediate	109	expresses gratitude and appreciation to others who have provided information, assistance or support.
Intermediate	110	takes time to get to know co-workers, to build rapport and establish a common bond.
Intermediate	111	knows marketing process, from assessing market needs to marketing products and services.
Intermediate	112	negotiates win-win outcomes by exploring different positions and building consensus.
Intermediate	113	demonstrates the ability to challenge existing practices in order to become more effective.
Intermediate	114	expresses pride in the group and encourages people to feel good about their accomplishments.

Level	Items	Descriptors
Intermediate	115	structures situations to create a desired impact and to maximize the chances of a favorable outcome.
Advanced	116	approves tax returns to ensure accuracy, completeness and statutory compliance.
Advanced	117	develops and implements solutions at an operational level to address actions emanating from insights.
Advanced	118	uses understanding of the organization's commercial business and markets to tailor offerings to current and future needs.
Advanced	119	devises information reporting tools to aid the understanding of regulatory stakeholders.
Advanced	120	assesses and understands customers' and competitors' strengths and limitations and uses insight to influence business decisions.
Advanced	121	sets up business processes to deliver successful outcomes, assesses their effectiveness and reviews performance measures relating to each.
Advanced	122	sets demanding and realistic targets for process improvement and ensures changes to existing processes are carried out in a systematic and logical way.
Advanced	123	works with stakeholders to develop and drive potential efficiency improvements.
Advanced	124	provides guidance on correct procedures to successfully run contracts.
Advanced	125	takes the lead in developing and implementing complex project plans that have implications across business units or the organization.
Advanced	126	identifies new and innovative ways to achieve required outputs of projects.
Advanced	127	provides recommendations to macroeconomic analysis.
Advanced	128	evaluates and properly interprets the influence of the external environment on the organization.
Advanced	129	identifies key environmental drivers and understands their impact upon business strategies and decisions.
Advanced	130	uses a combination of logic, personal passion, conviction and interpersonal skills to influence others.
Advanced	131	develops and makes use of a wide network of key relationships from both inside and outside the organization to influence others.

（续表）

Level	Items	Descriptors
Advanced	132	negotiates in tough situations with both external and internal stakeholders.
Advanced	133	demonstrates confidence, good political savvy and maintains credibility with third-party of key decision-makers.
Advanced	134	adjusts personal positions and style quickly if circumstances change favorably and unfavorably.
Advanced	135	wins concessions without damaging stakeholder relationship.
Advanced	136	assesses and leads fact-based decisions in high-risk situations.
Advanced	137	delivers presentation to senior management with confidence and acknowledge when the answer is unknown to a business question.
Advanced	138	encourages the sharing of ideas and best practices to ensure understanding and achieves best possible outcomes.
Advanced	139	leads cross-functional business initiatives and encourages team to cultivate relationships across the business.
Advanced	140	ensures customer service levels are maintained and improved upon.
Advanced	141	takes an active interest in setting high standards of customer care.
Advanced	142	collaborates to actively improve customers' experience of dealing with the organization.
Advanced	143	analyses customer requirements both short- and long-term and develops appropriate solutions.
Advanced	144	communicates to staff the work of other areas that contribute to business success.
Advanced	145	recognizes strengths and weaknesses of team members and plays to strengths.
Advanced	146	builds trust and seeks common ground.
Advanced	147	influences others through well-reasoned arguments.
Advanced	148	develops well researched business proposals.
Advanced	149	proactively encourages continuous improvements and commitments to change.
Advanced	150	evaluates the long-term cost benefit implications of change and their impact on customers- staff and the business.
Advanced	151	ensures the potential benefits and improvements of new initiatives are implemented and realized.
Advanced	152	uses marketing and financial tools to inform and analyse data to set direction.

（续表）

Level	Items	Descriptors
Advanced	153	identifies opportunities to use technology to improve processes, and implements systems effectively.
Advanced	154	analyses data from multiple sources to identify trends and makes recommendations for procedural or policy changes.
Advanced	155	translates data into summary charts and overviews to assist decision making.
Advanced	156	is fully conversant with financial accounts, accounting procedures and legislation.
Advanced	157	plans budgets and business activities from a financial perspective.
Advanced	158	interprets and analyses data by using marketing and financial tools to make sound, future decisions, policies and to set direction.
Advanced	159	follows established guidelines and procedures to ensure approval of funding for key initiatives.
Advanced	160	encourages and offers support for others' ideas and proposals.
Advanced	161	expresses disagreement in a tactful and constructive manner.
Advanced	162	provides positive and encouraging reinforcement to team members for their contributions.
Advanced	163	regularly seeks specific performance feedback from his/her manager and from others with whom he/she interacts on the job.
Advanced	164	takes significant action to develop skills needed for effectiveness in current or future job.
Advanced	165	efficiently presents several different arguments in clear support of a position that have a strong effect.
Advanced	166	asks about and demonstrates a sincere and genuine concern for the other person's personal experience, interests, and family.
Advanced	167	recognizes trends in business, industry and market information that may reveal business opportunities.
Advanced	168	actively seeks out feedback from others on own performance.
Advanced	169	motivates self and others to focused efforts on meeting deadlines even in demanding time frames.
Advanced	170	leads by collaboration and facilitates leadership in own areas of responsibility.
Advanced	171	focuses upon establishing and maintaining productive relationships with key internal groups to ensure collaborative work practices.
Advanced	172	actively fosters productive two-way flow of ideas.

（续表）

Level	Items	Descriptors
Advanced	173	seeks to understand clients' operating environment and their issues/problems.
Advanced	174	develops strategic alliances with external groups to enhance the quality of service.
Advanced	175	creates operational plans that realize strategic goals.
Expert	176	uses insights to lead and influence changes at strategic, tactical, team and individual levels across the organization.
Expert	177	develops finance strategy that is aligned with the organizational long-term plan.
Expert	178	identifies and focuses on future critical areas for the organization and devises strategy to maximize opportunity and minimize risk.
Expert	179	monitors and forecasts changes in customers' and competitors' behaviour and develops appropriate organization response.
Expert	180	determines impact of emerging business models and sponsors initiatives to deliver optimal response.
Expert	181	defines process improvement to achieve business performance.
Expert	182	manages key business processes from end-to-end such that they add value to the business.
Expert	183	identifies core competencies and builds strategic alliances with stakeholders to close gaps.
Expert	184	leads critical decisions between the organization and third-party regarding contract terms.
Expert	185	negotiates and develops complex contracts and/or agreements.
Expert	186	identifies projects that drive value creation and aligns them to organizational strategies.
Expert	187	champions projects that have broad implications across the organization by aligning and influencing all key stakeholders.
Expert	188	anticipates economic conditions and provides strategic insight on how to mitigate impact on the organization as a whole.
Expert	189	understands and applies the underlying theories behind macroeconomic behaviour to all levels of the organization.
Expert	190	influences and works effectively with organization numbers from different cultures.
Expert	191	negotiates effectively at senior levels through anticipating and managing objections and challenges.
Expert	192	communicates effectively and assertively in high risk situations to resolve complex and/or sensitive issues and build consensus.

（续表）

Level	Items	Descriptors
Expert	193	demonstrates the use of a direct and diplomatic style.
Expert	194	challenges information to detect discrepancies in reasoning.
Expert	195	leads the most complex negotiations and demonstrates expert closing skills and excellent political and cultural savvy
Expert	196	analyses the wider business and political implications when making decisions, including the effectiveness of outcome.
Expert	197	leads organization forums to obtain wide perspective of ideas.
Expert	198	confidently presents controversial and/or complex information to all levels of the organization.
Expert	199	drives cross-functional initiatives across the business that create value.
Expert	200	leverages a broader network across the business.
Expert	201	provides insight into the long-term implications for customers of strategic decisions
Expert	202	promotes a customer focused culture and drives through relevant strategies and business practices.
Expert	203	develops strategies to persuade others to develop and operate a constructive and collaborative team working environment.
Expert	204	collaborates to build high level team relationships to obtain desired results.
Expert	205	identifies opportunities for team synergies both within the team and among different teams across the group.
Expert	206	uses a wide range of different influencing styles effectively based on an assessment of the other party/the audience.
Expert	207	maintains positive expectations of others, even when provoked, and strives to create the conditions for successful collaborative working in the long term.
Expert	208	recognizes and effectively deals with complex, sensitive and political issues.
Expert	209	initiates strategic change and identifies and communicates the implications and consequences clearly.
Expert	210	recognizes changing internal and external strategic influences and is an advocate for proactive change.
Expert	211	ensures change is sustained and evaluated regularly to ensure the change is effective and still meets its original objective.

Level	Items	Descriptors
Expert	212	sets strategic direction in full recognition of economic and business challenges and opportunities.
Expert	213	evaluates commercial and business opportunities against potential short- and long-term risks.
Expert	214	uses performance indicators, internal/external business analysis, and a range of economic and global factors to inform sustainable decisions.
Expert	215	identifies the opportunities/needs for new technologies to improve the way the area works, and be work with ICT to formulate a business case for change.
Expert	216	takes a strategic view of how technology will enable the organization to fulfil its current/future customer and resident requirements.
Expert	217	uses data/info selectively to reinforce arguments without prejudice or lack of objectivity.
Expert	218	uses a range of data to analyse business effectiveness and make strategic decisions.
Expert	219	keeps abreast of emerging changes of info technology in functional area and organization wide.
Expert	220	uses financial information in an intuitive manner to inform business decisions.
Expert	221	develops strategies that enable business growth and is able to evaluate opportunities against risks.
Expert	222	sets the strategic agenda and initiates discussion of changing business priorities.
Expert	223	places organisational strategy within the context of the wider environment.
Expert	224	develops innovative customer service initiative which significantly improves quality and enhances customer satisfaction.
Expert	225	anticipates growing customer needs and expectations to continuously improve product development and service delivery.
Expert	226	develops and implements new procurement system to support agency program within time and budgetary constraints.
Expert	227	ensures financial commitments and deadlines are met by facilitating and assessing processes, situations, and issues and takes corrective action as needed.

（续表）

Level	Items	Descriptors
Expert	228	regularly provides assistance to others when they need it.
Expert	229	works for solutions that all team members can support.
Expert	230	seeks opportunities to become actively involved working on teams as a means to develop experience and knowledge.
Expert	231	provides valuable assistance, information, or other support to others, to build or maintain relationships with them and fosters a cooperative team spirit.
Expert	232	provides valuable and needed assistance, information and support to others, to build a basis for future reciprocity; makes others want to build a partnership.
Expert	233	builds long lasting relationships with people whose assistance, cooperation and support may be needed.
Expert	234	encourages and supports entrepreneurial behavior in others.
Expert	235	demonstrates an eager willingness to take very calculated risks to achieve business goals.
Expert	236	proposes innovative and cost-effective business deals to potential customers, suppliers, and business partners.
Expert	237	has credible depth of knowledge across a range of disciplines and business environments.
Expert	238	leads by example, applying management and business skills in own business.
Expert	239	actively promotes the consulting profession through a network of contacts.
Expert	240	influences business thinking and agenda in one or more sectors.
Expert	241	utilizes knowledge of external issues and depth of experience to inform, challenge and define scope of work.
Expert	242	owns, leads and manages complex client bids and proposal with teams, demonstrating depth of experience.
Expert	243	reviews and advises on project management to ensure priorities are maintained and the assignment stay "on track."
Expert	244	takes responsibility for the people working for them in a project and ensures that they have the required competences.
Expert	245	advises on use of a range of diagnostic tools, methods and techniques.
Expert	246	makes a holistic assessment using information and knowledge from tools, techniques and market experience.

（续表）

Level	Items	Descriptors
Expert	247	develops and selects appropriate methods in unclear situations.
Expert	248	acts as a role model for ethical behavior and contributes to the development and maintenance of ethical standards within the profession.
Expert	249	demonstrates responsibility for his/her own actions, and those of others who work for him/her.
Expert	250	sets challenging and realistic goals and clear measures of success for himself/herself and his/her teams.
Expert	251	identifies and handles impediments to achieving outcomes.
Expert	252	demonstrates a passion for excellence and celebrates achievements.
Expert	253	recognizes when and how to apply principles of commercialization in planning and decision-making.
Expert	254	understands and utilizes accepted financial planning models.
Expert	255	predicts changes that may impact upon long-term financial issues through analysis of trend.
Expert	256	understands market trends and applies principles to areas of responsibility.
Expert	257	creates comprehensive reports or other documents to communicate ideas or concepts related to complex or sensitive issues.
Expert	258	presents information persuasively, with skill and power, seeking to influence an audience of critical importance.
Expert	259	uses political astuteness to negotiate and reaches agreement at a senior level on complex issues.
Expert	260	encourages and supports others to take on new challenges and opportunities.
Expert	261	works effectively to reduce silos and encourages collaboration across group.
Expert	262	is continually aware of own emotions and manages them effectively to create an effective working environment.
Expert	263	develops and utilizes networks at a strategic level.
Expert	264	understands when and how to use personal power and relational power underpinned by integrity to influence outcomes.
Expert	265	manages operations with a continual focus on the impact of decisions and actions on client.
Expert	266	manages complex client relationships.

（续表）

Level	Items	Descriptors
Expert	267	demonstrates and promotes a quality service culture by consulting and involving clients, colleagues and stakeholders.
Expert	268	creates strategic plans to realize organizational goals.
Expert	269	establishes and maintains business relationships with the key stakeholders.
Expert	270	maintains a clear sense of strategic direction within the international, national, and state contexts.
Expert	271	provides feedback to team members on their performance and develops action plans to develop performance.
Expert	272	keeps team members informed of relevant issues impacting on them or their work.
Expert	273	is sought out by others for advice and solutions on how to best interpret and use information.
Expert	274	discerns the level of pressure or influence to apply in each aspect of the analysis in relation to the broader context.
Expert	275	assesses group performance against goals and identifies areas for improvement.
Expert	276	translates business opportunities into concrete measures that are beneficial for the organization.
Expert	277	evaluates the financial impact of decisions and develops strategies to address financial resource issues.
Expert	278	sets and redefines priorities and reorganizes staff to increase the group's response.
Expert	279	delegates authority to match responsibility, and holds staff accountable for agreed upon commitments.
Expert	280	promotes group morale and productivity by being clear about output expectations.
Expert	281	sees arising conflict and takes action at division/ directorate/ organization level.
Expert	282	builds client's confidence using own personal reputation in the international community and expertise.
Expert	283	uses a variety of data gathering, problem-solving and analytical techniques that take into account client and own values and objectives and the type of recommendations to be made.

（续表）

Level	Items	Descriptors
Expert	284	monitors, evaluates and, as needed, renews the client service models and service standards.
Expert	285	ensures professional advice is sound and relevant to client's needs.
Expert	286	knows when to stand firm and when to accommodate.
Expert	287	accurately hears and understands the unspoken thoughts or feelings of others and acts purposefully.
Expert	288	anticipates and builds on others' reactions to keep momentum and support for an approach.
Expert	289	takes well thought-out influential actions to win a point or reach an agreement.
Expert	290	constructively works towards a win-win solution during negotiations.
Expert	291	demonstrates an ability to step back when necessary from the negotiation process while staying focused on the objective.
Expert	292	understands the nature and limits of related organizations and government agencies, and uses that knowledge to influence and lead.
Expert	293	takes ownership of compliance, ethical and other issues in order to protect the organisation's reputation and respect its obligations.
Expert	294	uses a variety of means to communicate the organisation's needs and strategic directions.
Expert	295	develops a strategic direction for one's unit that connects the role of the team to the success of the organisation.
Expert	296	ensures the initiatives and priorities in one's area are integrated with one another and aligned with the strategic priorities of the broader organisation.
Expert	297	utilises established network of relationships to seek information of strategic importance and to seek a position of influence in key forum.
Expert	298	considers the bigger picture while setting priorities and the way forward.
Expert	299	is intellectually agile in response to challenges of internal and external environments.
Expert	300	identifies and promptly tackles morale problems.

（续表）

Level	Items	Descriptors
Expert	301	establishes or supports structures and processes to plan and manage the orderly implementation of change.
Expert	302	quickly identifies and understands the central or underlying issues in a complex situation.
Expert	303	anticipates how individuals and groups will react to situations and information well in advance.
Expert	304	frequently develops better, faster, or less expensive ways to do things that significantly improves the organization.
Expert	305	carefully reviews and checks the accuracy of information in work reports.

附录6：《普通高等学校本科专业类教学质量国家标准（外国语言文学类——商务英语专业）》

《国标》涵盖了普通高等学校本科专业目录中全部 92 个本科专业类、587 个专业，涉及全国高校 56 000 多个专业布点，商务英语专业（050262）也在其中。

前言

本标准依据《高等学校外语类专业本科教学质量国家标准》制定，是商务英语本科专业准入、建设和评价的依据。各高等学校应根据本标准、相关行业标准和人才需求，制定本校的商务英语专业培养方案。

适用专业

本标准适用于各类高等学校的商务英语本科专业。商务英语专业学制 4 年，授予文学学士学位，专业代码为 050262。

培养目标

商务英语专业旨在培养英语基本功扎实，具有国际视野和人文素养，掌握语言学、经济学、管理学、法学（国际商法）等相关基础理论与知识，熟悉国际商务的通行规则和惯例，具备英语应用能力、商务实践能力、跨文化交流能力、思辨与创新能力、自主学习能力，能从事国际商务工作的复合型、应用型人才。

一、培养规格

（一）素质要求

商务英语专业学生应具有高尚品德、人文与科学素养、国际视野、社会责任感、敬业与合作精神、创新创业精神、健康的身心。

（二）知识要求

商务英语专业学生应掌握语言知识、商务知识、跨文化知识、人文社科知识、跨学科知识。

（三）能力要求

商务英语专业学生应具备英语应用能力、跨文化交际能力、商务实践能力、思辨与创新能力、自主学习能力。

二、课程体系

（一）总体框架

商务英语专业课程体系包括公共课程、专业核心课程、专业方向课程、实践环节、毕业论文五个部分。

课程总学分和总学时应不少于 150 和 2 500。专业课程总学分和总学时应不少于 100 和 1 600（公共课程除外）。毕业论文与实习/实践不计入总学时。

（二）课程结构

公共课程应设置思想政治理论、信息技术、人文与艺术、军事理论与训练、现代汉语、社会科学、自然科学、体育与健康、职业规划、第二外国语等类别的课程。

三、专业核心课程

专业核心课程按四大模块设置。各模块占专业课程总学时的比例大体为：英语知识与技能模块为 50% ～ 60%；商务知识与技能模块为 25% ～ 35%；跨文化交际模块为 5% ～ 10%；人文素养模块为 5% ～ 10%。

英语知识与技能模块应开设语音、语法、综合商务英语、商务英语听说、商务英语阅读、商务英语写作、商务英语翻译等课程。

商务知识与技能模块应开设经济学、管理学、国际商法、国际营销、国际贸易实务、国际商务谈判、电子商务等课程。商务知识类课程可用汉语或英汉双语授课，学生也可通过跨专业辅修或攻读双学位完成。

跨文化交际模块应开设跨文化商务交际、英语演讲等课程。

人文素养模块应开设英美概况、欧美文化、英美文学等课程。

四、专业方向课程

专业方向课程按必修和选修设置，突出商务知识与技能、跨文化商务交际、人文素养等类别。各高等学校根据培养规格、专业特色和行业需求，自主设置和动态调整。

五、实践环节

实践环节涵盖实训、实践和实习，占总学分的10% ～ 25%（不包括教育部规定的社会实践学分），由专业教师和行业专家共同指导完成。鼓励学生取得外贸、金融、会计、人力资源管理、财务管理、司法等行业资格证书。

专业实训在商务实训室等模拟仿真教学环境中操练外贸、金融、财务、营销、法律等实务流程。

专业实践在第二课堂活动（如：商业创意、商务谈判、商务技能等类比赛）和涉外商务活动（如：经贸洽谈、招商引资、商品会展等）等课外环境中完成。

专业实习在已签约或定点的校外实习基地集中实施或自主完成。

六、毕业论文

毕业论文重点考查学生对商务英语和专业知识的综合运用，以及实践与创新能力。毕业论文可采用实践类或学术类形式，要求符合行业或学术规范，用英语撰写，正文长度不少于5 000词。

实践类包含项目报告（如：商业计划、营销方案、案例分析、翻译及评述等）和调研报告（如：企业、行业、市场调研分析等）。对实践类毕业论文的指导和考核应有企业或行业专家参与。

七、教学与评价

（一）教学要求

商务英语专业教学应按纲施教，因材施教，合理运用教学方法和教育技术，注重学生的思想品德、英语基本功、人文与科学素养、国际视野、商务知识、创新创业能力等方面的培养。

（二）评价要求

商务英语教学评价应注重形成性与终结性相结合，重点评价学生的素质、知识和能力，教师的职业道德、教研能力、实践能力等，以及专业教学的各个环节。

八、教师队伍

（一）师资结构

商务英语专业的生师比不超过 18∶1。教师的年龄、学缘、职称、专业等结构合理，一般应具有硕士以上学位，能满足教学需要。

专业教师中语言类、商务类、实践类师资的大体比例为 6∶3∶1，商务类教师除英语能力合格外，其本科、硕士或博士学历中至少有一个应为经济、管理或法律类专业。实践类教师从行业专家中兼职聘请。还需聘有外籍教师。

（二）教师素质

商务英语教师应师德高尚，具备合格的英语基本功、专业知识、教学能力、科研能力、实践能力，运用现代教育信息技术，开展课堂教学与教学改革。

（三）教师发展

商务英语专业应制定教师发展规划，通过学历教育、国内外进修和学术交流、行业兼职或挂职等方式，不断更新教师的教育观念和知识结构，提高理论素养、教研水平和实践能力。

九、教学条件

（一）教学设施

商务英语专业应配备足够数量的教学设备、教室、设施，实务流程和环境符合实训要求，安排专人日常管理和维护。

（二）图书资料

外语、商务、人文、科技类的中外文专业图书期刊、电子数据库、工具书等符合要求，能满足学生的学习和教师教学科研的需要。

（三）网络资源

网络系统和网络资源完备,能满足日常的专业学习、网络教学和课件开发等需要。

（四）经费投入

经费投入有保障,能满足本专业发展的需要。

十、质量保障体系

（一）教学质量监控机制要求

本专业应建立教学质量监控机制。各教学环节应有明确的质量要求,应定期进行课程设置和教学质量评价。

（二）毕业生跟踪反馈机制要求

本专业应建立毕业生跟踪反馈机制和社会评价机制,对培养方案是否有效、实现培养目标进行定期评价。

（三）专业持续改进机制要求

本专业应建立完善的持续改进机制,确保教学质量监控结果、毕业生跟踪反馈结果和社会评价结果及时有效地促进专业不断改进。

术语与释义

《高等学校商务英语专业本科教学质量国家标准》中下列术语和定义适用于本文件。

（1）**商务英语**（Business English）指国际商务活动通用的英语。

（2）**商务英语专业**（Business English Program）指英语类本科专业,是英语与商务复合的人才培养模式。

（3）**复合型人才**（Inter-disciplinary Talent）指掌握和综合应用跨学科知识和技能的专业人才。

（4）**应用型人才**（Applied Talent）指能综合应用专业知识与工作技能，完成岗位实际工作的专业人才。

（5）**商务实践能力**（Business Practice Ability）指在跨文化环境中，运用所学专业知识和技能，按照行业规范，成功开展国际商务活动的能力。

商务英语专业知识要求

知识模块	知识要求
语言知识	语音知识、词汇知识、语法知识、语篇知识、语用知识等
商务知识	经济学知识、管理学知识、国际商法知识、国际金融知识、国际营销知识、人力资源管理知识、财务管理知识、商务操作规程、信息技术知识等
跨文化知识	外国文学知识、欧美文化知识、商业文化知识、中国文化知识等
人文社科知识	区域国别知识、国际政治知识、世界历史知识、世界宗教知识、外交知识等
跨学科知识	学科交叉知识、学科整合知识等

商务英语专业能力要求

能力模块	能力构成	能力要求
英语应用能力	英语组织能力	语音语调识读能力、词汇拼读能力、造句能力、谋篇能力等
	英语运用能力	听、说、读、写、译技能、语用能力、纠误能力等
	学习策略能力	调控策略、学习策略、社交策略等
跨文化交际能力	跨文化交际能力	跨文化思维能力、跨文化适应能力、跨文化沟通能力
	跨文化商务交际能力	沟通能力、商务能力、跨文化能力
商务实践能力	通用商务技能	办公文秘技能、信息调研技能、公共演讲技能、商务礼仪等
	专业商务技能	商务技能、市场营销技能、人力资源管理技能、财务管理技能等
思辨与创新能力	认知能力	理解、推理、评价、分析、解释、自我调控、精确性、相关性、逻辑性、深刻性、灵活性等
	情感调适能力	好奇、开放、自信、坚毅、开朗、公正、诚实、谦虚、好学、包容等
自主学习能力	学科自学能力	自我规划能力、自我决策能力、自我监控能力、自我评价能力

商务英语专业核心课程要求

课程模块	专业核心课程	门数	占专业课学时比例
英语知识与技能	实用英语语音、英语语法实练	2	50%～60%
	综合商务英语、商务英语听说、商务英语阅读、商务英语写作、商务翻译	5	
商务知识与技能	经济学导论、管理学导论、国际商法导论、国际营销概论	4	25%～35%
	国际贸易实务、国际商务谈判、实用电子商务	3	
跨文化交际	跨文化商务交际导论、英语演讲	2	5%～10%
人文素养	英美概况、英美文学选读、欧美文化概论	3	5%～10%
实习/实践			不计入总学时
毕业论文			

附录7:《普通高等学校本科专业类教学质量国家标准（外国语言文学类——商务英语专业）》

一、实施方案

1. 培养目标

本专业旨在培养具有扎实的英语语言基本功和相关商务专业知识，拥有良好的人文素养、中国情怀与国际视野，熟悉文学、经济学、管理学和法学等相关理论知识，掌握国际商务的基础理论与实务，具备较强的跨文化能力、商务沟通能力与创新创业能力，能适应国家与地方经济社会发展、对外交流与合作需要，能熟练使用英语从事国际商务、国际贸易、国际会计、国际金融、跨境电子商务等涉外领域工作的国际化复合型人才。

2. 培养规格

（1）素质要求

本专业学生应具有正确的世界观、人生观、价值观，良好的道德品质，中国情怀与国际视野，人文与科学素养，合作精神，创新精神，创业意识和学科基本素养；具备良好的职业精神、商业伦理意识和社会责任感。

（2）知识要求

本专业学生应熟练掌握英语语言、文学、翻译、英语国家社会文化、跨文化研究等基本理论和基础知识；掌握商务活动的基本工作内容和运行机制；熟悉商务组织治理结构、战略规划、运营管理等方面的基本理论和基础知识；了解经济学、管理学、法学等相关学科基础知识；了解我国对外经贸政策法规、国际商务领域的规则和惯例，以及国际商务活动中的相关环境因素。

（3）能力要求

本专业学生应具有良好的商务英语运用能力和跨文化商务沟通能力；具有思辨能力、量化思维能力、数字化信息素养；具有基本的商务分析、决策和实践能力；具有良好的团队合作能力，较强的领导、管理、协调和沟通能力；具有终身学习能力；具有良好的汉语表达能力和基本的第二外语运用能力。

3. 学制、学分与学位

学制：四年

总学分：150～180学分。其中：公共基础类课程约占30%；专业核心课程约占38%；专业方向课程约占17%；

实践教学环节（含毕业论文）约占15%。

学位：文学学士。

4. 课程体系

本专业课程体系包括公共基础类课程、专业核心课程、专业方向课程、实践教学环节（含毕业论文）四个部分。

公共基础类课程包括公共必修课程和通识选修课程。公共必修课程一般包括思想政治理论、信息技术、体育与健康、军事理论与训练、创新创业教育、第二外语等课程；通识选修课程一般包括提升学生知识素养、道德品质与身心素质的人文社会科学和自然科学课程，各学校可根据自身办学定位、办学特色和人才培养需要开设。

专业核心课程分为语言技能课程和专业知识课程，主要包括综合商务英语、商务英语视听说、商务英语阅读、英语演讲与辩论、商务英语写作、商务翻译、英语文学导论、语言学导论、西方文明史、经济学导论、管理学导论、商务导论、跨文化商务交际导论、商业伦理、中国文化概要等课程。

专业方向课程分为必修课程和选修课程，主要包括国际商务、国际贸易、国际会计、国际金融、跨境电子商务等方向的系列课程。

实践教学环节开设的课程分为专业实践、创新创业实践、社会实践活动和国际交流活动等。毕业论文（设计）一般用英语撰写，正文不少于 5 000 词，可为学术论文、商务计划书、商务研究报告和商务案例分析报告等多种形式。按教育部有关文件要求，实践教学环节的学分应不低于商务英语专业总学分的 15%，其中毕业论文（设计）的学分不低于总学分的 3%。

5. 教学计划（参考）

（1）公共基础类课程

公共基础类课程开课计划表

课程类别		课程名称	总学时	学时分配		学分数	开课学期	周学时	备注
				讲授	实验（践）				
公共基础类课程	公共必修课程	按国家相关要求开设（含第二外语）							40 学分
	通识选修课程	学校可根据自身人才培养实际需要开设							10 学分

（2）专业核心课程

专业核心课程开课计划表

课程类别		课程名称	总学时	学时分配		学分	开课学期	周学时	备注
				讲授	实验（践）				
专业核心课程	必修课程	综合商务英语（一）	64	48	16	4	1	4	
		综合商务英语（二）	64	48	16	4	2	4	
		综合商务英语（三）	64	48	16	4	3	4	
		综合商务英语（四）	64	48	16	4	4	4	
		商务英语视听说（一）	32	24	8	2	1	2	
		商务英语视听说（二）	32	24	8	2	2	2	
		商务英语视听说（三）	32	24	8	2	3	2	
		商务英语视听说（四）	32	24	8	2	4	2	
		商务英语阅读（一）	32	32		2	1	2	
		商务英语阅读（二）	32	32		2	2	2	
		商务英语阅读（三）	32	32		2	3	2	
		西方文明史	32	32		2	1	2	
		商务导论	64	64		4	2	4	
		管理学导论（双语）	32	32		2	3	2	
		经济学导论（双语）	32	32		2	3	2	
		商务英语写作（一）	32	24	8	2	3	2	
		商务英语写作（二）	32	24	8	2	4	2	
		商务英语写作（三）	32	24	8	2	5	2	
		英语演讲与辩论（一）	32	16	16	2	4	2	
		英语演讲与辩论（二）	32	16	16	2	5	2	
		英语演讲与辩论（三）	32	16	16	2	6	2	
		商务翻译（英—汉）	32	8	24	2	5	2	
专业核心课程	必修课程	商务翻译（汉—英）	32	8	24	2	6	2	
		跨文化商务交际导论	32	16	16	2	5	2	
		语言学导论	32	32		2	5	2	
		中国文化概要	32	32		2	5	2	
		英语文学导论	32	32		2	6	2	
		商业伦理	32	24	8	2	6	2	
		……							

（3）专业方向课程

专业方向课程开课计划表

课程类别		课程名称	总学时	学时分配		学分数	开课学期	周学时	备注
				讲授	实验（践）				
国际商务方向课程	必修／选修课程	世界经济概论*	32	32		2	4	2	完整修读1个方向，至少修读28学分，其中标注"*"课程为必修课程。
		国际商务导论*	32	32		2	4	2	
		国际商务谈判*	32	24	8	2	6	2	
		国际商法导论*	32	32		2	6	2	
		战略管理	32	32		2	3	2	
		商务计划	32	28	4	2	3	2	
		国际金融	32	32		2	4	2	
		组织行为学	32	32		2	4	2	
		国际商务合同	32	32		2	4	2	
		国际贸易	32	32		2	5	2	
		财务管理	32	32		2	5	2	
		跨境电子商务	32	32		2	5	2	
		国际关系与国际政治基础	32	32		2	5	2	
		国际市场营销	32	32		2	6	2	
		国际项目管理	32	32		2	6	2	
		跨国公司管理	32	32		2	6	2	
		国际市场调查与预测	32	24	8	2	6	2	
		商务分析	32	24	8	2	7	2	
		国际商务模拟实践	32	16	16	2	7	2	
		……							
国际贸易方向课程	必修／选修课程	世界经济概论*	32	32		2	4	2	完整修读1个方向，至少修读28学分，其中标注"*"课程为必修课程
		国际贸易原理*	32	32		2	4	2	
		国际贸易实务*	32	24	8	2	5	2	
		国际商务导论*	32	32		2	5	2	
		国际结算	32	32		2	3	2	
		战略管理	32	32		2	3	2	

（续表）

课程类别		课程名称	总学时	学时分配		学分数	开课学期	周学时	备注
				讲授	实验（践）				
国际贸易方向课程	必修／选修课程	国际服务贸易	32	32		2	4	2	
		公司战略与风险管理	32	32		2	5	2	
		国际商务合同	32	32		2	5	2	
		跨境电子商务	32	32		2	5	2	
		国际商法导论	32	32		2	5	2	
		国际商务谈判	32	24	8	2	6	2	
		国际市场营销	32	32		2	6	2	
		商务分析	32	24	8	2	6	2	
		国际项目管理	32	32		2	6	2	
		物流管理	32	32		2	6	2	
		国际金融	32	32		2	6	2	
		国际关系与国际政治基础	32	32		2	7	2	
		外贸运输与保险	32	32		2	7	2	
		……							
国际会计方向课程	必修／选修课程	金融学*	32	32		2	3	2	完整修读1个方向，至少修读28学分，其中标注"*"课程为必修课程
		基础会计*	32	24	8	2	4	2	
		财务管理*	32	32		2	5	2	
		中级财务会计*	32	24	8	2	6	2	
		经济法	32	32		2	3	2	
		证券投资学	32	32		2	4	2	
		资产评估	32	32		2	4	2	
		会计信息系统	32	24	8	2	4	2	
		审计学	32	32		2	5	2	
		税法	32	32		2	5	2	
		成本会计	32	24	8	2	5	2	

（续表）

课程类别		课程名称	总学时	学时分配		学分数	开课学期	周学时	备注
				讲授	实验（践）				
国际会计方向课程	必修／选修课程	管理会计	32	24	8	2	5	2	
		公司战略与风险管理	32	32		2	6	2	
		财务报表编制与分析	32	24	8	2	6	2	
		税收筹划	32	32		2	6	2	
		政府与非营利性组织会计	32	32		2	6	2	
		内部控制	32	32		2	7	2	
		业绩管理	32	32		2	7	2	
		应用统计学	32	24	8	2	7	2	
		……							
国际金融方向课程	必修／选修课程	金融学*	32	32		2	4	2	完整修读1个方向，至少修读28学分，其中标注"*"课程为必修课程
		会计学*	32	24	8	2	5	2	
		国际金融*	32	32		2	6	2	
		国际投资学*	32	32		2	6	2	
		世界经济概论	32	32		2	3	2	
		保险学	32	32		2	3	2	
		国际市场营销	32	32		2	4	2	
		国际贸易	32	24	8	2	4	2	
		跨国公司与直接投资	32	32		2	4	2	
		公司理财	32	24	8	2	5	2	
		证券投资学	32	32		2	5	2	
		金融市场	32	32		2	5	2	
		金融风险管理	32	32		2	6	2	
		商业银行经营管理	32	32		2	6	2	

（续表）

课程类别		课程名称	总学时	学时分配		学分数	开课学期	周学时	备注
				讲授	实验（践）				
国际金融方向课程	必修/选修课程	国际结算	32	32		2	6	2	
		金融法	32	32		2	6	2	
		财务报表分析	32	24	8	2	7	2	
		信托与租赁	32	32		2	7	2	
		个人理财	32	24	8	2	7	2	
		……							
跨境电子商务方向课程	必修/选修课程	国际商务导论*	32	32		2	4	2	完整修读1个方向，至少修读28学分，其中标注"*"课程为必修课程
		跨境电子商务概论*	32	32		2	4	2	
		国际贸易*	32	24	8	2	5	2	
		国际市场网络营销*	32	24	8	2	5	2	
		应用统计学	32	32		2	3	2	
		新媒体营销	32	24	8	2	3	2	
		数据报表与信息管理	32	32		2	4	2	
		网络消费心理学	32	32		2	4	2	
		国际结算	32	32		2	5	2	
		国际商务合同	32	32		2	5	2	
		跨境电商客服	32	32		2	5	2	
		国际商务谈判	32	24	8	2	6	2	
		现代物流基础	32	32		2	6	2	
		电子商务法律	32	32		2	6	2	
		跨境电子商务实践	32	24	8	2	6	2	
		新媒体图文设计	32	24	8	2	6	2	

（续表）

课程类别		课程名称	总学时	学时分配		学分数	开课学期	周学时	备注
				讲授	实验（践）				
跨境电子商务方向课程	必修/选修课程	电子商务项目管理	32	32		2	7	2	
		跨境电商平台运营与管理	32	24	8	2	7	2	
		财务报表分析	32	24	8	2	7	2	
		……							
		说明：建议学校根据自身办学定位、办学条件和办学特色，设置专业方向选修课程。							

（4）实践教学环节

实践教学环节开课计划表

课程类别		课程名称	总学时	学时分配		学分	开课学期	周学时	备注
				讲授	实验（践）				
实践教学环节	专业实践课程	英语语音训练	28	20	8	1	1	2	
		笔译实训	32	10	22	2	5	2	
		口译实训	32	10	22	2	6	2	
		课外阅读				6	1–6	2	
		创业实践	32	10	22	2	7	2	
		专业实习	4周			4	8		
		……							
	创新创业实践	英语竞赛				1	3–8		至少修读2学分
		英语学习兴趣小组				1	3–8		
		创新项目				1	3–8		
		学术社团				1	3–8		
		……							

（续表）

课程类别		课程名称	总学时	学时分配		学分	开课学期	周学时	备注
				讲授	实验（践）				
实践教学环节	社会实践活动	社会调查				1	3–8		至少修读2学分
		志愿服务				1	3–8		
		勤工助学				1	3–8		
		支教活动				1	3–8		
		……							
	国际交流	出国（境）学习				1	3–8		至少修读1学分
		参加涉外活动				1	3–8		
		……							
	毕业论文（设计）	学术论文	10周			5	8		
		商务计划书							
		商务研究报告							
		商务案例分析报告							
		……							

6. 教学要求

贯彻学生中心、产出导向、持续改进的教育理念。合理设置课程教学目标和评价标准，做到课程教学目标可衡量、可达成、可评价。在教学过程中以能力培养为导向、以内容为依托，在实现语言技能训练和商务专业知识教学有机融合的基础上，综合运用交互式学习、讨论式学习、合作式学习、体验式学习、项目式学习等教学方式以及混合式教学、翻转课堂等教学方法，推进现代信息技术与专业教学的有效融合，突出语言综合运用能力、思辨能力、数字化信息素养、量化思维以及创新精神、创业意识、创造能力培养，注重专业素养和跨学科思维的养成。激发学生学习兴趣与潜能，鼓励学生独立思考，合理提升学业挑战度，积极倡导探究性学习、反思性学习和整合性学习，培养学生高阶性学习能力，营造适合学生专业学习与个人发展的学习环境。

7. 教学评价

建立基于产出的教学有效性评价机制，培育基于证据的评价文化。制定专业和课程教学评价方案，明确评价内容、标准和程序，保证评价的效度和信度。采取形成性评价和终结性评价相结合的评价方式，加强教学过程中的诊断性评价，突出形成性评价在教学评价中的重要作用。将语言综合运用能力有机融入专业课程教学评价中，突出专门用途英语（ESP）特色，并加强对学生解决复杂问题能力和高阶思维能力的评价，实现知识、能力、素质的有机融合。通过系统采集、分析、解释和反馈教学信息，充分发挥评价与反馈的积极作用，及时为学生和教师提供建设性反馈信息，促进学生学习和教师教学质量的持续改进。

8. 教师队伍

（1）师资结构

商务英语专业应有一支合格的专任教师队伍，形成教研团队。教师的年龄结构、学历结构、学缘结构、职称结构应合理。根据需要从行业或企业专家中聘请兼职教师。有条件的高等学校应聘请外籍教师。专业生师比不高于18:1。

（2）教师素质

专任教师应：①符合《中华人民共和国教师法》《中华人民共和国高等教育法》规定的资格和条件，履行相关义务；②具有外国语言文学类学科或相关学科研究生学历；③具有厚实的专业知识，熟悉外语教学与学习的理论和方法，对教育学、心理学等相关学科知识有一定了解；④具有扎实的英语语言基本功、评价素养、教学设计与实施能力、课堂组织与管理能力、现代教育技术和教学手段的应用能力以及教学反思和改革能力；⑤具有明确的学术研究方向和研究能力。外籍教师的聘任应根据岗位需要，达到上述条款中所有适用标准。

（3）教师发展

各高等学校应制定科学的教师发展规划与制度，通过学历教育、在岗培养、国内外进修与学术交流、行业实践等方式，使教师不断更新教育理念，优化知识结构，提高专业理论水平与教学和研究能力。教师应树立终身发展的观念，制定切实可行的发展计划，不断提高教学水平和研究能力。

9. 教学条件

（1）教学设施

教学场地和实践场所在数量和功能上应满足教学需要，并配备专职人员对教学设施进行日常管理和维护。拥有覆盖学习及生活场所的网络系统，具备实施现代化教学的软件和硬件条件。

（2）信息资源

图书资料能满足学生的学习和教师的教学与科研所需；管理规范，共享程度高；应有一定比例的外文图书和报刊；拥有本专业相关的电子资源。

（3）实践教学

具备满足人才培养需要的相对稳定的实践教学条件；应根据专业特点和需要建设专业实验室、实训中心、校内外实践教学基地等；应充分利用各种资源建设大学生创新创业教育平台。

（4）教学经费

教学和科研经费有保障，总量能满足教学需要。生均年教学日常运行支出不低于教育部对本科专业设置的要求。不同地区、不同类型的学校应根据实际情况合理提高教学经费的投入。

10. 质量管理

（1）内部保障机制要求

应建立完善的教学质量标准体系和校院两级教学质量保障机制。专业教学质量保障目标清晰，各教学环节质量标准科学明确，能开展常态化质量监测和专业自我评价，形成追求卓越的教学质量文化。

（2）外部评价机制要求

应引入第三方评价机构，建立毕业生跟踪反馈机制以及社会评价机制，能定期开展毕业生和用人单位调查，对培养方案是否有效达到培养目标进行定期评价。积极参加专业认证。

（3）持续改进机制要求

应建立完善的持续改进机制，能根据专业建设需要定期对校内外评价结果进行分析，确保教学过程质量监控、毕业生跟踪反馈和社会评价等分析结果及时用于专业的持续改进。

11. 术语与释义

（1）商务英语运用能力

在国际商务活动中，能理解英语口语和书面语传递的信息、观点、情感；能使用英语口语和书面语有效传递信息，表达思想、情感，再现生活经验，并能注意语言表达的得体性和准确性；能借助语言工具书和相关资源进行笔译工作，并能完成一般的口译任务；能有效使用交际策略提高交际效果；能运用语言学知识和基本研究方法对商务英语语言现象进行分析与解释。

（2）跨文化能力

尊重世界文化多样性，具有跨文化包容性和批判性意识；掌握基本的跨文化研究理论知识和分析方法，理解中外文化的基本特点和异同；能对不同文化现象、文本和制品进行阐释和评价；能有效和恰当地进行跨文化沟通；能帮助不同文化背景的人士进行有效的跨文化沟通。

（3）思辨能力

勤学好问，相信理性，尊重事实，谨慎判断，公正评价，敏于探究，持之以恒地追求真理；能对证据、概念、方法、标准、背景等要素进行阐述、分析、评价、推理与解释；能自觉反思和调节自己的思维过程。

（4）量化思维能力

能对国际商务环境中的主要因素进行评价和判断，在商务分析和决策中能有效运用图形、表格和数据量化、呈现、说明商务信息，并能运用文字对图形、表格和数据所表达的信息进行描述、分析、整合和评价。

（5）数字化信息素养

能安全、负责、恰当地使用数字工具、技术和设备，明确信息需求，有效获取、分析、整合、评估、管理和传递信息和数字资源，支撑数字化时代的学习、工作和沟通。

（6）终身学习能力

具有终身学习的意识，能自我规划、自我管理，通过不断学习，适应社会和个人高层次、可持续发展的需要。

（7）实践能力

能通过实践活动拓展知识，掌握技能，学会与他人沟通合作；能运用所学的理论和技能解决实际问题；能管理时间，规划和完成任务；能承受压力，适应新环境。

二、核心课程描述

1. 综合商务英语

英语名称：Comprehensive Business English

教学目标：本课程旨在以"语言技能—商务知识—商务技能—商务思维—商务应用"的学习路径为基础，培养学生在国际商务领域内综合运用英语语言技能进行商务交际的能力。通过课程学习，学生应做到：能准确理解商务领域的英语口语和书面语篇内容；能使用准确、清晰、流利、得体的英语口语完成商务领域口头沟通任务；能运用准确、连贯、简洁、得体的英语书面语完成不同内容和体裁的商务沟通任务。

教学内容：本课程按照以商务活动为主题的场景模拟和案例学习等交际任务组织教学单元，线上、线下深度融合，全方位配置"课前、课中、课后"教学资源。按照语言与内容难度分级，逐层递进。授课内容涵盖语言技能、商务知识，以及主要英语国家、"一带一路"沿线国家和中国的商业文化。语言技能包括对语音、词汇、句法、语篇和语用等知识与策略进行专项训练，通过商务交际任务促进听、说、读、写、译技能的综合运用，强调语言能力的整体性。商务知识包括商业文化、国际商务、企业管理、市场营销、财务管理、商业竞争、商务谈判、国际贸易、国际纠纷、国际投资、创新创业、电子商务、物流运输、客户服务、商务办公等领域。

2. 商务英语视听说

英语名称：Audio-Visual-Oral Business English

教学目标：本课程旨在培养学生在国际商务沟通中理解口头英语并就相关内容进行口头表达的能力。通过课程学习，学生应做到：能正确辨识标准英语及其常见变体的语音和语调；能识记基础英语词汇、商务英语词汇、句型表达；能分辨要义与细节，推断隐含意义，概括主旨大意；能利用笔记对视听内容进行转述、复述、概述和评价；能围绕单元主题就视听内容展开讨论，并对讨论结果进行口头总结和汇报；能运用信息技术进行有效沟通和准确获取信息；能理解主要英语国家及"一带一路"沿线国家的商业文化及中外商业文化差异，在商务沟通中运用国际商务基本概念和知识；能熟练运用英语视听说策略有效进行跨文化商务沟通。

教学内容：本课程使学生理解国际商务真实语境下不同题材、体裁、风格、交际模式、英语变体和语音的口语语篇，有效完成不同目的、主题和语域的国际商务交际任务。交际任务均参照真实的商务交际情景，内容涉及商业新闻报道、会议组织、工作报告、业务洽谈、市场开拓等商务话题，素材形式包括情景对话、专题讲话、商务谈判、演讲辩论、广播电视节目等语言材料，难度根据语言、话题和知识结构等进行分级。

3. 商务英语阅读

英语名称：Reading in Business English

教学目标：本课程旨在通过系统、全面地介绍英语阅读策略和技巧，帮助学生提升商务英语阅读能力，提高英语阅读速度。通过课程学习，学生应做到：能运用略读、速读、查读等阅读方法快速、准确地概括篇章和段落的主旨大意、分析逻辑结构、推断作者的态度和观点、掌握细节信息和隐含信息；具备较强的分析归纳能力，能对阅读材料进行概括、复述和评论；能运用语言知识和阅读技巧阅读各类题材和体裁的商务英语文本，拓宽商务知识。

教学内容：本课程使学生能在阅读商务文本的过程中运用各种策略与技巧有

效获取信息。阅读策略与技巧主要包括概括文章和段落的主旨大意、掌握段落的组织和布局、推理和判断主旨意图、猜测词义、区分事实和观点、掌握细节信息和隐含信息、进行快速阅读实践。阅读题材涉及商业文化、国际商务、企业管理、市场营销、财务管理、商业竞争、商务谈判、国际贸易、贸易纠纷、国际投资、创新创业、电子商务、物流运输、客户服务、商务办公等领域。体裁主要涉及商业新闻报道、产品发布、商务文书、公司年报、商务信函、法律文书、报刊（网站）等，根据语言和内容的难度进行分级。

4. 英语演讲与辩论

英语名称：English Public Speaking and Debating

教学目标：本课程旨在培养学生运用英语在公开场合进行演讲和辩论的能力。通过课程学习，学生应做到：具有比较扎实的英语语言功底，知识面广，视野宽阔；具有较强的逻辑推理、批判性思维和临场应变能力；能就某一话题广泛收集素材，撰写演讲稿并脱稿进行演讲；能在经过短时准备（一般为五分钟）后就给定话题进行即席演讲（一般三分钟左右）；熟悉辩论的一般规则，能参与主题发言、抗辩、问题挑战、总结陈词等辩论环节；能熟练运用演讲和辩论策略。

教学内容：本课程主要包括英语演讲与辩论的内容准备和策略训练两个方面的内容。内容准备主要指根据演讲和辩论的主题、目的、听众／对手等广泛收集素材，并归纳整理、拟列提纲、撰写演讲稿或发言稿。策略训练重点训练提高口头表达效果的方法和技巧，主要包括：如何开场、过渡和总结；如何阐述观点、抒发情感、活跃气氛；如何运用表情、眼神、手势等肢体语言；如何把控音量、音高、语气和语调；如何克服紧张情绪、调整即时心态、改正不良习惯等。根据口头表达任务的特点和难度，有备演讲和即兴演讲的训练各有侧重，英语演讲和英语辩论的训练由易到难、循序渐进。

5. 商务英语写作

英语名称：Business English Writing

教学目标：本课程旨在培养学生在国际商务环境下选用适当写作策略进行有效沟通的能力。通过课程学习，学生应做到：能掌握商务写作基本理论、原则和技巧，了解商务沟通过程和参与要素；能辨识商务英语沟通环境与条件，选用有效的沟通策略；能分析商务沟通常见文件的体裁特征和语言特征；能有效利用数字化技术，提高商务写作的有效性；能了解求职应聘过程，改进求职沟通效果；能理解人际沟通在商务沟通中的重要性。

教学内容：本课程主要包括商务沟通与跨文化商务沟通、商务写作策略与技巧、商务沟通体裁分析和信息技术应用四个方面的内容。商务沟通与跨文化商务沟通主要指商务沟通的目的、过程和要素；商务写作策略与技巧重点训练信息收集、分析和表达，积极信息、消极信息和说服性信息传达，数字化技术使用技巧；商务沟通体裁分析主要包括商务信函、备忘录、新闻发布稿、会议纪要、商务合同、商务报告、建议书、求职文件等常用体裁特征分析；信息技术应用侧重训练图表设计制作和评述、演示文稿设计、视觉辅助工具使用等。

6. 商务翻译

英语名称：Business Translation

教学目标：本课程旨在培养学生掌握商务翻译的基本概念和理论基础，训练英汉互译常用策略和技巧，具备常见商务文本的翻译能力。通过课程学习，学生应做到：能在翻译实践中运用理论知识进行文本分析和体裁分析；能熟练运用翻译策略和技巧，完成不同类型商务文本的翻译任务；能在商务翻译实践中识别并尊重文化间的差异，体现较好的跨文化翻译能力；能够熟练运用现代信息技术手段解决翻译实践问题，具备良好的信息素养。

教学内容：本课程主要包括翻译理论学习和翻译实践能力培养两部分内容。理论部分包括商务翻译相关概念、理论、标准、过程、常用策略与技巧，英汉语言与文化对比等。实践部分通过示例分析和笔译实训，让学生根据翻译的标准以及英汉两种语言在词汇、句法、篇章及社会文化等方面的异同，熟练运用直译、意译、归化、异化等翻译方法、技巧和策略。翻译素材包括商务信函、商务合同、商业广告、产品说明、企业介绍、商务文书等常用商务体裁。

7. 英语文学导论

英语名称：Introduction to English Literature

教学目标：本课程旨在帮助学生掌握英语文学基础知识，提高理解、欣赏和评价英语文学作品的能力。通过课程学习，学生应做到：理解英语文学的基本要素；熟悉英国和美国的文学传统，并对其他英语国家的文学以及后殖民英语文学的多元发展有一定了解；能通过文学作品深入了解英语国家的语言、社会、文化及其历史传承；掌握文学研究的基础理论和基本方法，对英语文学作品进行分析和评论。

教学内容：本课程内容主要包括文学作品导读、西方文论与文学批评等方面。文学作品导读以英美文学史上的经典名作为主，重点介绍小说、诗歌、戏剧三类文学体裁的要素特征、主要流派及相关文学史知识，并将加拿大、澳大利亚、新西兰等英美以外英语国家的文学作品穿插在课程中进行讨论，以体现当代英语文学发展的新格局和趋势。西方文论与文学批评着重介绍马克思主义、精神分析、女性主义、接受美学、后殖民批评等现代西方文学分析与批评理论，以及学术论文撰写的基本规范和常见体例，指导学生运用有关理论进行初步、规范的文学批评写作。

8. 语言学导论

英语名称：Introduction to Linguistics

教学目标：本课程旨在培养学生对人类语言的理性认识，提高学生的语言文化意识和批判性思维能力。通过课程学习，学生应做到：初步掌握语言学的基本概念、原则和方法；了解语言学的基本分支和主要理论流派；了解语言学跨学科应用与研究的主要领域、课题和发展趋势；能运用语言学知识观察和分析语言现象，促进外语学习。

教学内容：本课程主要包括语言与语言学、语言学的基本分支和语言学的跨学科研究等方面的内容。语言与语言学主要突出语言的甄别性特征、语言的功能和语言学基本概念；语言学基本分支重点介绍语音学、音位学、词汇学、句法学、语义学、语用学等分支的基本内容及研究方法，以及现代语言学主要流派的基本观点；语言学的跨学科研究简要介绍语言与社会、语言与文化、语言与大脑、语言学与外语教学等方面的基本知识和主要研究课题。

9. 西方文明史

英语名称：History of Western Civilisation

教学目标：本课程旨在帮助学生了解西方文明的发展历程，同时夯实英语语言基础、拓展文化视野、提升人文素养和逻辑思辨能力。通过课程学习，学生应做到：熟悉与西方政治、经济、宗教、文艺、科技等相关的特殊词汇与特定表达方式；了解西方文明的历史发展脉络，掌握各历史时期的重大历史事件及主要人文思想；能运用所学知识对西方文明进行理性分析，同时结合东方文明进行比较和思辨，并形成自己独到的见解。

教学内容：本课程主要按照西方文明的发展历史，分阶段组织教学内容。主要阶段包括早期中东文明、希腊罗马时期、中世纪、文艺复兴、宗教改革、地理大发现、启蒙运动、欧洲政治革命与美国革命、现代西方文明等。讲授内容以各阶段的重大历史事件、主要人文思想，以及政治、经济、宗教、科技等的发展状况为主，同时兼顾各历史阶段之间的相关性和西方文明史的整体性。难度按文本的语言难度分为初级、中级和高级三个等级。初级和中级分别为难度较小和有一定难度的英文读本，高级应为难度较大且为英语国家权威专家所著的英文原版著作，同时辅以一定数量的英语视听材料和参考书作为补充。

10. 经济学导论

英语名称：**Introduction to Economics**

教学目标：本课程旨在帮助学生通过对经济学基本概念和基本原理的学习，形成基本的经济学思维，具有分析、判断市场经济运行机制的基本能力。通过课程学习，学生应做到：了解现代市场经济的基本运行机制，从微观和宏观两个层面增进对主要经济现象和经济问题的理解；掌握经济学的基本思想、概念与分析方法；对经济新闻和经济事件具有较强的敏感性，能运用所学理论对社会生活中常见的经济问题、经济现象进行分析，增强对现实经济行为与经济现象的观察和分析能力。

教学内容：本课程内容分为微观经济学和宏观经济学两部分。微观经济学主要研究单个经济主体如何作出决策，内容包括供求理论、消费者选择理论、企业行为理论，着重介绍消费者的效用水平和消费决策、企业的生产成本和市场决策。宏观经济学主要研究总体经济如何运行，内容包括国民收入核算理论、宏观经济政策、失业与通货膨胀理论，重点讲授政府如何运用财政政策、货币政策实现宏观经济目标。

11. 管理学导论

英语名称：Introduction to Management

教学目标：本课程旨在培养学生熟练掌握组织管理的基本概念与理论，认知、识别商务实践中的管理问题，具备运用相关管理理论与方法从事国际商务实践的能力。通过课程学习，学生应能做到：结合国际商务环境，识别并描述计划与决策、组织设计与组织文化、员工激励与沟通、生产诸方面控制等主要管理问题；能运用决策理论、企业文化理论、沟通理论、激励理论等相关理论与方法在跨文化商务活动中实现有关管理目标；能主动适应国际商务环境演变与技术进步条件下的管理实践变革。

教学内容：本课程按照管理职能的知识体系组织教学内容，主要包括古典决策理论、行为决策理论以及定性与定量的决策方法；企业计划以及战略规划的制定与实施；组织结构的层级与幅度设计、人力资源规划以及招聘、培训、绩效评价，组织文化结构与建设；领导理论、需要激励理论与过程激励理论以及组织、团队及个人沟通方法；控制理论以及生产、财务等控制方法。

12. 商务导论

英语名称：Introduction to Business

教学目标：本课程旨在帮助学生掌握从事商务活动所需的基本理论和知识，提升管理能力和市场分析能力，培养风险意识，有效解决商务实践中的具体问题。通过课程学习，学生应做到：能全面、系统地掌握商务组织运作的基本概念和知识；能系统地了解商务活动所涵盖的范围，掌握公司经营的外部环境、公司的经营、管理、财务管理等方面的运作机制，为从事商务活动和进行相关理论研究奠定基础。

教学内容：本课程内容融合了西方商务管理基本理论和我国的具体商务实践。课程内容包括商务环境、商务运行和企业创办等，重点介绍市场经济的基本运行规律和运行机制，商务组织运行环境对企业经营决策的影响，商务组织的战略管理、运营管理、财务管理、风险管理、商业伦理与社会责任等。

13. 跨文化商务交际导论

英语名称：Introduction to Intercultural Business Communication

教学目标：本课程旨在帮助学生掌握跨文化交际理论知识，并具备将理论与实践有效结合的能力。通过课程学习，学生应做到：能在跨文化交际意识及在跨文化商务语境中解决实际问题；能建立良好的元认知并在跨文化交际中具备策略使用意识；能探究跨文化交际现象背后的问题。

教学内容：本课程内容主要涵盖跨文化交际理论和跨文化交际实践两部分。理论部分包括跨文化交际能力、文化模式、语言和非言语交际等理论知识；实践部分包括跨文化交际理论在市场营销、商务谈判、书面商务沟通、跨文化商务礼仪、跨文化商务伦理等方面的实践应用。

14. 商业伦理

英语名称：Business Ethics

教学目标：本课程旨在帮助学生理解商业活动中各主体间的伦理关系及其基本规律；理解和掌握商业活动中应遵循的伦理原则和道德规范；引导学生思考企业管理行为和经营决策的伦理正当性，在此过程中建立伦理意识，培养道德判断和伦理决策能力。通过课程学习，学生应做到：能理解企业社会责任的伦理内涵；能理解和掌握中西文化中商业文化的差异及其产生的根源；能以跨文化的视角审视国际商务活动中商业伦理、价值观、决策方式、思维模式和社会责任等方面的差异，并进行有效沟通。

教学内容：本课程主要内容包括商业伦理与商业文化、中西商业文化与商业伦理的差异、商业伦理与社会责任、企业商业伦理规范与伦理决策、企业内部管理与对外经营中的商业伦理与道德规范、全球化背景下国际商务活动中的商业伦理与社会责任、基于价值观的商业决策过程模型、商业伦理规范的形成与构建、商业伦理与企业文化建设等。

15. 中国文化概要

英语名称：Introduction to Chinese Culture

教学目标：本课程旨在使学生对中国悠久的历史、灿烂的文化和优秀的文学传统有深入的了解，培养学生对中国文化的自豪和热爱，扩展文化视野，丰富文化内涵。通过本课程的学习，学生应能做到：向世界介绍中国的历史发展轨迹、基本国情、风土人情、民俗习惯等一般人文知识，并具备较强的跨文化交际、交流意识，能在未来的国际交流中灵活处理文化差异，掌握交际的主动权。

教学内容：本课程可以根据历史年代（古代、近代、现代）组织教学内容，也可以根据主题组织教学内容。教学主题可以包括且不限于：历史、政体、宗教、人文地理、法律制度、伦理价值观、少数民族政策、语言文字、哲学、教育、科技、艺术、民俗等。在教学材料的选择上注意材料的代表性、包容性、多样性和时代性，讲究古今结合、南北兼顾，并突出跨文化交际的视角。

中国人民大学出版社读者信息反馈表

尊敬的读者：

感谢您购买和使用中国人民大学出版社的 _____ 一书，我们希望通过这张小小的反馈表来获得您更多的建议和意见，以改进我们的工作，加强我们双方的沟通和联系。我们期待着能为更多的读者提供更多的好书。

请您填妥下表后，寄回或传真回复我们，对您的支持我们不胜感激！

1. 您是从何种途径得知本书的：
   □书店　　　　□网上　　　　□报纸杂志　　　　□朋友推荐
2. 您为什么决定购买本书：
   □工作需要　　□学习参考　　□对本书主题感兴趣　　□随便翻翻
3. 您对本书内容的评价是：
   □很好　　　　□好　　　　□一般　　　　□差　　　　□很差
4. 您在阅读本书的过程中有没有发现明显的专业及编校错误，如果有，它们是：

   _____

   _____

   _____

5. 您对哪些专业的图书信息比较感兴趣：

   _____

   _____

   _____

6. 如果方便，请提供您的个人信息，以便于我们和您联系（您的个人资料我们将严格保密）：

   您供职的单位：_____

   您教授的课程（教师填写）：_____

   您的通信地址：_____

   您的电子邮箱：_____

请联系我们：黄婷　程子殊　王新文　王琼

电话：010-62512737，62513265，62515580，62515573

传真：010-62514961

E-mail：huangt@crup.com.cn　　chengzsh@crup.com.cn　　wangxw@crup.com.cn
　　　　crup_wy@163.com

通信地址：北京市海淀区中关村大街甲59号文化大厦15层　　　邮编：100872

中国人民大学出版社